托福高频
真词表

北京新东方研发中心
刘娟　　编著

海豚出版社
DOLPHIN BOOKS
中国国际出版集团

图书在版编目（CIP）数据

托福高频真词表 / 北京新东方研发中心，刘娟编著.
— 北京：海豚出版社，2018.7
ISBN 978-7-5110-4216-3

Ⅰ.①托… Ⅱ.①北… ②刘… Ⅲ.①TOEFL—词汇—
自学参考资料 Ⅳ.①H313

中国版本图书馆CIP数据核字（2018）第112664号

托福高频真词表
北京新东方研发中心　刘娟　编著

出 版 人	蔡剑峰
责任编辑	慕君黎　张嫣然
封面设计	大愚设计
责任印制	于浩杰　蔡　丽
出　　版	海豚出版社
网　　址	http://www.dolphin-books.com.cn
地　　址	北京市西城区百万庄大街24号
邮　　编	100037
电　　话	010-68325006（销售）　010-68996147（总编室）
邮　　箱	dywh@xdf.cn
印　　刷	三河市良远印务有限公司
经　　销	新华书店及网络书店
开　　本	710mm×1000mm　1/16
印　　张	21.75
字　　数	269千字
版　　次	2018年7月第1版　2018年7月第1次印刷
标准书号	ISBN 978-7-5110-4216-3
定　　价	50.00元

献给奋斗在托福备考前线的你们

在托福考试的阅读部分中，词汇题的比重大约占了 1/4，每篇文章有 3~5 道词汇题，词汇对阅读部分的提分至关重要。做词汇题时，基本上不太需要上下文的理解，看到单词，认识意思，可以秒选。所以如果对阅读词汇题非常熟悉的话，可以给其他题目省下大量的做题时间。

从 2014 年开始，在每场考试之后，我都有意识地去收集考到的词汇题，汇总在一个专门的 excel 表格中，配上词性和中文注释，上课给学生们补充，慢慢也积累了不少。但真正开始系统地汇总历年所有的词汇题，是从 2015 年 10 月开始的。那时我还在新东方北美研发中心的托福阅读组做研发工作，整理词汇题也是我工作的一部分。通过各种途径，我最早找到了 2010 年考过的词汇题，把每一年的词汇题都存在一个单独的表格里，每一个词对都有对应的确切来源。到 2016 年年初，我整理的词对总量共有上千对，经过查重、合并归类，最终保留了 1310 对，形成了"托福佛脚词 1.0"，在新东方内部的班课开始使用。同时，"托福佛脚词 1.0"也在乐词上线了。接下来的半年，我和其他几位老师一起，给乐词上的"佛脚词表"录制了单词的讲解视频。

在这个过程中，我从来没有停止过词汇题的汇总和深度处理。我把每一个词都匹配了韦氏字典中的英文释义，然而最终去掉英文释义是因为我发现，词对对应的正确选项基本都来源于韦氏字典的解释，为了减少对大家记忆的干扰，最终去掉了。另外，在每年年底，我都会按过去一年中考查的次数，给学生提供过去一年的词汇题整理。同时，我也发现一个中文释义会对应很多考过的词对，这些词会在不同考试中串着考。比如，如果我问表示"分散、传播"含义的英文单词，在词汇题中出现过哪些词，这些词来回串着考了多少次，你是否能答得上来？答不上来就在书中寻找答案吧。

通过不断地深度处理，我对词汇题越来越熟悉，似乎也摸到了一些规律，所以从 2016 年 4 月，我开始在公众号"X 大仙"上负责阅读词汇的预测。经过一年的时间，在 2017 年 7 月，终于更新到了"托福佛脚词 2.0"。在 1.0 版本的基础上，2.0 版本更进一步地将词汇合理汇总，将一个主词曾经考过的多个同义词放在一组，最终浓缩出 1000 组词汇题，降低了记忆的难度。同时，2.0 版本还加入了词汇题的练习。这就是本书的雏形。截至出版，本书涵盖了 50 多套 TPO 和截止到目前所有我能找到的词汇题，并且词表仍然在不断更新中。

我更加推荐在备考后期使用本书，大量、反复地去背诵和练习。这 1000 组词汇题，在考前两周至少要过三遍，达到看到左边的词就能想到右边的词，这样上考场才能做到秒选。本书的词表按照考试时间倒序排列，Word List 1 是近期考试的新词，越往后时间越靠前，最后几个 List 是 TPO 中的词对。建议同学们在背诵的时候，有效地使用"记忆尺"做好标记，把不熟悉的词记录下来，重点背诵。

最后，要感谢韩冰和潘晨光老师的《GRE 高频真词表》给《托福高频真词表》开了个好头。特别感谢韩冰老师给我提供了很多建议和帮助。感谢在使用过程中提出过改进意见的老师和同学。希望这本书能帮助到你。感恩，在你备考的路上，我曾陪伴过。

刘 娟
于北京新东方大厦

目 录

词汇部分

音频

| **occasionally** | 释 *adv.* 偶尔 | 记忆尺 |
| [ə'keɪʒnəli] | 同 sometimes / once in a while | □□□□□ |

| **segregate** | 释 *v.* 隔离 | 记忆尺 |
| ['segrɪgeɪt] | 同 separate | □□□□□ |

| **apparent** | 释 *adj.* 明显的 | 记忆尺 |
| [ə'pærənt] | 同 evident / noticeable / clearly seen in / obvious | □□□□□ |

| **apparently** | 释 *adv.* 显然 | 记忆尺 |
| [ə'pærəntli] | 同 seemingly | □□□□□ |

| **leftover** | 释 *adj.* 剩余的 | 记忆尺 |
| ['leftoʊvər] | 同 remaining | □□□□□ |

| **ensure/insure** | 释 *v.* 确保 | 记忆尺 |
| [ɪn'ʃʊr] | 同 guarantee | □□□□□ |

| **match** | 释 *v.* 相匹配 | 记忆尺 |
| [mætʃ] | 同 agree with / equal | □□□□□ |

rival	释 *n.* 对手	记忆尺
['raɪvl]	同 competitor	□□□□□
	释 *v.* 对抗	
	同 compete	

| **unrivaled** | 释 *adj.* 无与伦比的 | 记忆尺 |
| [ʌn'raɪvld] | 同 unequaled | □□□□□ |

| **be susceptible to** | 易受…影响的 | 记忆尺 |
| | be subject to / likely to be affected by | □ □ □ □ □ |

| **faithfully** ['feɪθfəli] | adv. 准确地 | 记忆尺 |
| | accurately | □ □ □ □ □ |

| **faithful** ['feɪθfl] | adj. 正确的 | 记忆尺 |
| | exact | □ □ □ □ □ |

| **admiration for** | 钦佩 | 记忆尺 |
| | high opinion of | □ □ □ □ □ |

| **fragile** ['frædʒl] | adj. 脆弱的 | 记忆尺 |
| | delicate / easily damaged / brittle | □ □ □ □ □ |

| **perceive** [pər'siːv] | v. 察觉 | 记忆尺 |
| | see | □ □ □ □ □ |

| **garment** ['gɑːrmənt] | n. 服装 | 记忆尺 |
| | article of clothing | □ □ □ □ □ |

| **obtain** [əb'teɪn] | v. 获得 | 记忆尺 |
| | gather | □ □ □ □ □ |

| **be preserved** | 保留 | 记忆尺 |
| | survive | □ □ □ □ □ |

| **a wealth of** | 大量的 | 记忆尺 |
| | a lot of / an abundance of | □ □ □ □ □ |

| **put up with** | 忍受 | 记忆尺 |
| | tolerate | □ □ □ □ □ |

| **entail** [ɪn'teɪl] | v. 牵涉 | 记忆尺 |
| | involve | □ □ □ □ □ |

essential	adj. 主要的	记忆尺
[ɪ'senʃl]	main	☐ ☐ ☐ ☐ ☐

encompass	v. 包含	记忆尺
[ɪn'kʌmpəs]	include	☐ ☐ ☐ ☐ ☐

lethal	adj. 致命的	记忆尺
['liːθl]	deadly	☐ ☐ ☐ ☐ ☐

appeal	n. 吸引力	记忆尺
[ə'piːl]	attraction	☐ ☐ ☐ ☐ ☐

annual	adj. 每年的	记忆尺
['ænjuəl]	yearly	☐ ☐ ☐ ☐ ☐

subsequent	adj. 随后的	记忆尺
['sʌbsɪkwənt]	later / following	☐ ☐ ☐ ☐ ☐

observation	n. 发现	记忆尺
[ˌɑːbzər'veɪʃn]	finding	☐ ☐ ☐ ☐ ☐

vulnerable	adj. 脆弱的	记忆尺
['vʌlnərəbl]	unprotected / easily attacked by / easily damaged by / open to attack	☐ ☐ ☐ ☐ ☐

verify	v. 证实	记忆尺
['verɪfaɪ]	confirm	☐ ☐ ☐ ☐ ☐

ascend	v. 上升	记忆尺
[ə'send]	go up / climb	☐ ☐ ☐ ☐ ☐

converge on	汇集	记忆尺
	meet at	☐ ☐ ☐ ☐ ☐

vanish	v. 消失	记忆尺
['vænɪʃ]	disappear	☐ ☐ ☐ ☐ ☐

4

| **feature** | 譯 *n.* 方面 | 记忆尺 |
| ['fiːtʃər] | 同 aspect | ☐☐☐☐☐ |

| **merely** | 譯 *adv.* 仅仅 | 记忆尺 |
| ['mɪrli] | 同 only | ☐☐☐☐☐ |

| **exclusively** | 譯 *adv.* 仅仅 | 记忆尺 |
| [ɪk'skluːsɪvli] | 同 solely / only | ☐☐☐☐☐ |

| **verging** | 譯 *n.* 边缘 | 记忆尺 |
| ['vɜːrdʒɪŋ] | 同 bordering | ☐☐☐☐☐ |

| **admirably** | 譯 *adv.* 极好地 | 记忆尺 |
| ['ædmərəbli] | 同 very well | ☐☐☐☐☐ |

| **continuously** | 譯 *adv.* 连续地 | 记忆尺 |
| [kən'tɪnjuəsli] | 同 constantly | ☐☐☐☐☐ |

| **almost universal among** | 譯 在…中很普遍 | 记忆尺 |
| | 同 used by almost all | ☐☐☐☐☐ |

| **identifiable** | 譯 *adj.* 可识别的 | 记忆尺 |
| [aɪ,dentɪ'faɪəbl] | 同 recognizable | ☐☐☐☐☐ |

| **attest** | 譯 *v.* 证实 | 记忆尺 |
| [ə'test] | 同 confirm | ☐☐☐☐☐ |

| **inherent** | 譯 *adj.* 内在的 | 记忆尺 |
| [ɪn'hɪrənt] | 同 built-in | ☐☐☐☐☐ |

| **fluid** | 譯 *adj.* 流动的 | 记忆尺 |
| ['fluːɪd] | 同 liquid | ☐☐☐☐☐ |

| **onset** | 譯 *n.* 发生，开始 | 记忆尺 |
| ['ɑːnset] | 同 start | ☐☐☐☐☐ |

| **comprehensive** | 譯 *adj.* 全面的 | 记忆尺 |
| [,kɑːmprɪ'hensɪv] | 同 completed / thorough | ☐☐☐☐☐ |

insist [ɪn'sɪst]	v. 坚持 state forcefully	记忆尺 □ □ □ □ □
interpret [ɪn'tɜːrprɪt]	v. 理解 understand	记忆尺 □ □ □ □ □
copious ['koʊpiəs]	adj. 大量的 abundant	记忆尺 □ □ □ □ □
assertion [ə'sɜːrʃn]	n. 宣称 claim	记忆尺 □ □ □ □ □
speculate ['spekjuleɪt]	v. 推测 put forward as a possibility / think about / guess	记忆尺 □ □ □ □ □
tremendous [trə'mendəs]	adj. 巨大的 enormous / huge	记忆尺 □ □ □ □ □
remnant ['remnənt]	n. 剩余 remains	记忆尺 □ □ □ □ □
anchor ['æŋkər]	v. 固定 hold in place	记忆尺 □ □ □ □ □

音频

exotic	释 *adj.* 异国的	记忆尺
[ɪgˈzɑːtɪk]	同 foreign	☐☐☐☐☐
dominate	释 *v.* 处于支配地位	记忆尺
[ˈdɑːmɪneɪt]	同 control	☐☐☐☐☐
obsolete	释 *adj.* 过时的	记忆尺
[ˌɑːbsəˈliːt]	同 out of date	☐☐☐☐☐
suitable	释 *adj.* 合适的	记忆尺
[ˈsuːtəbl]	同 appropriate	☐☐☐☐☐
ambitious	释 *adj.* 有抱负的，费力的	记忆尺
[æmˈbɪʃəs]	同 impressive but difficult to achieve	☐☐☐☐☐
take precedence over	释 优先于	记忆尺
	同 have greater importance than / be more important than	☐☐☐☐☐
little short of miraculous	释 奇迹般的	记忆尺
	同 amazing because almost impossible	☐☐☐☐☐
designation	释 *n.* 标志	记忆尺
[ˌdezɪgˈneɪʃn]	同 identification	☐☐☐☐☐
lateral	释 *adj.* 侧面的	记忆尺
[ˈlætərəl]	同 side	☐☐☐☐☐
be expelled from	释 被驱逐	记忆尺
	同 be left by	☐☐☐☐☐

proximity [prɑːkˈsɪməti]	n. 接近 closeness	记忆尺 ☐☐☐☐☐
intense [ɪnˈtens]	adj. 强烈的 strong	记忆尺 ☐☐☐☐☐
pierce [pɪrs]	v. 穿过 break through	记忆尺 ☐☐☐☐☐
penetrate [ˈpenətreɪt]	v. 穿过 pass through / pierce	记忆尺 ☐☐☐☐☐
determinant [dɪˈtɜːrmɪnənt]	n. 决定因素 cause	记忆尺 ☐☐☐☐☐
perfect [pərˈfekt]	v. 完善 improve / complete	记忆尺 ☐☐☐☐☐
predominate [prɪˈdɑːmɪneɪt]	v.（数量上）占优势 be in the majority	记忆尺 ☐☐☐☐☐
account for	解释 explain	记忆尺 ☐☐☐☐☐
considerably [kənˈsɪdərəbli]	adv. 极大地 significantly	记忆尺 ☐☐☐☐☐
striking [ˈstraɪkɪŋ]	adj. 明显的 noteworthy / attention getting / noticeable	记忆尺 ☐☐☐☐☐
precise [prɪˈsaɪs]	adj. 精确的 accurate / exact	记忆尺 ☐☐☐☐☐
imitator [ˈɪmɪteɪtər]	n. 模仿者 the person who copied someone	记忆尺 ☐☐☐☐☐

exercise ['eksərsaɪz]	v. 运用 apply	记忆尺 ☐☐☐☐☐
emerge [i'mɜːrdʒ]	v. 出现 appear / arise	记忆尺 ☐☐☐☐☐
emergence [i'mɜːrdʒəns]	n. 出现 rise	记忆尺 ☐☐☐☐☐
tactic ['tæktɪk]	n. 策略 strategy	记忆尺 ☐☐☐☐☐
thus [ðʌs]	adv. 因此 consequently / in this way	记忆尺 ☐☐☐☐☐
hence [hens]	adv. 因此 thus	记忆尺 ☐☐☐☐☐
consequently ['kaːnsəkwentli]	adv. 因此 thereby / therefore / as a result	记忆尺 ☐☐☐☐☐
sentimental [ˌsentɪ'mentl]	adj. 情感的 emotional	记忆尺 ☐☐☐☐☐
assimilate [ə'sɪməleɪt]	v. 吸收 absorb	记忆尺 ☐☐☐☐☐
devastating ['devəsteɪtɪŋ]	adj. 破坏性极大的 extremely destructive	记忆尺 ☐☐☐☐☐
devastate ['devəsteɪt]	v. 毁坏 destroy	记忆尺 ☐☐☐☐☐
point out	指出 state	记忆尺 ☐☐☐☐☐
favor ['feɪvər]	v. 偏爱 prefer	记忆尺 ☐☐☐☐☐

contain [kən'teɪn]	释 *v.* 包括 同 include	记忆尺 ☐☐☐☐☐
further ['fɜːrðər]	释 *adv.* 更进一步地 同 additionally 释 *adj.* 更进一步的 同 additional	记忆尺 ☐☐☐☐☐
furthermore [ˌfɜːrðər'mɔːr]	释 *adv.* 此外 同 in addition	记忆尺 ☐☐☐☐☐
approach [ə'proʊtʃ]	释 *v.* 接近 同 come close	记忆尺 ☐☐☐☐☐
anonymous [ə'nɑːnɪməs]	释 *adj.* 匿名的 同 unidentifiable	记忆尺 ☐☐☐☐☐
culminate ['kʌlmɪneɪt]	释 *v.* 达到顶点 同 reach a high point with 释 *v.* 结束 同 reach completion	记忆尺 ☐☐☐☐☐
culmination [ˌkʌlmɪ'neɪʃn]	释 *n.* 告终 同 end	记忆尺 ☐☐☐☐☐
decisive [dɪ'saɪsɪv]	释 *adj.* 决定性的 同 determining	记忆尺 ☐☐☐☐☐
beneficial [ˌbenɪ'fɪʃl]	释 *adj.* 有利的 同 helpful	记忆尺 ☐☐☐☐☐
rely [rɪ'laɪ]	释 *v.* 依靠 同 depend	记忆尺 ☐☐☐☐☐
or so	释 大约 同 roughly	记忆尺 ☐☐☐☐☐

focus	□ *v.* 集中	记忆尺
['foʊkəs]	□ concentrate	□□□□□
imminent	□ *adj.* 即将发生的	记忆尺
['ɪmɪnənt]	□ about to happen	□□□□□
refinement	□ *n.* 改善	记忆尺
[rɪ'faɪnmənt]	□ improvement	□□□□□
refine	□ *v.* 改善	记忆尺
[rɪ'faɪn]	□ improve	□□□□□
virtually	□ *adv.* 几乎	
	□ almost completely / nearly / almost	记忆尺
['vɜːrtʃuəli]	□ *adv.* 事实上	□□□□□
	□ in fact	
startled	□ *adj.* 受惊的	记忆尺
['stɑːrtld]	□ surprised	□□□□□
disrupt	□ *v.* 打断	记忆尺
[dɪs'rʌpt]	□ disturb / destroy / upset	□□□□□
exhibit	□ *v.* 展示	记忆尺
[ɪg'zɪbɪt]	□ display / show	□□□□□
compensate for	□ 弥补	记忆尺
	□ make up for	□□□□□
crude	□ *adj.* 低级的	记忆尺
[kruːd]	□ primitive / rough	□□□□□
eventual	□ *adj.* 最终的	记忆尺
[ɪ'ventʃuəl]	□ later / final	□□□□□
eventually	□ *adv.* 最终	记忆尺
[ɪ'ventʃuəli]	□ in the end / at a later time / over time	□□□□□

11

initially

[ɪˈnɪʃəli]

adv. 最初

at first

记忆尺

☐ ☐ ☐ ☐ ☐

initial

[ɪˈnɪʃl]

adj. 最初的

first

记忆尺

☐ ☐ ☐ ☐ ☐

adjacent [əˈdʒeɪsnt]	释 *adj.* 毗邻的 同 next to / neighboring / nearby	记忆尺 ☐☐☐☐☐
dependable [dɪˈpendəbl]	释 *adj.* 可靠的 同 reliable	记忆尺 ☐☐☐☐☐
chronology [krəˈnɑːlədʒi]	释 *n.* 年表 同 a list that pairs past events with dates	记忆尺 ☐☐☐☐☐
remarkably close	释 极为接近 同 extremely close	记忆尺 ☐☐☐☐☐
competence [ˈkɑːmpɪtəns]	释 *n.* 才能 同 ability	记忆尺 ☐☐☐☐☐
supplement [ˈsʌplɪmənt]	释 *v.* 补充 同 add to	记忆尺 ☐☐☐☐☐
supplementary [ˌsʌplɪˈmentri]	释 *adj.* 补充的 同 additional	记忆尺 ☐☐☐☐☐
assert [əˈsɜːrt]	释 *v.* 断言 同 declare	记忆尺 ☐☐☐☐☐
integrate [ˈɪntɪɡreɪt]	释 *v.* 结合 同 connect / coordinate / combine / unify	记忆尺 ☐☐☐☐☐
integrity [ɪnˈteɡrəti]	释 *n.* 整体性 同 unity	记忆尺 ☐☐☐☐☐

integration [ˌɪntɪˈɡreɪʃn]	*n.* 整体性 unity	记忆尺 ☐☐☐☐☐
experiment with	尝试做 try to	记忆尺 ☐☐☐☐☐
vacate [ˈveɪkeɪt]	*v.* 腾空 empty / abandon	记忆尺 ☐☐☐☐☐
compelling [kəmˈpelɪŋ]	*adj.* 有说服力的 convincing / persuasive	记忆尺 ☐☐☐☐☐
essential [ɪˈsenʃl]	*adj.* 重要的 principal / fundamental	记忆尺 ☐☐☐☐☐
unprecedented [ʌnˈpresɪdentɪd]	*adj.* 前所未有的 never seen before / not previously experienced / unlike anything in the past	记忆尺 ☐☐☐☐☐
permanent [ˈpɜːrmənənt]	*adj.* 永久的 constant / forever	记忆尺 ☐☐☐☐☐
rudimentary [ˌruːdɪˈmentri]	*adj.* 基本的 primitive / simple / elementary / basic	记忆尺 ☐☐☐☐☐
surge [sɜːrdʒ]	*v.* 激增 to suddenly increase	记忆尺 ☐☐☐☐☐
a surge of	猛增 a suddenly increase in	记忆尺 ☐☐☐☐☐
vicinity [vəˈsɪnəti]	*n.* 周边地区 surrounding area/region	记忆尺 ☐☐☐☐☐
ceaselessly [ˈsiːsləsli]	*adv.* 不断地 continually	记忆尺 ☐☐☐☐☐

| **undoubtedly** | adv. 毫无疑问 | 记忆尺 |
| [ʌn'daʊtɪdli] | certainly | ☐☐☐☐☐ |

| **doubtlessly** | adv. 无疑 | 记忆尺 |
| ['daʊtləsli] | certainly | ☐☐☐☐☐ |

| **exceed** | v. 超过 | 记忆尺 |
| [ɪk'siːd] | be more than / go beyond | ☐☐☐☐☐ |

| **compose of** | 由···组成 | 记忆尺 |
| | make up of | ☐☐☐☐☐ |

| **extract** | v. 提取 | 记忆尺 |
| ['ekstrækt] | remove | ☐☐☐☐☐ |

| **pioneering** | adj. 先驱的 | 记忆尺 |
| [ˌpaɪə'nɪrɪŋ] | original | ☐☐☐☐☐ |

pioneer	v. 开拓	记忆尺
[ˌpaɪə'nɪr]	introduce	
	n. 先锋	☐☐☐☐☐
	leader	

| **bare** | adj. 光秃秃的 | 记忆尺 |
| [ber] | be not covered by leaves | ☐☐☐☐☐ |

| **intrigue** | v. 激起兴趣 | 记忆尺 |
| [ɪn'triːg] | interest | ☐☐☐☐☐ |

| **intriguing** | adj. 引人入胜的 | 记忆尺 |
| [ɪn'triːgɪŋ] | fascinating | ☐☐☐☐☐ |

| **revered** | adj. 崇敬的 | 记忆尺 |
| [rɪ'vɪrd] | greatly admired / honored | ☐☐☐☐☐ |

| **impulse to** | 刺激 | 记忆尺 |
| | push toward | ☐☐☐☐☐ |

15

| **impulse** | *n.* 刺激 | 记忆尺 |
| [ˈɪmpʌls] | basic motive | □ □ □ □ □ |

| **potential** | *adj.* 可能的 | 记忆尺 |
| [pəˈtenʃl] | promising / possible / likely | □ □ □ □ □ |

| **appreciably** | *adv.* 显著地 | 记忆尺 |
| [əˈpriːʃəbli] | significantly | □ □ □ □ □ |

| **fluctuation** | *n.* 波动 | 记忆尺 |
| [ˌflʌktʃuˈeɪʃn] | variation | □ □ □ □ □ |

maintain	*v.* 宣称	记忆尺
[meɪnˈteɪn]	claim	□ □ □ □ □
	v. 保持	
	keep	

| **abrupt** | *adj.* 突然的 | 记忆尺 |
| [əˈbrʌpt] | sudden | □ □ □ □ □ |

| **abruptly** | *adv.* 突然 | 记忆尺 |
| [əˈbrʌptli] | suddenly | □ □ □ □ □ |

| **scatter** | *v.* 分散 | 记忆尺 |
| [ˈskætər] | widely separate / spread apart / distribute | □ □ □ □ □ |

| **presume** | *v.* 假定 | 记忆尺 |
| [prɪˈzuːm] | suppose / assume | □ □ □ □ □ |

| **presumably** | *adv.* 大概 | 记忆尺 |
| [prɪˈzuːməbli] | supposedly / most likely / probably / it is reasonable that / it can be assumed | □ □ □ □ □ |

| **drastically** | *adv.* 大幅度地 | 记忆尺 |
| [ˈdræstɪkli] | extremely / severely / extensively | □ □ □ □ □ |

| **conceive** | v. 构思 | 记忆尺 |
| [kən'siːv] | imagine | ☐☐☐☐☐ |

| **conceivable** | adj. 可想象的 | 记忆尺 |
| [kən'siːvəbl] | imaginable | ☐☐☐☐☐ |

advocate	['ædvəkət] n. 支持者	
	supporter	记忆尺
	['ædvəkeɪt] v. 提倡	☐☐☐☐☐
	support / promote	

elaborate	[ɪ'læbərət] adj. 复杂的	
	complex	记忆尺
	[ɪ'læbəreɪt] v. 详细说明	☐☐☐☐☐
	develop	

| **elaborately** | adv. 详细阐述地 | 记忆尺 |
| [ɪ'læbərətli] | with great detail / in detail | ☐☐☐☐☐ |

| **abandon** | v. 放弃 | 记忆尺 |
| [ə'bændən] | give up | ☐☐☐☐☐ |

| **abandoned** | adj. 被抛弃的 | 记忆尺 |
| [ə'bændənd] | left / no longer occupied | ☐☐☐☐☐ |

| **keen** | adj. 敏锐的 | 记忆尺 |
| [kiːn] | sharp / intense | ☐☐☐☐☐ |

| **intend** | v. 打算 | 记忆尺 |
| [ɪn'tend] | plan | ☐☐☐☐☐ |

| **intended** | adj. 渴望的 | 记忆尺 |
| [ɪn'tendɪd] | desired | ☐☐☐☐☐ |

| **secrete** | v. 分泌 | 记忆尺 |
| [sɪ'kriːt] | create | ☐☐☐☐☐ |

formulate ['fɔːrmjuleɪt]	v. 提出 state / construct	记忆尺 ☐☐☐☐☐
feat [fiːt]	n. 功绩 achievement / remarkable achievement	记忆尺 ☐☐☐☐☐
bizarre [bɪ'zɑːr]	adj. 奇怪的 strange	记忆尺 ☐☐☐☐☐
unpredictable [ˌʌnprɪ'dɪktəbl]	adj. 不确定的 uncertain	记忆尺 ☐☐☐☐☐
alter ['ɔːltər]	v. 改变 change / transform	记忆尺 ☐☐☐☐☐
alternate ['ɔːltərnət]	v. 轮流 take turns at	记忆尺 ☐☐☐☐☐
alteration [ˌɔːltə'reɪʃn]	n. 改变 modification / change	记忆尺 ☐☐☐☐☐
alternative [ɔːl'tɜːrnətɪv]	n. 选择 option	记忆尺 ☐☐☐☐☐
unaltered [ʌn'ɔːltərd]	adj. 不变的 unchanged	记忆尺 ☐☐☐☐☐
subdue [səb'duː]	v. 征服 defeat	记忆尺 ☐☐☐☐☐
coincide [ˌkoʊɪn'saɪd]	v. 巧合 take place at the same time	记忆尺 ☐☐☐☐☐
coincide with	与…一致 occur at the same time as / correspond to	记忆尺 ☐☐☐☐☐

coincidence
[koʊˈɪnsɪdəns]

n. 巧合

at the same time and by chance

记忆尺

☐ ☐ ☐ ☐ ☐

self-sufficient
[ˌselfsəˈfɪʃnt]

adj. 自立的

independent

记忆尺

☐ ☐ ☐ ☐ ☐

property ['prɑːpərti]	释 *n.* 特征 同 characteristic	记忆尺 ☐☐☐☐☐
substantially [səb'stænʃəli]	释 *adv.* 极大地 同 significantly / largely / considerably	记忆尺 ☐☐☐☐☐
allege [ə'ledʒ]	释 *v.* 断言 同 assert / suppose	记忆尺 ☐☐☐☐☐
allegedly [ə'ledʒɪdli]	释 *adv.* 据说 同 supposedly	记忆尺 ☐☐☐☐☐
ideal [aɪ'diːəl]	释 *adj.* 理想的 同 perfect	记忆尺 ☐☐☐☐☐
ideally [aɪ'diːəli]	释 *adv.* 理想地 同 perfectly	记忆尺 ☐☐☐☐☐
capacity [kə'pæsəti]	释 *n.* 能力 同 ability 释 *n.* 容量 同 available storage space	记忆尺 ☐☐☐☐☐
durable ['dʊrəbl]	释 *adj.* 耐用的 同 existing for a long time without significant damage / long lasting	记忆尺 ☐☐☐☐☐
hasten ['heɪsn]	释 *v.* 催促 同 speed up / hurry / rush / accelerate	记忆尺 ☐☐☐☐☐

| allied | adj. 联合的 | 记忆尺 |
| ['ælaɪd] | related | ☐ ☐ ☐ ☐ ☐ |

| compilation | n. 编纂 | 记忆尺 |
| [ˌkɑːmpɪ'leɪʃn] | collection | ☐ ☐ ☐ ☐ ☐ |

| disperse | v. 扩散 | 记忆尺 |
| [dɪ'spɜːrs] | spread / scatter / spread out | ☐ ☐ ☐ ☐ ☐ |

| dispersal | n. 扩散 | 记忆尺 |
| [dɪ'spɜːrsl] | distribution | ☐ ☐ ☐ ☐ ☐ |

| elevate | v. 举起 | 记忆尺 |
| ['elɪveɪt] | raise | ☐ ☐ ☐ ☐ ☐ |

| elevated | adj. 高的 | 记忆尺 |
| ['elɪveɪtɪd] | high | ☐ ☐ ☐ ☐ ☐ |

| inconclusive | adj. 非决定性的 | 记忆尺 |
| [ˌɪnkən'kluːsɪv] | not definitive / not decisive | ☐ ☐ ☐ ☐ ☐ |

| unethical | adj. 不道德的 | 记忆尺 |
| [ʌn'eθɪkl] | improper | ☐ ☐ ☐ ☐ ☐ |

| cycle | n. 循环 | 记忆尺 |
| ['saɪkl] | pattern of events that repeat themselves | ☐ ☐ ☐ ☐ ☐ |

| succeeding | adj. 以后的 | 记忆尺 |
| [sək'sidɪŋ] | following | ☐ ☐ ☐ ☐ ☐ |

| persuasive | adj. 有说服力的 | 记忆尺 |
| [pər'sweɪsɪv] | convincing | ☐ ☐ ☐ ☐ ☐ |

| corroborate | v. 确认 | 记忆尺 |
| [kə'rɑːbəreɪt] | confirm | ☐ ☐ ☐ ☐ ☐ |

install [ɪnˈstɔːl]	*v.* 安装 put in place	记忆尺 □□□□□
hierarchy [ˈhaɪəraːrki]	*n.* 等级制度 system of ranking	记忆尺 □□□□□
hierarchical [ˌhaɪəˈraːrkɪkl]	*adj.* 等级（制度）的 having several levels of authority	记忆尺 □□□□□
initiate [ɪˈnɪʃieɪt]	*v.* 开始 introduce / begin / start	记忆尺 □□□□□
related to	关于 in proportion to	记忆尺 □□□□□
be distracted by an unfamiliar stimulus	干扰 the stimulus shifts attention of	记忆尺 □□□□□
distinct [dɪˈstɪŋkt]	*adj.* 不同的 separate / clear	记忆尺 □□□□□
distinction [dɪˈstɪŋkʃn]	*n.* 差别 difference	记忆尺 □□□□□
promote [prəˈmoʊt]	*v.* 推动 encourage	记忆尺 □□□□□
favorable [ˈfeɪvərəbl]	*adj.* 有利的 advantageous	记忆尺 □□□□□
unfavorable [ʌnˈfeɪvərəbl]	*adj.* 不利的 disadvantageous / negative	记忆尺 □□□□□
reinforce [ˌriːɪnˈfɔːrs]	*v.* 加强 make stronger / support / strengthen	记忆尺 □□□□□

22

| **superficially** | *adv.* 浅薄地 | 记忆尺 |
| [ˌsuːpərˈfɪʃəli] | on the first impression / without deeper analysis | ☐☐☐☐☐ |

| **mutual** | *adj.* 相互的 | 记忆尺 |
| [ˈmjuːtʃuəl] | shared | ☐☐☐☐☐ |

| **specified** | *adj.* 指定的 | 记忆尺 |
| [ˈspesɪfaɪd] | stated / typical | ☐☐☐☐☐ |

| **booming** | *adj.* 激增的 | 记忆尺 |
| [buːmɪŋ] | rapidly growing | ☐☐☐☐☐ |

| **anticipate** | *v.* 预期 | 记忆尺 |
| [ænˈtɪsɪpeɪt] | expect / predict | ☐☐☐☐☐ |

| **unanticipated** | *adj.* 意料之外的 | 记忆尺 |
| [ˌʌnænˈtɪsɪpeɪtɪd] | not expected | ☐☐☐☐☐ |

| **intrusive** | *adj.* 侵入的 | 记忆尺 |
| [ɪnˈtruːsɪv] | unwelcome | ☐☐☐☐☐ |

| **constituent** | *n.* 构成部分 | 记忆尺 |
| [kənˈstɪtʃuənt] | component | ☐☐☐☐☐ |

| **gradual** | *adj.* 渐进的 | 记忆尺 |
| [ˈɡrædʒuəl] | slow | ☐☐☐☐☐ |

| **diffuse** | *v.* 扩散 | 记忆尺 |
| [dɪˈfjuːs] | spread | ☐☐☐☐☐ |

| **diffusion** | *n.* 扩散 | 记忆尺 |
| [dɪˈfjuːʒn] | dispersal | ☐☐☐☐☐ |

| **customarily** | *adv.* 通常来讲 | 记忆尺 |
| [ˌkʌstəˈmerəli] | commonly / usually | ☐☐☐☐☐ |

artificial [ˌɑːrtɪˈfɪʃl]	*adj.* 人造的 manmade / made by humans / human-made / not real	记忆尺 □ □ □ □ □
barring [ˈbɑːrɪŋ]	*prep.* 除了 except for	记忆尺 □ □ □ □ □
classic [ˈklæsɪk]	*adj.* 经典的、典型的 typical	记忆尺 □ □ □ □ □
collective [kəˈlektɪv]	*n.* 集体 group	记忆尺 □ □ □ □ □
fabricate [ˈfæbrɪkeɪt]	*v.* 制造 produce	记忆尺 □ □ □ □ □
intact [ɪnˈtækt]	*adj.* 完整的 in complete form / whole / complete / undamaged / without breaking into pieces	记忆尺 □ □ □ □ □
ringed [rɪŋd]	*adj.* 环形的 ring-shaped / surrounded	记忆尺 □ □ □ □ □
contract to	缩减 reduce to	记忆尺 □ □ □ □ □
evolve [iˈvɑːlv]	*v.* 进化 develop	记忆尺 □ □ □ □ □
exclude [ɪkˈskluːd]	*v.* 排除 keep out / remove	记忆尺 □ □ □ □ □
fortunately [ˈfɔːrtʃənətli]	*adv.* 幸运地 luckily	记忆尺 □ □ □ □ □

mundane

[mʌn'deɪn]

adj. 平凡的

ordinary

记忆尺

☐ ☐ ☐ ☐ ☐

resolve

[rɪ'zaːlv]

v. 解决

settle

记忆尺

☐ ☐ ☐ ☐ ☐

seldom

['seldəm]

adv. 很少

rarely / not often

记忆尺

☐ ☐ ☐ ☐ ☐

| **sparse** | adj. 稀疏的 | 记忆尺 |
| [spɑːrs] | thinly distributed | ☐ ☐ ☐ ☐ ☐ |

| **sparsely** | adv. 稀疏地 | 记忆尺 |
| ['spɑːrsli] | thinly | ☐ ☐ ☐ ☐ ☐ |

| **advantageous** | adj. 有利的 | 记忆尺 |
| [ˌædvən'teɪdʒəs] | favorable / beneficial | ☐ ☐ ☐ ☐ ☐ |

| **congestion** | n. 拥挤 | 记忆尺 |
| [kən'dʒestʃən] | overcrowding | ☐ ☐ ☐ ☐ ☐ |

| **continually** | adv. 持续地 | 记忆尺 |
| [kən'tɪnjuəli] | regularly | ☐ ☐ ☐ ☐ ☐ |

| **discontent** | adj. 不满的 | 记忆尺 |
| [ˌdɪskən'tent] | unhappy | ☐ ☐ ☐ ☐ ☐ |

| **eradicate** | v. 消除 | 记忆尺 |
| [ɪ'rædɪkeɪt] | eliminate | ☐ ☐ ☐ ☐ ☐ |

| **facilitate** | v. 使…容易 | 记忆尺 |
| [fə'sɪlɪteɪt] | make easier / ease | ☐ ☐ ☐ ☐ ☐ |

| **obvious** | adj. 明显的 | 记忆尺 |
| ['ɑːbviəs] | visible / clear | ☐ ☐ ☐ ☐ ☐ |

| **retain** | v. 保留 | 记忆尺 |
| [rɪ'teɪn] | keep / preserve / maintain | ☐ ☐ ☐ ☐ ☐ |

vigorous	adj. 有活力的	记忆尺
['vɪgərəs]	energetic / strong / lively	☐☐☐☐☐

vigorously	adv. 有活力地	记忆尺
['vɪgərəsli]	strongly and healthily	☐☐☐☐☐

compact	[kəm'pækt] v. 压紧	记忆尺
	press together	
	['kɑːmpækt] adj. 紧密的	☐☐☐☐☐
	hard	

construct	v. 建造	记忆尺
[kən'strʌkt]	create	☐☐☐☐☐

distort	v. 曲解	记忆尺
[dɪ'stɔːrt]	misinterpret	☐☐☐☐☐

distortion	n. 扭曲	记忆尺
[dɪ'stɔːrʃn]	irregularity	☐☐☐☐☐

explicit	adj. 明确的	记忆尺
[ɪk'splɪsɪt]	clearly stated / clearly expressed / clear	☐☐☐☐☐

lucrative	adj. 有利可图的	记忆尺
['luːkrətɪv]	profitable	☐☐☐☐☐

peculiar	adj. 独特的	记忆尺
[pɪ'kjuːliər]	unusual / unique	☐☐☐☐☐

precede	v. 在…之前发生	记忆尺
[prɪ'siːd]	occur before	☐☐☐☐☐

sensitive to	敏感的	记忆尺
	affected by	☐☐☐☐☐

suspicion	n. 怀疑	记忆尺
[sə'spɪʃn]	distrust	☐☐☐☐☐

| **temporarily** | *adv.* 暂时 | 记忆尺 |
| [ˌtempə'rerəli] | briefly | ☐ ☐ ☐ ☐ ☐ |

| **temporary** | *adj.* 暂时的 | 记忆尺 |
| ['tempəreri] | short-term | ☐ ☐ ☐ ☐ ☐ |

aggregation	*n.* 聚集	记忆尺
[ˌægrɪ'geɪʃn]	collection / accumulation	☐ ☐ ☐ ☐ ☐
	n. 集体	
	group	

| **cluster** | *v.* 簇拥 | 记忆尺 |
| ['klʌstər] | group | ☐ ☐ ☐ ☐ ☐ |

| **continuous** | *adj.* 连续的 | 记忆尺 |
| [kən'tɪnjuəs] | unceasing / uninterrupted | ☐ ☐ ☐ ☐ ☐ |

| **exploit** | *v.* 利用 | 记忆尺 |
| [ɪk'splɔɪt] | make use of / use / take advantage of / utilize | ☐ ☐ ☐ ☐ ☐ |

implement	['ɪmplɪmənt] *n.* 工具	记忆尺
	tool	
	['ɪmplɪment] *v.* 实施	☐ ☐ ☐ ☐ ☐
	put into effect	

| **instrument** | *n.* 工具 | 记忆尺 |
| ['ɪnstrəmənt] | tool | ☐ ☐ ☐ ☐ ☐ |

| **be entitled to** | 有资格… | 记忆尺 |
| | be given the right to | ☐ ☐ ☐ ☐ ☐ |

| **justifiable** | *adj.* 正当的 | 记忆尺 |
| [ˌdʒʌstɪ'faɪəbl] | reasonable | ☐ ☐ ☐ ☐ ☐ |

| **justification** | *n.* 理由 | 记忆尺 |
| [ˌdʒʌstifi'keɪʃn] | reason | ☐ ☐ ☐ ☐ ☐ |

repulse [rɪ'pʌls]	v. 击退 drive back	记忆尺 ☐☐☐☐☐	

repulse
[rɪ'pʌls]
v. 击退
drive back
记忆尺 ☐☐☐☐☐

strenuous
['strenjuəs]
adj. 费力的
arduous
记忆尺 ☐☐☐☐☐

transparent
[træns'pærənt]
adj. 透明的
visible / can be seen through
记忆尺 ☐☐☐☐☐

allow for
允许
make possible
记忆尺 ☐☐☐☐☐

assume
[ə'suːm]
v. 承担
take on
v. 假定
believe / suppose
记忆尺 ☐☐☐☐☐

attribute
[ə'trɪbjuːt] v. 把…归因于
ascribe / credit / be responsible for
['ætrɪbjuːt] n. 特征
property / characteristic
记忆尺 ☐☐☐☐☐

critical
['krɪtɪkl]
adj. 极重要的
essential / crucial
记忆尺 ☐☐☐☐☐

furnish
['fɜːrnɪʃ]
v. 装备
equip
记忆尺 ☐☐☐☐☐

implication
[ˌɪmplɪ'keɪʃn]
n. 影响
consequence / significance
记忆尺 ☐☐☐☐☐

unceasing
[ʌn'siːsɪŋ]
adj. 连续的
continual
记忆尺 ☐☐☐☐☐

witness
['wɪtnəs]
v. 见证
experience
记忆尺 ☐☐☐☐☐

autonomy

[ɔːˈtɑːnəmi]

n. 自治

independence / self-rule

记忆尺

☐ ☐ ☐ ☐ ☐

autonomous

[ɔːˈtɑːnəməs]

adj. 自主的

independent

记忆尺

☐ ☐ ☐ ☐ ☐

besides

[bɪˈsaɪdz]

prep. 除…之外

in addition

记忆尺

☐ ☐ ☐ ☐ ☐

comprise

[kəmˈpraɪz]

v. 构成

consist of

记忆尺

☐ ☐ ☐ ☐ ☐

congregate

[ˈkɑːŋɡrɪɡeɪt]

v. 聚集

gather

记忆尺

☐ ☐ ☐ ☐ ☐

consequence

[ˈkɑːnsəkwens]

n. 结果

result

记忆尺

☐ ☐ ☐ ☐ ☐

couple with

与…相结合

combine with / add to

记忆尺

☐ ☐ ☐ ☐ ☐

preoccupation

[pri,ɑːkjuˈpeɪʃn]

n. 关注

concern

记忆尺

☐ ☐ ☐ ☐ ☐

prevail

[prɪˈveɪl]

v. 占优势

dominate

记忆尺

☐ ☐ ☐ ☐ ☐

prevailing

[prɪˈveɪlɪŋ]

adj. 盛行的

dominant / generally accepted / convincing

记忆尺

☐ ☐ ☐ ☐ ☐

absolutely

[ˈæbsəluːtli]

adv. 绝对

definitely

记忆尺

☐ ☐ ☐ ☐ ☐

acute

[əˈkjuːt]

adj. 剧烈的

severe

记忆尺

☐ ☐ ☐ ☐ ☐

adversely
[əd'vɜːrsli]

adv. 不利地
negatively

记忆尺
☐ ☐ ☐ ☐ ☐

characteristic
[ˌkærəktə'rɪstɪk]

adj. 独特的
typical

记忆尺
☐ ☐ ☐ ☐ ☐

音频

induce [ɪn'duːs]	v. 导致 cause / cause the formation of / increase / stimulate	记忆尺 ☐ ☐ ☐ ☐ ☐
inevitable [ɪn'evitəbl]	adj. 不可避免的 unavoidable / certain / necessary	记忆尺 ☐ ☐ ☐ ☐ ☐
accommodate [ə'kɑːmədeɪt]	v. 顺应 allow	记忆尺 ☐ ☐ ☐ ☐ ☐
modest ['mɑːdɪst]	adj. 适度的 reasonable / small / moderate / not large	记忆尺 ☐ ☐ ☐ ☐ ☐
persistently [pər'sɪstəntli]	adv. 持续地 constantly	记忆尺 ☐ ☐ ☐ ☐ ☐
be persistently viewed	被持续观看 continue to be viewed	记忆尺 ☐ ☐ ☐ ☐ ☐
prerequisite [ˌpriː'rekwəzɪt]	adj. 必要的 necessary n. 必要条件 requirement	记忆尺 ☐ ☐ ☐ ☐ ☐
rigid ['rɪdʒɪd]	adj. 死板的 fixed	记忆尺 ☐ ☐ ☐ ☐ ☐
straightforward [ˌstreɪt'fɔːrwərd]	adj. 简单的 simple	记忆尺 ☐ ☐ ☐ ☐ ☐

| **sustain** | *v.* 支持 | 记忆尺 |
| [sə'steɪn] | support / maintain | ☐☐☐☐☐ |

| **underlying** | *adj.* 基本的 | 记忆尺 |
| ['ʌndər‚laɪɪŋ] | basic | ☐☐☐☐☐ |

| **with regard for** | 关注 | 记忆尺 |
| | concern for | ☐☐☐☐☐ |

| **dismiss** | *v.* 驳回 | 记忆尺 |
| [dɪs'mɪs] | reject | ☐☐☐☐☐ |

| **flee** | *v.* 逃走 | 记忆尺 |
| [fliː] | run away | ☐☐☐☐☐ |

| **nevertheless** | *conj.* 然而 | 记忆尺 |
| [‚nevərðə'les] | even so / however | ☐☐☐☐☐ |

parallel	*v.* 与…同时发生	
	happen at the same time and rate	记忆尺
['pærəlel]	*v.* 比得上	☐☐☐☐☐
	match	

| **sabotage** | *v.* （故意）伤害 | 记忆尺 |
| ['sæbətɑːʒ] | intentionally damage / damage | ☐☐☐☐☐ |

| **systematically** | *adv.* 系统地 | 记忆尺 |
| [‚sɪstə'mætɪkli] | methodically | ☐☐☐☐☐ |

| **burgeoning** | *adj.* 迅速发展的 | 记忆尺 |
| ['bɜːrdʒənɪŋ] | increasingly expanding | ☐☐☐☐☐ |

| **confirm** | *v.* 证实 | 记忆尺 |
| [kən'fɜːrm] | prove | ☐☐☐☐☐ |

| **decipher** | *v.* 破译 | 记忆尺 |
| [dɪ'saɪfər] | figure out | ☐☐☐☐☐ |

| **derive from** | v. 获取 | 记忆尺 |
| | obtain/gain from | ☐ ☐ ☐ ☐ ☐ |

| **fleeting** | adj. 短暂的 | 记忆尺 |
| ['fliːtɪŋ] | brief | ☐ ☐ ☐ ☐ ☐ |

| **fluctuation** | n. 变动 | 记忆尺 |
| [ˌflʌktʃu'eɪʃn] | variation | ☐ ☐ ☐ ☐ ☐ |

| **fluctuate** | v. 波动 | 记忆尺 |
| ['flʌktʃueɪt] | vary | ☐ ☐ ☐ ☐ ☐ |

| **impede** | v. 限制 | 记忆尺 |
| [ɪm'piːd] | restrict / inhibit | ☐ ☐ ☐ ☐ ☐ |

| **inhibit** | v. 限制 | 记忆尺 |
| [ɪn'hɪbɪt] | slow down / restrict | ☐ ☐ ☐ ☐ ☐ |

| **restrict** | v. 限制 | 记忆尺 |
| [rɪ'strɪkt] | limit | ☐ ☐ ☐ ☐ ☐ |

| **keep in check** | 限制 | 记忆尺 |
| | limit | ☐ ☐ ☐ ☐ ☐ |

| **check** | n. 阻碍 | 记忆尺 |
| [tʃek] | limit | ☐ ☐ ☐ ☐ ☐ |

| **in profile** | 从侧面看 | 记忆尺 |
| | view from the side | ☐ ☐ ☐ ☐ ☐ |

| **appreciation** | n. 理解 | 记忆尺 |
| [əˌpriːʃi'eɪʃn] | recognition | ☐ ☐ ☐ ☐ ☐ |

| **ornament** | v. 装饰 | 记忆尺 |
| ['ɔːrnəmənt] | decorate | ☐ ☐ ☐ ☐ ☐ |

| **peak** | n. 巅峰 | 记忆尺 |
| [piːk] | the highest point / maximum | ☐ ☐ ☐ ☐ ☐ |

| **proliferate** | v. 猛增 | 记忆尺 |
| [prəˈlɪfəreɪt] | increase quickly | ☐☐☐☐☐ |

| **proliferation** | n. 猛增 | 记忆尺 |
| [prəˌlɪfəˈreɪʃn] | increase / growth | ☐☐☐☐☐ |

| **sleek** | adj. 光滑的 | 记忆尺 |
| [sliːk] | smooth | ☐☐☐☐☐ |

| **seek** | v. 寻求 | 记忆尺 |
| [siːk] | try to obtain | ☐☐☐☐☐ |

| **see for** | 寻求 | 记忆尺 |
| | desire | ☐☐☐☐☐ |

| **spectacular** | adj. 引人入胜的 | 记忆尺 |
| [spekˈtækjələr] | remarkable | ☐☐☐☐☐ |

| **stamina** | n. 耐力 | 记忆尺 |
| [ˈstæmɪnə] | endurance | ☐☐☐☐☐ |

| **subtly** | adv. 微妙地 | 记忆尺 |
| [ˈsʌtli] | slightly | ☐☐☐☐☐ |

| **uniformly** | adv. 一致地 | 记忆尺 |
| [ˈjuːnɪfɔːrmli] | consistently / completely | ☐☐☐☐☐ |

| **worshiper** | n. 崇拜者 | 记忆尺 |
| [ˈwɜːrʃɪpər] | who visit the temples | ☐☐☐☐☐ |

| **aim to do** | 打算做… | 记忆尺 |
| | intend to do | ☐☐☐☐☐ |

| **enduring** | adj. 持久的 | 记忆尺 |
| [ɪnˈdʊrɪŋ] | lasting | ☐☐☐☐☐ |

		记忆尺
endure	*v.* 持续存在	
[ɪnˈdʊr]	survive	☐ ☐ ☐ ☐ ☐
	v. 承受	
	withstand	
foundation	*n.* 基本	记忆尺
[faʊnˈdeɪʃn]	basis	☐ ☐ ☐ ☐ ☐
a foundation in	基础	记忆尺
	a basis in	☐ ☐ ☐ ☐ ☐
fulfill	*v.* 完成	记忆尺
[fʊlˈfɪl]	perform / achieve	☐ ☐ ☐ ☐ ☐
function	*n.* 作用	记忆尺
[ˈfʌŋkʃn]	role / purpose	☐ ☐ ☐ ☐ ☐
mask	*v.* 隐藏	记忆尺
[mæsk]	hide	☐ ☐ ☐ ☐ ☐
motive	*n.* 动力	记忆尺
[ˈmoʊtɪv]	reason	☐ ☐ ☐ ☐ ☐
recommend	*v.* 推荐	记忆尺
[ˌrekəˈmend]	support	☐ ☐ ☐ ☐ ☐
sophisticated	*adj.* 复杂的	记忆尺
[səˈfɪstɪkeɪtɪd]	complex	☐ ☐ ☐ ☐ ☐
	adj. 高级的	
	highly developed	
controversial	*adj.* 有争议的	记忆尺
[ˌkɑːntrəˈvɜːrʃl]	debated / producing disagreement / debatable	☐ ☐ ☐ ☐ ☐
diminish	*v.* 减少	记忆尺
[dɪˈmɪnɪʃ]	reduce	☐ ☐ ☐ ☐ ☐

divert

[daɪ'vɜːrt]

v. 转移

redirect / shift

记忆尺

☐ ☐ ☐ ☐ ☐

excessive

[ɪk'sesɪv]

adj. 过量的

too much

记忆尺

☐ ☐ ☐ ☐ ☐

音 频

| **live in strictly aquatic habitat** | 翻 只生活在水生环境中 | 记忆尺 |
| | 同 only live in aquatic environment | ▢▢▢▢▢ |

readily ['redli]	翻 *adv.* 迅速地	
	同 quickly	记忆尺
	翻 *adv.* 轻易地	▢▢▢▢▢
	同 easily	

| **widespread** ['waɪdspred] | 翻 *adj.* 普遍的 | 记忆尺 |
| | 同 common / prevalent / pervasive | ▢▢▢▢▢ |

| **as opposed to** | 翻 对比 | 记忆尺 |
| | 同 in contrast to | ▢▢▢▢▢ |

| **associate (with)** | 翻 *v.* 联系 | 记忆尺 |
| | 同 relate (to) / connect (to) | ▢▢▢▢▢ |

| **attest to** | 翻 证实 | 记忆尺 |
| | 同 provide evidence of / confirm | ▢▢▢▢▢ |

| **configuration** [kən,fɪgjə'reɪʃn] | 翻 *n.* 结构 | 记忆尺 |
| | 同 arrangement / shape | ▢▢▢▢▢ |

| **distinctive** [dɪ'stɪŋktɪv] | 翻 *adj.* 独特的 | 记忆尺 |
| | 同 recognizable / characteristic | ▢▢▢▢▢ |

| **fragment** ['frægmənt] | 翻 *n.* 碎片 | 记忆尺 |
| | 同 piece | ▢▢▢▢▢ |

painstaking	adj. 不辞辛苦的	记忆尺	
['peɪnzteɪkɪŋ]	with great effort	☐☐☐☐☐	
baffle	v. 使困惑	记忆尺	
['bæfl]	puzzle	☐☐☐☐☐	
discard	v. 抛弃	记忆尺	
[dɪ'skaːrd]	abandon / throw away	☐☐☐☐☐	
impressive	adj. 令人印象深刻的	记忆尺	
[ɪm'presɪv]	striking	☐☐☐☐☐	
periodically	adv. 周期性地	记忆尺	
[ˌpɪri'aːdɪkli]	at regular intervals of time / regularly	☐☐☐☐☐	
rule out	排除	记忆尺	
	exclude	☐☐☐☐☐	
enable	v. 使能够	记忆尺	
[ɪ'neɪbl]	allow	☐☐☐☐☐	
irritating	adj. 令人恼怒的	记忆尺	
['ɪrɪteɪtɪŋ]	annoying	☐☐☐☐☐	
renew	v. 恢复	记忆尺	
[rɪ'nuː]	restore	☐☐☐☐☐	
skepticism	n. 怀疑	记忆尺	
['skeptɪsɪzəm]	doubt	☐☐☐☐☐	
skeptical	adj. 怀疑的	记忆尺	
['skeptɪkl]	doubtful	☐☐☐☐☐	
slightly	adv. 少量地	记忆尺	
['slaɪtli]	by very small amounts	☐☐☐☐☐	
slight	adj. 轻微的	记忆尺	
[slaɪt]	small	☐☐☐☐☐	

ardent	*adj.* 热烈的	记忆尺	
[ˈɑːrdnt]	enthusiastic	☐☐☐☐☐	
back up	支持	记忆尺	
	support	☐☐☐☐☐	
confine	*v.* 限制	记忆尺	
[kənˈfaɪn]	restrict	☐☐☐☐☐	
in essence	本质上	记忆尺	
	basically	☐☐☐☐☐	
lone	*adj.* 单个的	记忆尺	
[loʊn]	single	☐☐☐☐☐	
resemble	*v.* 相似	记忆尺	
[rɪˈzembl]	look like	☐☐☐☐☐	
scanty	*adj.* 少的	记忆尺	
[ˈskænti]	few / thin	☐☐☐☐☐	
conducive	*adj.* 有助于…的	记忆尺	
[kənˈduːsɪv]	favorable to	☐☐☐☐☐	
dramatic	*adj.* 显著的	记忆尺	
[drəˈmætɪk]	striking / powerful	☐☐☐☐☐	
dramatically	*adv.* 显著地	记忆尺	
[drəˈmætɪkli]	greatly	☐☐☐☐☐	
exceptional	*adj.* 特别的	记忆尺	
[ɪkˈsepʃənl]	extraordinary	☐☐☐☐☐	
generally	*adv.* 通常	记忆尺	
[ˈdʒenrəli]	usually	☐☐☐☐☐	
generate	*v.* 产生	记忆尺	
[ˈdʒenəreɪt]	produce	☐☐☐☐☐	

perplex [pər'pleks]	v. 使…迷惑 puzzle	记忆尺 ☐ ☐ ☐ ☐ ☐
quest [kwest]	v. 探索 search	记忆尺 ☐ ☐ ☐ ☐ ☐
tend [tend]	v. 照料 take care of	记忆尺 ☐ ☐ ☐ ☐ ☐
adapt [ə'dæpt]	v. 适应 adjust	记忆尺 ☐ ☐ ☐ ☐ ☐
component [kəm'poʊnənt]	n. 构成部分 piece / part	记忆尺 ☐ ☐ ☐ ☐ ☐
invariably [ɪn'veriəbli]	adv. 一贯 always	记忆尺 ☐ ☐ ☐ ☐ ☐
constraint [kən'streɪnt]	n. 限制 limitation	记忆尺 ☐ ☐ ☐ ☐ ☐
consumption [kən'sʌmpʃn]	n. 消耗 use of products and services / utilization	记忆尺 ☐ ☐ ☐ ☐ ☐
in principle	原则上 theoretically	记忆尺 ☐ ☐ ☐ ☐ ☐
prosperous ['prɑːspərəs]	adj. 富裕的 wealthy	记忆尺 ☐ ☐ ☐ ☐ ☐
surely ['ʃʊrli]	adv. 确定地 certainly	记忆尺 ☐ ☐ ☐ ☐ ☐
the aftermath of a founder event	结果 the situation that results from a founder event	记忆尺 ☐ ☐ ☐ ☐ ☐

| **advent** | n. 到来 | 记忆尺 |
| ['ædvent] | arrival / beginning | □ □ □ □ □ |

| **main component** | 主要部分 | 记忆尺 |
| | steam makes up most of the matter | □ □ □ □ □ |

| **proponent** | n. 支持者 | 记忆尺 |
| [prə'poʊnənt] | supporter | □ □ □ □ □ |

| **scrutiny** | n. 仔细观察 | 记忆尺 |
| ['skruːtəni] | close observation | □ □ □ □ □ |

| **swift** | adj. 快速的 | 记忆尺 |
| [swɪft] | quick / fast | □ □ □ □ □ |

音 频

a good candidate for past life	圃 有早期生命形式 圙 originally had some earthlike forms of life	记忆尺 ☐☐☐☐☐
adequate ['ædɪkwət]	圃 *adj.* 充足的；适当的 圙 suitable	记忆尺 ☐☐☐☐☐
adequately ['ædɪkwətli]	圃 *adv.* 充分地 圙 sufficiently	记忆尺 ☐☐☐☐☐
assess [ə'ses]	圃 *v.* 评估 圙 evaluate	记忆尺 ☐☐☐☐☐
era ['ɪrə]	圃 *n.* 时代 圙 period	记忆尺 ☐☐☐☐☐
founding ['faʊndɪŋ]	圃 *n.* 建立 圙 establishment	记忆尺 ☐☐☐☐☐
massively ['mæsɪvli]	圃 *adv.* 大量地 圙 extensively	记忆尺 ☐☐☐☐☐
massive ['mæsɪv]	圃 *adj.* 巨大的 圙 very large / enormous / huge	记忆尺 ☐☐☐☐☐
pragmatic [præg'mætɪk]	圃 *adj.* 实际的 圙 practical	记忆尺 ☐☐☐☐☐
spurt [spɜːrt]	圃 *n.* 突然爆发 圙 sudden increase	记忆尺 ☐☐☐☐☐

suffice [sə'faɪs]	v. 足够 be enough	记忆尺 ☐ ☐ ☐ ☐ ☐
sufficient [sə'fɪʃnt]	adj. 足够的 enough	记忆尺 ☐ ☐ ☐ ☐ ☐
embrace [ɪm'breɪs]	v. 采用 adopt	记忆尺 ☐ ☐ ☐ ☐ ☐
ignore [ɪg'nɔːr]	v. 忽略 pay no attention to	记忆尺 ☐ ☐ ☐ ☐ ☐
inadvertently [ˌɪnəd'vɜːrtəntli]	adv. 非故意地 unintentionally	记忆尺 ☐ ☐ ☐ ☐ ☐
nominal ['nɑːmɪnl]	adj. 名义上的 named someone as the person in charge but did not give her/him power	记忆尺 ☐ ☐ ☐ ☐ ☐
substantial [səb'stænʃl]	adj. 大量的 large / considerable adj. 重要的 significant	记忆尺 ☐ ☐ ☐ ☐ ☐
a case in point	恰当的例子 a good example	记忆尺 ☐ ☐ ☐ ☐ ☐
bar [bɑːr]	v. 排除 exclude	记忆尺 ☐ ☐ ☐ ☐ ☐
courteous ['kɜːrtiəs]	adj. 礼貌的 polite	记忆尺 ☐ ☐ ☐ ☐ ☐
recognize ['rekəgnaɪz]	v. 承认 accept	记忆尺 ☐ ☐ ☐ ☐ ☐
simultaneously [ˌsaɪml'teɪniəsli]	adv. 同时 at the same time	记忆尺 ☐ ☐ ☐ ☐ ☐

the course of change	变化过程	记忆尺
	the way the change developed	▢▢▢▢▢

appreciate [ə'priːʃieɪt]	v. 了解	记忆尺
	understand	▢▢▢▢▢

margin ['maːrdʒən]	n. 边界	记忆尺
	limit	▢▢▢▢▢

stimulate ['stɪmjuleɪt]	v. 促进	记忆尺
	encourage	▢▢▢▢▢

conduct [kən'dʌkt]	v. 实施	记忆尺
	carry out	▢▢▢▢▢

confine [kən'faɪn]	v. 限制	记忆尺
	limit	▢▢▢▢▢

duration [du'reɪʃn]	n. 持续时间	记忆尺
	length	▢▢▢▢▢

found wanting	缺乏的	记忆尺
	judged inadequate	▢▢▢▢▢

harsh [haːrʃ]	adj. 严酷的	记忆尺
	severe	▢▢▢▢▢

remote [rɪ'moʊt]	adj. 偏远的	记忆尺
	distant / isolated	▢▢▢▢▢

profound [prə'faʊnd]	adj. 强烈的	记忆尺
	very strong / intense	
	adj. 深刻的	▢▢▢▢▢
	far-reaching	

resultant [rɪ'zʌltənt]	adj. 结果的	记忆尺
	consequent	▢▢▢▢▢

result	*n.* 结果	记忆尺
[rɪ'zʌlt]	consequence	☐ ☐ ☐ ☐ ☐
shallow	*adj.* 浅的	记忆尺
['ʃælou]	having little depth	☐ ☐ ☐ ☐ ☐
evenly	*adv.* 平均地	记忆尺
['iːvnli]	equally	☐ ☐ ☐ ☐ ☐
hitherto	*adv.* 直到某时	记忆尺
[ˌhɪðər'tuː]	up till then	☐ ☐ ☐ ☐ ☐
incentive	*n.* 刺激	记忆尺
[ɪn'sentɪv]	motivation	☐ ☐ ☐ ☐ ☐
investigate	*v.* 调查	记忆尺
[ɪn'vestɪgeɪt]	study / examine / look into	☐ ☐ ☐ ☐ ☐
unique	*adj.* 特有的	记忆尺
[ju'niːk]	one-of-a-kind / different from all other	☐ ☐ ☐ ☐ ☐
anxiety	*n.* 忧虑	记忆尺
[æŋ'zaɪəti]	worry	☐ ☐ ☐ ☐ ☐
erase	*v.* 消除	记忆尺
[ɪ'reɪs]	eliminate	☐ ☐ ☐ ☐ ☐
highlight	*v.* 强调	记忆尺
['haɪlaɪt]	emphasize	☐ ☐ ☐ ☐ ☐
trait	*n.* 特征	记忆尺
[treɪt]	feature	☐ ☐ ☐ ☐ ☐
admit	*v.* 承认	记忆尺
[əd'mɪt]	accept the truth of	☐ ☐ ☐ ☐ ☐

| **edible** | *adj.* 可食用的 | 记忆尺 |
| ['edəbl] | fit to be eaten | □□□□□ |

| **indicator** | *n.* 指示 | 记忆尺 |
| ['ɪndɪkeɪtər] | sign | □□□□□ |

| **moreover** | *adv.* 此外 | 记忆尺 |
| [mɔːr'ouvər] | in addition | □□□□□ |

| **propose** | *v.* 提出 | 记忆尺 |
| [prə'pouz] | suggest / offer the theory | □□□□□ |

| **trace** | *n.* 踪迹 | 记忆尺 |
| [treɪs] | evidence | □□□□□ |

accumulate	*v.* 积累	
	build up / increase / gather	记忆尺
[ə'kjuːmjəleɪt]	*v.* 聚集	□□□□□
	collect	

| **commonplace** | *adj.* 普通的 | 记忆尺 |
| ['kaːmənpleɪs] | ordinary | □□□□□ |

| **compatible** | *adj.* 一致的 | 记忆尺 |
| [kəm'pætəbl] | consistent | □□□□□ |

eminent	adj. 卓越的	记忆尺
['emɪnənt]	distinguished	☐☐☐☐☐
excrete	v. 分泌	记忆尺
[ɪk'skriːt]	release	☐☐☐☐☐
hazardous	adj. 冒险的	记忆尺
['hæzərdəs]	dangerous	☐☐☐☐☐
impractical	adj. 不切实际的	记忆尺
[ɪm'præktɪkl]	unrealistic	☐☐☐☐☐
notion	n. 观念	记忆尺
['noʊʃn]	idea	☐☐☐☐☐
optimal	adj. 最佳的	记忆尺
['ɑːptɪməl]	most favorable	☐☐☐☐☐
relatively	adv. 相对地	记忆尺
['relətɪvli]	comparatively	☐☐☐☐☐
relative	adj. 比较的	记忆尺
['relətɪv]	comparable	☐☐☐☐☐
relative to	相对的	记忆尺
	comparable to	☐☐☐☐☐
significant	adj. 重要的	记忆尺
[sɪg'nɪfəkənt]	important / considerable	☐☐☐☐☐

| **stationary** | *adj.* 静止的 | 记忆尺 |
| ['steɪʃəneri] | fixed / unmoving | ☐☐☐☐☐ |

| **accordingly** | *adv.* 相应地 | 记忆尺 |
| [ə'kɔːrdɪŋli] | correspondingly | ☐☐☐☐☐ |

| **conspicuous** | *adj.* 显而易见的 | 记忆尺 |
| [kən'spɪkjuəs] | easily noticed / clearly visible / noticeable | ☐☐☐☐☐ |

| **enormous** | *adj.* 巨大的 | 记忆尺 |
| [ɪ'nɔːrməs] | huge / vast / extremely large | ☐☐☐☐☐ |

| **severely** | *adv.* 严重地 | 记忆尺 |
| [sɪ'vɪrli] | greatly / very seriously | ☐☐☐☐☐ |

severe	*adj.* 极端的	记忆尺
[sɪ'vɪr]	extreme	☐☐☐☐☐
	adj. 严酷的	
	intense	

| **severity** | *n.* 严重（性） | 记忆尺 |
| [sɪ'verəti] | harshness / seriousness | ☐☐☐☐☐ |

surplus	*adj.* 多余的	记忆尺
['sɜːrplʌs]	extra	☐☐☐☐☐
	n. 过剩	
	excess / extra goods / excess quantity	

| **task** | *n.* 任务 | 记忆尺 |
| [tæsk] | job | ☐☐☐☐☐ |

| **trigger** | *v.* 触发 | 记忆尺 |
| ['trɪgər] | initiate / cause | ☐☐☐☐☐ |

conventional [kən'venʃənl]	*adj.* 常规的 standard / traditional / usual	记忆尺 ☐☐☐☐☐
be drawn to	被吸引到 be attracted toward	记忆尺 ☐☐☐☐☐
flourish ['flɜːrɪʃ]	*v.* 繁荣 prosper / do very well / succeed	记忆尺 ☐☐☐☐☐
mimic ['mɪmɪk]	*v.* 模仿 reproduce	记忆尺 ☐☐☐☐☐
stagnation [stæg'neɪʃn]	*n.* 停滞 lack of growth	记忆尺 ☐☐☐☐☐
sustained [sə'steɪnd]	*adj.* 持续的 continued / uninterrupted	记忆尺 ☐☐☐☐☐
considerable [kən'sɪdərəbl]	*adj.* 重大的 significant *adj.* 相当（多、大）的 a large amount of	记忆尺 ☐☐☐☐☐
discrepancy [dɪs'krepənsi]	*n.* 差异 inconsistency	记忆尺 ☐☐☐☐☐
integral ['ɪntɪgrəl]	*adj.* 不可缺少的 essential	记忆尺 ☐☐☐☐☐
mean [miːn]	*adj.* 平均的 average	记忆尺 ☐☐☐☐☐
proper ['prɑːpər]	*adj.* 合适的 appropriate	记忆尺 ☐☐☐☐☐
the lowest effective temperature	最低有效温度 the lowest temperature at which distillation can be accomplished	记忆尺 ☐☐☐☐☐

| **accelerate** | *v.* 加速 | 记忆尺 |
| [ək'seləreɪt] | speed up | ☐☐☐☐☐ |

| **detect** | *v.* 发觉 | 记忆尺 |
| [dɪ'tekt] | sense / discover / find / identify / notice / reveal | ☐☐☐☐☐ |

| **elusive** | *adj.* 难以捉摸的 | 记忆尺 |
| [i'luːsɪv] | hard to identify | ☐☐☐☐☐ |

| **isolate** | *v.* 隔离 | 记忆尺 |
| ['aɪsəleɪt] | separate | ☐☐☐☐☐ |

| **launch** | *v.* 发起 | 记忆尺 |
| [lɔːntʃ] | start | ☐☐☐☐☐ |

| **maintenance of** | 维持 | 记忆尺 |
| | supporting of | ☐☐☐☐☐ |

| **methodically** | *adv.* 有条理地 | 记忆尺 |
| [mə'θɑːdɪkli] | systematically | ☐☐☐☐☐ |

| **overwhelm** | *v.* 压倒 | 记忆尺 |
| [ˌoʊvər'welm] | be too large for | ☐☐☐☐☐ |

| **overwhelming** | *adj.* 压倒性的 | 记忆尺 |
| [ˌoʊvər'welmɪŋ] | powerful | ☐☐☐☐☐ |

| **overwhelmingly** | *adv.* 压倒性地 | 记忆尺 |
| [ˌoʊvər'welmɪŋli] | without doubts | ☐☐☐☐☐ |

| **particular** | *adj.* 特别的 | 记忆尺 |
| [pər'tɪkjələr] | specific | ☐☐☐☐☐ |

| **persuasively** | *adv.* 令人信服地 | 记忆尺 |
| [pər'sweɪsɪvli] | convincingly | ☐☐☐☐☐ |

duplicate ['duːplɪkeɪt]	*v.* 重复 copy / repeat	记忆尺	☐ ☐ ☐ ☐ ☐
extract [ɪk'strækt]	*v.* 提取 remove / take out of	记忆尺	☐ ☐ ☐ ☐ ☐
ingenuity [ˌɪndʒə'nuːəti]	*n.* 机智 cleverness *n.* 心灵手巧，创造性 inventiveness	记忆尺	☐ ☐ ☐ ☐ ☐
ingenious [ɪn'dʒiːniəs]	*adj.* 有独创性的 inventive / clever	记忆尺	☐ ☐ ☐ ☐ ☐
inspect [ɪn'spekt]	*v.* 检查 examine / check	记忆尺	☐ ☐ ☐ ☐ ☐
monotonous [mə'nɑːtənəs]	*adj.* 单调的 unchanging	记忆尺	☐ ☐ ☐ ☐ ☐
replicate ['replɪkeɪt]	*v.* 复制 copy	记忆尺	☐ ☐ ☐ ☐ ☐
typical ['tɪpɪkl]	*adj.* 典型的 common	记忆尺	☐ ☐ ☐ ☐ ☐
authority [ə'θɔːrəti]	*n.* 权威 expert	记忆尺	☐ ☐ ☐ ☐ ☐
magnitude ['mæɡnɪtuːd]	*n.* 大小 size	记忆尺	☐ ☐ ☐ ☐ ☐
proportion [prə'pɔːrʃn]	*n.* 尺寸 size	记忆尺	☐ ☐ ☐ ☐ ☐

Word List 10

音频

remarkable [rɪˈmɑːrkəbl]	圖 *adj.* 非凡的 回 extraordinary	记忆尺 ☐☐☐☐☐
combination [ˌkɑːmbɪˈneɪʃn]	圖 *n.* 结合 回 mix	记忆尺 ☐☐☐☐☐
criterion [kraɪˈtɪriən]	圖 *n.* 标准 回 standard	记忆尺 ☐☐☐☐☐
deliberately [dɪˈlɪbərətli]	圖 *adv.* 故意地 回 intentionally / purposely	记忆尺 ☐☐☐☐☐
intermittent [ˌɪntərˈmɪtənt]	圖 *adj.* 间歇性的 回 start and stop often	记忆尺 ☐☐☐☐☐
intermittently [ˌɪntərˈmɪtəntli]	圖 *adv.* 断断续续地 回 periodically	记忆尺 ☐☐☐☐☐
predominant [prɪˈdɑːmɪnənt]	圖 *adj.* 主要的 回 major / principal	记忆尺 ☐☐☐☐☐
predominantly [prɪˈdɑːmɪnəntli]	圖 *adv.* 主要地 回 mainly	记忆尺 ☐☐☐☐☐
breakthrough [ˈbreɪkθruː]	圖 *n.* 突破 回 development	记忆尺 ☐☐☐☐☐
contradictory [ˌkɑːntrəˈdɪktəri]	圖 *adj.* 相互矛盾的 回 conflicting	记忆尺 ☐☐☐☐☐

counter ['kaʊntər]	v. 对抗 combat / act against / argue back	记忆尺 ☐ ☐ ☐ ☐ ☐
manifestation [ˌmænɪfe'steɪʃn]	n. 表现 expression	记忆尺 ☐ ☐ ☐ ☐ ☐
invite [ɪn'vaɪt]	v. 引发 encourage	记忆尺 ☐ ☐ ☐ ☐ ☐
suspect [sə'spekt]	v. 怀疑 doubt	记忆尺 ☐ ☐ ☐ ☐ ☐
ambiguous [æm'bɪgjuəs]	adj. 模糊的 unclear	记忆尺 ☐ ☐ ☐ ☐ ☐
annihilate [ə'naɪəleɪt]	v. 消灭 destroy / conquer	记忆尺 ☐ ☐ ☐ ☐ ☐
augment [ɔːg'ment]	v. 增加 add to / increase	记忆尺 ☐ ☐ ☐ ☐ ☐
convey [kən'veɪ]	v. 传播 transmit	记忆尺 ☐ ☐ ☐ ☐ ☐
cumulative ['kjuːmjəleɪtɪv]	adj. 积累的 combined	记忆尺 ☐ ☐ ☐ ☐ ☐
cumulatively ['kjuːmjəleɪtɪvli]	adv. 累积地 altogether	记忆尺 ☐ ☐ ☐ ☐ ☐
at intervals	有间隔地 periodically	记忆尺 ☐ ☐ ☐ ☐ ☐
correspond to	相当于 equal / match	记忆尺 ☐ ☐ ☐ ☐ ☐
episode ['epɪsoʊd]	n. 事件 occurrence / event	记忆尺 ☐ ☐ ☐ ☐ ☐

| prolific | adj. 多产的 | 记忆尺 |
| [prə'lɪfɪk] | highly productive | ☐☐☐☐☐ |

| the norm | 常态 | 记忆尺 |
| | common | ☐☐☐☐☐ |

| complexity | n. 复杂（性） | 记忆尺 |
| [kəm'pleksəti] | sophistication | ☐☐☐☐☐ |

complex	n. 复合体	记忆尺
[kɑːm'pleks]	system	
	adj. 复杂的	☐☐☐☐☐
	elaborate	

| ongoing | adj. 持续的 | 记忆尺 |
| ['ɑːngoʊɪŋ] | continuing | ☐☐☐☐☐ |

| scarcity of | 缺乏 | 记忆尺 |
| | lack in | ☐☐☐☐☐ |

| scarcity | n. 缺乏 | 记忆尺 |
| ['skersəti] | lack | ☐☐☐☐☐ |

| scarce | adj. 缺乏的 | 记忆尺 |
| [skers] | rare / short in supply | ☐☐☐☐☐ |

| mobilize | v. 发动 | 记忆尺 |
| ['moʊbəlaɪz] | put into action | ☐☐☐☐☐ |

| akin to | 与…类似的 | 记忆尺 |
| | similar to | ☐☐☐☐☐ |

| plentiful | adj. 大量的 | 记忆尺 |
| ['plentɪfl] | numerous | ☐☐☐☐☐ |

| routinely | adv. 常规地 | 记忆尺 |
| [ruː'tiːnli] | regularly | ☐☐☐☐☐ |

altogether [ˌɔːltə'geðər]	*adv.* 完全 fully	记忆尺 ☐☐☐☐☐
approximate [ə'prɑːksɪmeɪt]	*v.* 近似 resemble	记忆尺 ☐☐☐☐☐
in profusion	大量地 abundantly	记忆尺 ☐☐☐☐☐
convert [kən'vɜːrt]	*v.* 转变 change	记忆尺 ☐☐☐☐☐
equivalent [ɪ'kwɪvələnt]	*adj.* 可比较的 comparable	记忆尺 ☐☐☐☐☐
obscure [əb'skjʊr]	*v.* 掩盖 hide *adj.* 不清楚的 little known	记忆尺 ☐☐☐☐☐
sculpt [skʌlpt]	*v.* 雕刻 shape	记忆尺 ☐☐☐☐☐
steadily ['stedili]	*adv.* 连续地 at an unvarying rate / continuously	记忆尺 ☐☐☐☐☐
steady ['stedi]	*adj.* 不变的 continual	记忆尺 ☐☐☐☐☐
tangible ['tændʒəbl]	*adj.* 有形的 physical	记忆尺 ☐☐☐☐☐
comparable ['kɑːmpərəbl]	*adj.* 可比较的 similar	记忆尺 ☐☐☐☐☐
consult [kən'sʌlt]	*v.* 咨询 ask	记忆尺 ☐☐☐☐☐

| **extreme** [ɪk'striːm] | *adj.* 非常的 | 记忆尺 |
| | great | ☐ ☐ ☐ ☐ ☐ |

| **imply** [ɪm'plaɪ] | *v.* 暗示 | 记忆尺 |
| | suggest | ☐ ☐ ☐ ☐ ☐ |

| **permeable** ['pɜːrmiəbl] | *adj.* 能渗透的 having places where crossings could occur | 记忆尺 ☐ ☐ ☐ ☐ ☐ |

| **prompt** [prɑːmpt] | *v.* 促使 | 记忆尺 |
| | stimulate | ☐ ☐ ☐ ☐ ☐ |

| **upon reflection** | 反思之后 | 记忆尺 |
| | after consideration | ☐ ☐ ☐ ☐ ☐ |

| **astonishment** [ə'stɑːnɪʃmənt] | *n.* 惊讶 | 记忆尺 |
| | surprise | ☐ ☐ ☐ ☐ ☐ |

| **exert** [ɪg'zɜːrt] | *v.* 施加 put forth *v.* 运用 utilize | 记忆尺 ☐ ☐ ☐ ☐ ☐ |

| **in retrospect** | 回顾 | 记忆尺 |
| | looking back | ☐ ☐ ☐ ☐ ☐ |

| **recall** [rɪ'kɔːl] | *v.* 回忆 | 记忆尺 |
| | remember | ☐ ☐ ☐ ☐ ☐ |

| **adhesive** | adj. 黏的 | 记忆尺 |
| [əd'hiːsɪv] | sticky | ☐☐☐☐☐ |

| **engage** | v. 参加 | 记忆尺 |
| [ɪn'ɡeɪdʒ] | participate in | ☐☐☐☐☐ |

| **needless to say** | 毫无疑问地 | 记忆尺 |
| | obviously | ☐☐☐☐☐ |

| **remnant** | n. 残余 | 记忆尺 |
| ['remnənt] | remain / remainder | ☐☐☐☐☐ |

| **embody** | v. 包含 | 记忆尺 |
| [ɪm'bɑːdi] | incorporate | ☐☐☐☐☐ |

| **incredible** | adj. 不可思议的 | 记忆尺 |
| [ɪn'kredəbl] | impossible to believe / unbelievable | ☐☐☐☐☐ |

| **rapport** | n. （友好）关系 | 记忆尺 |
| [ræ'pɔːr] | bond | ☐☐☐☐☐ |

| **replenish** | v. 补充 | 记忆尺 |
| [rɪ'plenɪʃ] | restore | ☐☐☐☐☐ |

| **suspend** | v. 悬浮 | 记忆尺 |
| [sə'spend] | float / hang | ☐☐☐☐☐ |

| **suspended** | adj. 悬浮的 | 记忆尺 |
| [sə'spendɪd] | hung | ☐☐☐☐☐ |

| **thrill** | *n.* 激动 | 记忆尺 |
| [θrɪl] | excitement | ☐ ☐ ☐ ☐ ☐ |

| **ultimately** | *adv.* 最终地 | 记忆尺 |
| [ˈʌltɪmətli] | eventually / in the end / finally | ☐ ☐ ☐ ☐ ☐ |

| **vitality** | *n.* 活力 | 记忆尺 |
| [vaɪˈtæləti] | energy | ☐ ☐ ☐ ☐ ☐ |

| **fuel** | *v.* 供以燃料 | 记忆尺 |
| [ˈfjuːəl] | provide energy for | ☐ ☐ ☐ ☐ ☐ |

| **particularly** | *adv.* 特别 | 记忆尺 |
| [pərˈtɪkjələrli] | especially | ☐ ☐ ☐ ☐ ☐ |

| **principally** | *adv.* 主要地 | 记忆尺 |
| [ˈprɪnsəpli] | mainly | ☐ ☐ ☐ ☐ ☐ |

| **principal** | *adj.* 主要的 | 记忆尺 |
| [ˈprɪnsəpl] | major | ☐ ☐ ☐ ☐ ☐ |

| **justify** | *v.* 证明…正当 | 记忆尺 |
| [ˈdʒʌstɪfaɪ] | provide a rational basis for / support | ☐ ☐ ☐ ☐ ☐ |

| **pertinent** | *adj.* 相关的 | 记忆尺 |
| [ˈpɜːrtnənt] | relevant | ☐ ☐ ☐ ☐ ☐ |

| **several simultaneous developments** | 若干同步的进展 | 记忆尺 |
| | developments that occur at the same time | ☐ ☐ ☐ ☐ ☐ |

| **subdue** | *v.* 打败 | 记忆尺 |
| [səbˈduː] | defeat | ☐ ☐ ☐ ☐ ☐ |

| **excavate** | *v.* 挖掘 | 记忆尺 |
| [ˈekskəveɪt] | dig from the ground / dig out | ☐ ☐ ☐ ☐ ☐ |

henceforth	adv. 从此以后	记忆尺
[ˌhens'fɔːrθ]	from this time on	☐☐☐☐☐

incite	v. 刺激	记忆尺
[ɪn'saɪt]	stimulate	☐☐☐☐☐

oblige	v. 强制	记忆尺
[ə'blaɪdʒ]	force	☐☐☐☐☐

outweigh	v. 超过	记忆尺
[ˌaʊt'weɪ]	exceed	☐☐☐☐☐

erect	v. 建立	记忆尺
[ɪ'rekt]	construct / build	☐☐☐☐☐

regime	n. 政权	记忆尺
[reɪ'ʒiːm]	government	☐☐☐☐☐

synthesize	v. 综合	记忆尺
['sɪnθəsaɪz]	combine / integrate	☐☐☐☐☐

cite	v. 引用	记忆尺
[saɪt]	mention	☐☐☐☐☐

extensive	adj. 广大的	记忆尺
[ɪk'stensɪv]	large / considerable / widespread	☐☐☐☐☐

feasible	adj. 可行的	记忆尺
['fiːzəbl]	practical / achievable	☐☐☐☐☐

foster	v. 促进	记忆尺
['fɔːstər]	encourage	☐☐☐☐☐

frigid	adj. 寒冷的	记忆尺
['frɪdʒɪd]	cold	☐☐☐☐☐

scale	n. 规模	记忆尺
[skeɪl]	size	☐☐☐☐☐

be deficient in	缺乏 not have enough	记忆尺 ☐☐☐☐☐
curious ['kjʊriəs]	*adj.* 奇怪的 strange	记忆尺 ☐☐☐☐☐
preservative [prɪ'zɜːrvətɪv]	*n.* 防腐剂 something that keeps food fresh	记忆尺 ☐☐☐☐☐
preservation [ˌprezər'veɪʃn]	*n.* 保存 conservation	记忆尺 ☐☐☐☐☐
preserve [prɪ'zɜːrv]	*v.* 保留 maintain	记忆尺 ☐☐☐☐☐
edge [edʒ]	*n.* 优势 advantage	记忆尺 ☐☐☐☐☐
tie [taɪ]	*n.* 联系 connection	记忆尺 ☐☐☐☐☐
chaotic [keɪ'ɑːtɪk]	*adj.* 混乱的 disorganized	记忆尺 ☐☐☐☐☐
coalesce [ˌkoʊə'les]	*v.* 结合 join	记忆尺 ☐☐☐☐☐
constant ['kɑːnstənt]	*adj.* 稳定的 continual / unchanging / occurring periodically	记忆尺 ☐☐☐☐☐
domestic [də'mestɪk]	*adj.* 家庭的 household	记忆尺 ☐☐☐☐☐
emit [i'mɪt]	*v.* 释放 release / give off / send out	记忆尺 ☐☐☐☐☐

61

| **obligate** | v. 规定 | 记忆尺 |
| ['ɑːblɪɡeɪt] | require | ☐ ☐ ☐ ☐ ☐ |

| **relentless** | adj. 不停的 | 记忆尺 |
| [rɪ'lentləs] | unceasing | ☐ ☐ ☐ ☐ ☐ |

| **cease** | v. 停止 | 记忆尺 |
| [siːs] | stop | ☐ ☐ ☐ ☐ ☐ |

| **fundamental** | adj. 基础的 | 记忆尺 |
| [ˌfʌndə'mentl] | basic | ☐ ☐ ☐ ☐ ☐ |

| **mandate** | v. 命令 | 记忆尺 |
| ['mændeɪt] | require | ☐ ☐ ☐ ☐ ☐ |

| **ponder** | v. 沉思 | 记忆尺 |
| ['pɑːndər] | think about / think of | ☐ ☐ ☐ ☐ ☐ |

| **signify** | v. 表明 | 记忆尺 |
| ['sɪɡnɪfaɪ] | indicate | ☐ ☐ ☐ ☐ ☐ |

Word
List 12

音频

irreversible	adj. 无法挽回的，永久的	记忆尺
[ˌɪrɪ'vɜːrsəbl]	permanent	☐☐☐☐☐
exposed	adj. 暴露的	记忆尺
[ɪk'spoʊzd]	unprotected / visible	☐☐☐☐☐
manipulate	v. 操纵	记忆尺
[mə'nɪpjuleɪt]	skillfully used / handle	☐☐☐☐☐
monumental	adj. 极大的	记忆尺
[ˌmaːnju'mentl]	enormous / great and significant	☐☐☐☐☐
pursue	v. 从事	记忆尺
[pər'suː]	practice / engage in	☐☐☐☐☐
retard	v. 放缓	记忆尺
[rɪ'taːrd]	slow	☐☐☐☐☐
subsistence	n. 生存	记忆尺
[səb'sɪstəns]	survival	☐☐☐☐☐
with no warning	毫无预警的	记忆尺
	without any indication beforehand	☐☐☐☐☐
deficiency	n. 缺乏	记忆尺
[dɪ'fɪʃnsi]	shortage	☐☐☐☐☐
distribute	v. 散发	记忆尺
[dɪ'strɪbjuːt]	spread	☐☐☐☐☐

			记忆尺
devoid of	缺乏的		☐☐☐☐☐
	lack of / lacking		
contradict	*v.* 与…有矛盾		记忆尺
[ˌkɑːntrəˈdɪkt]	conflict		☐☐☐☐☐
hostile	*adj.* 敌对的		记忆尺
[ˈhɑːstl]	unfavorable		☐☐☐☐☐
unpromising	*adj.* 不利的		记忆尺
[ʌnˈprɑːmɪsɪŋ]	unfavorable		☐☐☐☐☐
perpetual	*adj.* 永恒的		记忆尺
[pərˈpetʃuəl]	constant		☐☐☐☐☐
dense	*adj.* 密集的		记忆尺
[dens]	thick / crowded		☐☐☐☐☐
novel	*adj.* 新的		记忆尺
[ˈnɑːvl]	new		☐☐☐☐☐
subject to	遭受		记忆尺
	experience / expose to		☐☐☐☐☐
activate	*v.* 启动		记忆尺
[ˈæktɪveɪt]	switch on		☐☐☐☐☐
current	*adj.* 目前的		记忆尺
[ˈkɜːrənt]	present		☐☐☐☐☐
currently	*adv.* 目前		记忆尺
[ˈkɜːrəntli]	at the present time		☐☐☐☐☐
experimental	*adj.* 实验的		记忆尺
[ɪkˌsperɪˈmentl]	trial		☐☐☐☐☐
find	*v.* 发现		记忆尺
[faɪnd]	locate		☐☐☐☐☐

retrieve [rɪ'triːv]	*v.* 找回 recover	记忆尺 ☐☐☐☐☐
indefinite [ɪn'defɪnət]	*adj.* 无限期的 endless	记忆尺 ☐☐☐☐☐
indefinitely [ɪn'defɪnətli]	*adv.* 无限期地 without limit	记忆尺 ☐☐☐☐☐
indefinite period	无限期 a period whose end has not been determined	记忆尺 ☐☐☐☐☐
invertebrate [ɪn'vɜːrtɪbrət]	*adj.* 无脊椎的 spineless	记忆尺 ☐☐☐☐☐
renovate ['renəveɪt]	*v.* 革新 invent	记忆尺 ☐☐☐☐☐
residue ['rezɪduː]	*n.* 残留物 remains	记忆尺 ☐☐☐☐☐
sedimentation [ˌsedɪmen'teɪʃn]	*n.* 沉积 deposit	记忆尺 ☐☐☐☐☐
concentration [ˌkaːnsn'treɪʃn]	*n.* 浓缩（物） dense grouping	记忆尺 ☐☐☐☐☐
consume [kən'suːm]	*v.* 消耗 use up / destroy	记忆尺 ☐☐☐☐☐
continued [kən'tɪnjuːd]	*adj.* 持续的 ongoing	记忆尺 ☐☐☐☐☐
contribute to	有助于 add to	记忆尺 ☐☐☐☐☐

delicately	adv. 巧妙地	记忆尺
['delɪkətli]	finely	☐ ☐ ☐ ☐ ☐

delicate	adj. 脆弱的	记忆尺
['delɪkət]	fragile	☐ ☐ ☐ ☐ ☐

indispensable	adj. 必不可少的	记忆尺
[ˌɪndɪ'spensəbl]	essential	☐ ☐ ☐ ☐ ☐

ingest	v. 摄取	记忆尺
[ɪn'dʒest]	eat	☐ ☐ ☐ ☐ ☐

ingestion	n. 摄入	记忆尺
[ɪn'dʒestʃən]	swallow	☐ ☐ ☐ ☐ ☐

rapid	adj. 快的	记忆尺
['ræpɪd]	fast	☐ ☐ ☐ ☐ ☐

ambiguity	n. 模棱两可的话	记忆尺
[ˌæmbɪ'gjuːəti]	statements that can be interpreted in more than one way	☐ ☐ ☐ ☐ ☐

detach	v. 分离	记忆尺
[dɪ'tætʃ]	separate	☐ ☐ ☐ ☐ ☐

discrete	adj. 分离的	记忆尺
[dɪ'skriːt]	separate	☐ ☐ ☐ ☐ ☐

diverge	v. 分散	记忆尺
[daɪ'vəːrdʒ]	separate	☐ ☐ ☐ ☐ ☐

minute	adj. 非常小的	记忆尺
[maɪ'nuːt]	tiny / small	☐ ☐ ☐ ☐ ☐

portray	v. 描绘	记忆尺
[pɔːr'treɪ]	represent	☐ ☐ ☐ ☐ ☐

traumatic [trɔʊˈmætɪk]	*adj.* 痛苦的 upsetting / highly stressful	记忆尺 ☐ ☐ ☐ ☐ ☐
plague [pleɪg]	*v.* 折磨 cause trouble for	记忆尺 ☐ ☐ ☐ ☐ ☐
susceptible to	易受影响的 likely to be affected by	记忆尺 ☐ ☐ ☐ ☐ ☐
perspective [pərˈspektɪv]	*n.* 观点 viewpoint / point of view	记忆尺 ☐ ☐ ☐ ☐ ☐
reflect [rɪˈflekt]	*v.* 体现 show / indicate	记忆尺 ☐ ☐ ☐ ☐ ☐
traditional [trəˈdɪʃənl]	*adj.* 传统的 conventional	记忆尺 ☐ ☐ ☐ ☐ ☐
traditionally [trəˈdɪʃənəli]	*adv.* 传统上 originally	记忆尺 ☐ ☐ ☐ ☐ ☐
commodity [kəˈmɑːdəti]	*n.* 商品 product	记忆尺 ☐ ☐ ☐ ☐ ☐
indigenous [ɪnˈdɪdʒənəs]	*adj.* 本土的 native	记忆尺 ☐ ☐ ☐ ☐ ☐
namely [ˈneɪmli]	*adv.* 也就是 that is to say	记忆尺 ☐ ☐ ☐ ☐ ☐

Word List 13

音频

to some degree	从某种程度上	记忆尺
	in some places / to a certain extent	☐ ☐ ☐ ☐ ☐
to some extent	从某种程度上	记忆尺
	within limitation	☐ ☐ ☐ ☐ ☐
outlying	*adj.* 偏远的	记忆尺
['aʊtlaɪɪŋ]	far / far from the center	☐ ☐ ☐ ☐ ☐
posterity	*n.* 后代	记忆尺
[pɑːˈsterəti]	further generation	☐ ☐ ☐ ☐ ☐
premise	*n.* 假定	记忆尺
[ˈpremɪs]	assumption	☐ ☐ ☐ ☐ ☐
redundancy	*n.* 多余	记忆尺
[rɪˈdʌndənsi]	duplication	☐ ☐ ☐ ☐ ☐
beneficial	*adj.* 有益的	记忆尺
[ˌbenɪˈfɪʃl]	helpful / advantageous	☐ ☐ ☐ ☐ ☐
entirely	*adv.* 全部地	记忆尺
[ɪnˈtaɪərli]	completely	☐ ☐ ☐ ☐ ☐
key	*adj.* 至关重要的	记忆尺
[kiː]	essential / crucial / important	☐ ☐ ☐ ☐ ☐
now and then	偶尔	记忆尺
	occasionally	☐ ☐ ☐ ☐ ☐

virtue ['vɜːrtʃuː]	*n.* 美德 desirable quality	记忆尺 ☐☐☐☐☐
plausible ['plɔːzəbl]	*adj.* 合情理的 believable / reasonable	记忆尺 ☐☐☐☐☐
insensitive to	不敏感的 not affected by	记忆尺 ☐☐☐☐☐
consider [kən'sɪdər]	*v.* 认为 believe	记忆尺 ☐☐☐☐☐
execute ['eksɪkjuːt]	*v.* 完成 accomplish	记忆尺 ☐☐☐☐☐
infusion [ɪn'fjuːʒn]	*n.* 注入 combination	记忆尺 ☐☐☐☐☐
respective [rɪ'spektɪv]	*adj.* 各自的 separate	记忆尺 ☐☐☐☐☐
uniform ['juːnɪfɔːrm]	*adj.* 一致的 standard / without variation	记忆尺 ☐☐☐☐☐
adjoin [ə'dʒɔɪn]	*v.* 毗邻 border	记忆尺 ☐☐☐☐☐
damage ['dæmɪdʒ]	*v.* 损害 mutilate	记忆尺 ☐☐☐☐☐
decorate ['dekəreɪt]	*v.* 装饰 camouflage / ornament	记忆尺 ☐☐☐☐☐
camouflage ['kæməflaːʒ]	*v.* 掩饰 hide	记忆尺 ☐☐☐☐☐
enhance [ɪn'hæns]	*v.* 提高 increase / improve	记忆尺 ☐☐☐☐☐

formidable [ˈfɔːrmɪdəbl]	*adj.* 令人生畏的 impressive	记忆尺 ☐☐☐☐☐
originate from	来源于 come into existence from	记忆尺 ☐☐☐☐☐
repeat [rɪˈpiːt]	*v.* 重复 recur	记忆尺 ☐☐☐☐☐
reproduce [ˌriːprəˈduːs]	*v.* 繁殖 breed / propagate	记忆尺 ☐☐☐☐☐
terminate [ˈtɜːrmɪneɪt]	*v.* 终止 end	记忆尺 ☐☐☐☐☐
counterpart [ˈkaʊntərpɑːrt]	*n.* 对应物 equivalent	记忆尺 ☐☐☐☐☐
pronouncement [prəˈnaʊnsmənt]	*n.* 声明 statement	记忆尺 ☐☐☐☐☐
rekindle [ˌriːˈkɪndl]	*v.* 重新点燃，使复苏 renew	记忆尺 ☐☐☐☐☐
initiative [ɪˈnɪʃətɪv]	*n.* 行动 action	记忆尺 ☐☐☐☐☐
many-segmented [ˈmeniˈsegməntɪd]	分成多个部分的 divided into many parts	记忆尺 ☐☐☐☐☐
prior to	在…之前 before	记忆尺 ☐☐☐☐☐
set in motion	开始 start	记忆尺 ☐☐☐☐☐
acquire [əˈkwaɪər]	*v.* 获取 obtain	记忆尺 ☐☐☐☐☐

persuade	v. 说服	记忆尺
[pər'sweɪd]	talk into	□ □ □ □ □

random	adj. 随机的	记忆尺
['rændəm]	chance	□ □ □ □ □

underlie	v. 是…的基础	记忆尺
[ˌʌndər'laɪ]	on the basis of	□ □ □ □ □

approach	v. 接近	记忆尺
[ə'proʊtʃ]	come nearer to / near	□ □ □ □ □

beautifully preserved	保存完好的	记忆尺
	with no damage	□ □ □ □ □

indicative	adj. 表明的	记忆尺
[ɪn'dɪkətɪv]	suggesting	□ □ □ □ □

identical	adj. 相同的	记忆尺
[aɪ'dentɪkl]	the same / look alike	□ □ □ □ □

intensive	adj. 强烈的	记忆尺
[ɪn'tensɪv]	strong	□ □ □ □ □

reach consensus on	达成共识	记忆尺
	agree on	□ □ □ □ □

successive	adj. 连续的	记忆尺
[sək'sesɪv]	following	□ □ □ □ □

a glimpse into	一瞥	记忆尺
	a brief view of	□ □ □ □ □

evade	v. 逃避	记忆尺
[ɪ'veɪd]	escape	□ □ □ □ □

habit	n. 习惯	记忆尺
['hæbɪt]	usual behavior	□ □ □ □ □

notably	*adv.* 显著地	记忆尺
['noʊtəbli]	particularly / especially	▢ ▢ ▢ ▢ ▢
overall	*adv.* 总体来说	记忆尺
[ˌoʊvər'ɔːl]	generally / considered as a whole	▢ ▢ ▢ ▢ ▢
anarchy	*n.* 无政府状态	记忆尺
['ænərki]	lawlessness	▢ ▢ ▢ ▢ ▢

| **perishable** | *adj.* 易腐蚀的 | 记忆尺 |
| ['perɪʃəbl] | likely to decay | ☐☐☐☐☐ |

| **define** | *v.* 确定 | 记忆尺 |
| [dɪ'faɪn] | identify | ☐☐☐☐☐ |

| **discern** | *v.* 辨别 | 记忆尺 |
| [dɪ's3ːrn] | identify | ☐☐☐☐☐ |

| **meticulously** | *adv.* 细致地 | 记忆尺 |
| [mə'tɪkjələsli] | carefully | ☐☐☐☐☐ |

| **mechanism** | *n.* 机制 | 记忆尺 |
| ['mekənɪzəm] | means | ☐☐☐☐☐ |

| **secure** | *v.* 争取到 | 记忆尺 |
| [səkjʊr] | get | ☐☐☐☐☐ |

| **observe** | *v.* 观察 | 记忆尺 |
| [əb'z3ːrv] | monitor | ☐☐☐☐☐ |

| **oversee** | *v.* 监督 | 记忆尺 |
| [,oʊvər'siː] | supervise | ☐☐☐☐☐ |

| **surpass** | *v.* 超过 | 记忆尺 |
| [sər'pæs] | exceed / be higher than | ☐☐☐☐☐ |

| **heighten** | *v.* 提高 | 记忆尺 |
| ['haɪtn] | increase | ☐☐☐☐☐ |

radical [ˈrædɪkl]	adj. 极端的 extreme / drastic adj. 根本的 fundamental	记忆尺 ☐☐☐☐☐
abundant [əˈbʌndənt]	adj. 丰富的 plentiful	记忆尺 ☐☐☐☐☐
abundance [əˈbʌndəns]	n. 丰富 plenty	记忆尺 ☐☐☐☐☐
adverse [ədˈvɜːrs]	adj. 不利的 harmful	记忆尺 ☐☐☐☐☐
detrimental [ˌdetrɪˈmentl]	adj. 有害的 harmful	记忆尺 ☐☐☐☐☐
indiscriminate [ˌɪndɪˈskrɪmɪnət]	adj. 任意的 random	记忆尺 ☐☐☐☐☐
resistance [rɪˈzɪstəns]	n. 反对 opposition	记忆尺 ☐☐☐☐☐
deflect [dɪˈflekt]	v. 偏离 change direction	记忆尺 ☐☐☐☐☐
disguise [dɪsˈɡaɪz]	v. 隐藏 hide	记忆尺 ☐☐☐☐☐
evident [ˈevɪdənt]	adj. 明显的 obvious	记忆尺 ☐☐☐☐☐
inventive [ɪnˈventɪv]	adj. 有创造力的 creative	记忆尺 ☐☐☐☐☐
moral [ˈmɔːrəl]	n. 教训 lesson	记忆尺 ☐☐☐☐☐

| **viability** | *n.* 生命力 | 记忆尺 |
| [ˌvaɪəˈbɪləti] | ability to exist | ☐☐☐☐☐ |

| **catastrophic** | *adj.* 灾难的 | 记忆尺 |
| [ˌkætəˈstrɑːfɪk] | disastrous / extremely harmful | ☐☐☐☐☐ |

propagate	*v.* 传播	
	spread	记忆尺
[ˈprɑːpəgeɪt]	*v.* 繁殖	☐☐☐☐☐
	multiply	

| **deter** | *v.* 制止 | 记忆尺 |
| [dɪˈtɜːr] | stop | ☐☐☐☐☐ |

| **intricate** | *adj.* 复杂的 | 记忆尺 |
| [ˈɪntrɪkət] | complex | ☐☐☐☐☐ |

| **portable** | *adj.* 便携的 | 记忆尺 |
| [ˈpɔːrtəbl] | moveable | ☐☐☐☐☐ |

project	*v.* 展示	
	show	记忆尺
[prəˈdʒekt]	*v.* 预计	☐☐☐☐☐
	estimate	

| **exhaust** | *v.* 耗尽 | 记忆尺 |
| [ɪgˈzɔːst] | use up | ☐☐☐☐☐ |

| **exhausting** | *adj.* 精疲力尽的 | 记忆尺 |
| [ɪgˈzɔːstɪŋ] | extremely tiring | ☐☐☐☐☐ |

| **mortality** | *n.* （大量）死亡 | 记忆尺 |
| [mɔːrˈtæləti] | death | ☐☐☐☐☐ |

| **on balance** | 总体来说 | 记忆尺 |
| | overall | ☐☐☐☐☐ |

modify	*v.* 修改	记忆尺
[ˈmɑːdɪfaɪ]	change	▢ ▢ ▢ ▢ ▢
prohibit	*v.* 阻止	记忆尺
[prəˈhɪbɪt]	prevent	▢ ▢ ▢ ▢ ▢
reliance	*n.* 依赖	记忆尺
[rɪˈlaɪəns]	dependence	▢ ▢ ▢ ▢ ▢
cope with	应对	记忆尺
	manage / adapt	▢ ▢ ▢ ▢ ▢
domain	*n.* 领域	记忆尺
[doʊˈmeɪn]	field of expertise	▢ ▢ ▢ ▢ ▢
flexible	*adj.* 灵活的	记忆尺
[ˈfleksəbl]	adaptable / bendable	▢ ▢ ▢ ▢ ▢
no wonder	不足为奇	记忆尺
	unsurprisingly	▢ ▢ ▢ ▢ ▢
assorted	*adj.* 各种各样的	记忆尺
[əˈsɔːrtəd]	various	▢ ▢ ▢ ▢ ▢
burdensome work rhythm	工作节奏快的	记忆尺
	frequent work rhythm	▢ ▢ ▢ ▢ ▢
compound	*v.* 增加	记忆尺
[ˈkɑːmpaʊnd]	add to	▢ ▢ ▢ ▢ ▢
roughly	*adv.* 大约	记忆尺
[ˈrʌfli]	approximately	▢ ▢ ▢ ▢ ▢
vast	*adj.* 巨大的	记忆尺
[væst]	enormous / huge	▢ ▢ ▢ ▢ ▢
contour	*v.* 概述	记忆尺
[ˈkɑːntʊr]	outline	▢ ▢ ▢ ▢ ▢

strut

[strʌt]

v. 支撑

support

记忆尺

☐ ☐ ☐ ☐ ☐

valid

['vælɪd]

adj. 合理的

reasonable

记忆尺

☐ ☐ ☐ ☐ ☐

collectively

[kə'lektɪvli]

adv. 共同地

jointly

记忆尺

☐ ☐ ☐ ☐ ☐

envelop

[ɪn'veləp]

v. 包围

surround

记忆尺

☐ ☐ ☐ ☐ ☐

supplant

[sə'plænt]

v. 取代

replace

记忆尺

☐ ☐ ☐ ☐ ☐

| **homogeneous** | adj. 同质的 | 记忆尺 |
| [ˌhoʊməˈdʒiːniəs] | uniform | ☐☐☐☐☐ |

| **homogenize** | v. 同质化 | 记忆尺 |
| [həˈmɑːdʒəˌnaɪz] | eliminate distinction | ☐☐☐☐☐ |

| **astonishing** | adj. 惊人的 | 记忆尺 |
| [əˈstɑːnɪʃɪŋ] | incredible | ☐☐☐☐☐ |

| **commence** | v. 开始 | 记忆尺 |
| [kəˈmens] | begin | ☐☐☐☐☐ |

| **negligible** | adj. 可忽略的 | 记忆尺 |
| [ˈneglɪdʒəbl] | minor | ☐☐☐☐☐ |

| **unexpectedly** | adv. 出乎意料地 | 记忆尺 |
| [ˌʌnɪkˈspektɪdli] | surprisingly | ☐☐☐☐☐ |

| **resilient** | adj. 有弹性的，易复原的 | 记忆尺 |
| [rɪˈzɪliənt] | easy to recover | ☐☐☐☐☐ |

| **drawback** | n. 弱点 | 记忆尺 |
| [ˈdrɔːbæk] | disadvantage / problem / fault | ☐☐☐☐☐ |

| **just** | adj. 公正的 | 记忆尺 |
| [dʒʌst] | fair | ☐☐☐☐☐ |

| **sequentially** | adv. 连续地 | 记忆尺 |
| [sɪˈkwenʃəli] | one after another | ☐☐☐☐☐ |

asset ['æset]	*n.* 财富（尤指优势、资源、人才等） advantage	记忆尺 ☐☐☐☐☐
precipitate [prɪ'sɪpɪteɪt]	*v.* 造成 bring about	记忆尺 ☐☐☐☐☐
vital ['vaɪtl]	*adj.* 事关重大的 crucial / essential	记忆尺 ☐☐☐☐☐
mature [mə'tʃʊr]	*adj.* 成熟的 developed	记忆尺 ☐☐☐☐☐
prominent ['prɑːmɪnənt]	*adj.* 卓越的 eminent / outstanding / principal / important	记忆尺 ☐☐☐☐☐
free-standing [ˌfriː'stændɪŋ]	*adj.* 独立（支撑）的 separate	记忆尺 ☐☐☐☐☐
ostentatious [ˌɑːsten'teɪʃəs]	*adj.* 卖弄的 showy	记忆尺 ☐☐☐☐☐
trap [træp]	*v.* 设圈套 catch	记忆尺 ☐☐☐☐☐
strategy ['strætədʒi]	*n.* 策略 plan	记忆尺 ☐☐☐☐☐
accompany [ə'kʌmpəni]	*v.* 伴随 occur along with / be associated with	记忆尺 ☐☐☐☐☐
converge [kən'vɜːrdʒ]	*v.* 汇集 come together / move closer	记忆尺 ☐☐☐☐☐
cushion ['kʊʃn]	*v.* 缓冲 protect	记忆尺 ☐☐☐☐☐

doctrine ['dɑːktrɪn]	*n.* 教义 principle	记忆尺 ☐☐☐☐☐	
intercourse ['ɪntərkɔːrs]	*n.* 交流 exchange	记忆尺 ☐☐☐☐☐	
outbreak ['aʊtbreɪk]	*n.* 爆发 sudden increase	记忆尺 ☐☐☐☐☐	
firmly ['fɜːrmli]	*adv.* 稳固地 securely	记忆尺 ☐☐☐☐☐	
rupture ['rʌptʃər]	*v.* 破裂 break	记忆尺 ☐☐☐☐☐	
concede [kən'siːd]	*v.* 承认（某事属实） accept	记忆尺 ☐☐☐☐☐	
have priority	优先 have advantages	记忆尺 ☐☐☐☐☐	
maximum ['mæksɪməm]	*adj.* 最大值的 the greatest size	记忆尺 ☐☐☐☐☐	
simulated ['sɪmjuleɪtəd]	*adj.* 模仿的 artificial	记忆尺 ☐☐☐☐☐	
stable ['steɪbl]	*adj.* 稳定的 constant / steady	记忆尺 ☐☐☐☐☐	
timid ['tɪmɪd]	*adj.* 胆怯的 fearful	记忆尺 ☐☐☐☐☐	
dormant ['dɔːrmənt]	*adj.* 静止的 inactive	记忆尺 ☐☐☐☐☐	
drive [draɪv]	*n.* 动力 incentive	记忆尺 ☐☐☐☐☐	

impetus ['ɪmpɪtəs]	*n.* 刺激 incentive / stimulus	记忆尺 ☐☐☐☐☐	
inhospitable [ˌɪnhɑːˈspɪtəbl]	*adj.* 不适宜居住的 not suitable to live in	记忆尺 ☐☐☐☐☐	
objective [əbˈdʒektɪv]	*adj.* 客观的 unbiased *n.* 目标 purpose	记忆尺 ☐☐☐☐☐	
bombard [bɑːmˈbɑːrd]	*v.* 轰炸，攻击 strike / assail / assault	记忆尺 ☐☐☐☐☐	
adopt [əˈdɑːpt]	*v.* 采用 start to use	记忆尺 ☐☐☐☐☐	
hint [hɪnt]	*n.* 线索 clue	记忆尺 ☐☐☐☐☐	
merge [mɜːrdʒ]	*v.* 合并 combine	记忆尺 ☐☐☐☐☐	
miniature ['mɪnətʃər]	*adj.* 微小的 small	记忆尺 ☐☐☐☐☐	
pinpoint ['pɪnpɔɪnt]	*v.* 准确指出 identify precisely / locate exactly	记忆尺 ☐☐☐☐☐	
relic ['relɪk]	*n.* 遗迹 remains	记忆尺 ☐☐☐☐☐	
obsession with	迷恋 fixation on	记忆尺 ☐☐☐☐☐	
ritual ['rɪtʃuəl]	*adj.* 仪式的 ceremonial	记忆尺 ☐☐☐☐☐	

score

[skɔːr]

n. 许多

large numbers

记忆尺

☐ ☐ ☐ ☐ ☐

sphere

[sfɪr]

n. 范围

area

记忆尺

☐ ☐ ☐ ☐ ☐

turbulent

['tɜːrbjələnt]

adj. 骚乱的

violent

记忆尺

☐ ☐ ☐ ☐ ☐

critically

['krɪtɪkli]

adv. 严重地

fundamentally

记忆尺

☐ ☐ ☐ ☐ ☐

Word List 16

音频

vastly ['væstli]	*adv.* 极大地 greatly	记忆尺 ☐☐☐☐☐
diversification [daɪˌvɜːrsɪfɪ'keɪʃn]	*n.* 多样化 emergence of many varieties	记忆尺 ☐☐☐☐☐
mutually exclusive	相互排斥的 if one of the theories is true, then all the others must be false	记忆尺 ☐☐☐☐☐
undisputed [ˌʌndɪ'spjuːtɪd]	*adj.* 无争议的 acknowledged	记忆尺 ☐☐☐☐☐
attain [ə'teɪn]	*v.* 实现 achieve / reach	记忆尺 ☐☐☐☐☐
lavishly ['lævɪʃli]	*adv.* 丰富地 richly	记忆尺 ☐☐☐☐☐
renowned [rɪ'naʊnd]	*adj.* 著名的 famous	记忆尺 ☐☐☐☐☐
renown [rɪ'naʊn]	*n.* 名望 fame	记忆尺 ☐☐☐☐☐
sacred ['seɪkrɪd]	*adj.* 神圣的 holy	记忆尺 ☐☐☐☐☐
alliance [ə'laɪəns]	*n.* 同盟 partnership	记忆尺 ☐☐☐☐☐

tolerant of	容忍…	记忆尺
	able to withstand	☐☐☐☐☐
decline [dɪ'klaɪn]	v. 衰落	记忆尺
	weaken	☐☐☐☐☐
encounter [ɪn'kaʊntər]	v. 遇见	记忆尺
	meet / come into contact with	☐☐☐☐☐
exceptionally [ɪk'sepʃənəli]	adv. 异乎寻常地	记忆尺
	unusually / extraordinarily	☐☐☐☐☐
jointly ['dʒɔɪntli]	adv. 共同地	记忆尺
	together	☐☐☐☐☐
crisis ['kraɪsɪs]	n. 危机	记忆尺
	critical situation	☐☐☐☐☐
halt [hɔːlt]	v. 阻止	记忆尺
	stop	☐☐☐☐☐
managed ['mænɪdʒd]	adj. 设法完成的	记忆尺
	be able	☐☐☐☐☐
signature ['sɪɡnətʃər]	n. 符号	记忆尺
	identifying mark	☐☐☐☐☐
strictly ['strɪktli]	adv. 严格地	记忆尺
	exclusively	☐☐☐☐☐
undergo [ˌʌndər'ɡoʊ]	v. 经历	记忆尺
	experience	☐☐☐☐☐
ancestor ['ænsestər]	n. 祖先	记忆尺
	relative from an earlier generation	☐☐☐☐☐
diversify [daɪ'vɜːrsɪfaɪ]	v. 多样化	记忆尺
	vary	☐☐☐☐☐

enlist [ɪnˈlɪst]	v. 招募 recruit	记忆尺 ☐ ☐ ☐ ☐ ☐
luminous [ˈluːmɪnəs]	adj. 明亮的 bright	记忆尺 ☐ ☐ ☐ ☐ ☐
persist [pərˈsɪst]	v. 持续 continue	记忆尺 ☐ ☐ ☐ ☐ ☐
prime [praɪm]	adj. 优质的 high-quality	记忆尺 ☐ ☐ ☐ ☐ ☐
abolish [əˈbaːlɪʃ]	v. 废除 eliminate / end	记忆尺 ☐ ☐ ☐ ☐ ☐
dwell [dwel]	v. 居住 live	记忆尺 ☐ ☐ ☐ ☐ ☐
dwelling [dwelɪŋ]	n. 住所 home	
dweller [ˈdwelər]	n. 居民 inhabitant	记忆尺 ☐ ☐ ☐ ☐ ☐
embellish [ɪmˈbelɪʃ]	v. 美化 make more attractive	记忆尺 ☐ ☐ ☐ ☐ ☐
stunning [ˈstʌnɪŋ]	adj. 令人震惊的 impressive	记忆尺 ☐ ☐ ☐ ☐ ☐
foul [faʊl]	v. 污染 pollute	记忆尺 ☐ ☐ ☐ ☐ ☐
in the same breath	同时 immediately	记忆尺 ☐ ☐ ☐ ☐ ☐
marked [maːrkt]	adj. 显著的 considerable	记忆尺 ☐ ☐ ☐ ☐ ☐

| **markedly** | adv. 显著地 | 记忆尺 |
| ['mɑːrkɪdli] | noticeably | ☐☐☐☐☐ |

| **rebound** | n. 回升 | 记忆尺 |
| [rɪ'baʊnd] | recovery | ☐☐☐☐☐ |

| **slope** | n. 倾斜 | 记忆尺 |
| [sloʊp] | incline | ☐☐☐☐☐ |

| **trappings** | n. 装饰 | 记忆尺 |
| ['træpɪŋz] | decorations | ☐☐☐☐☐ |

| **abound** | v. 充满 | 记忆尺 |
| [ə'baʊnd] | be numerous | ☐☐☐☐☐ |

| **foremost** | adj. 最重要的 | 记忆尺 |
| ['fɔːrmoʊst] | most important | ☐☐☐☐☐ |

| **regrettably** | adv. 令人遗憾地 | 记忆尺 |
| [rɪ'gretəbli] | unfortunately | ☐☐☐☐☐ |

| **consistently** | adv. 持续不断地 | 记忆尺 |
| [kən'sɪstəntli] | increasingly | ☐☐☐☐☐ |

| **giant** | adj. 巨大的 | 记忆尺 |
| ['dʒaɪənt] | huge | ☐☐☐☐☐ |

| **nonetheless** | adv. 然而 | 记忆尺 |
| [ˌnʌnðə'les] | however | ☐☐☐☐☐ |

| **perpetuate** | v. 使永存 | 记忆尺 |
| [pər'petʃueɪt] | continue | ☐☐☐☐☐ |

| **persistent** | adj. 持续的 | 记忆尺 |
| [pər'sɪstənt] | lasting / enduring | ☐☐☐☐☐ |

| **scenario** | n. 方案，情况 | 记忆尺 |
| [sə'nærioʊ] | situation | ☐☐☐☐☐ |

boost
[buːst]

v. 推动

raise

记忆尺

☐ ☐ ☐ ☐ ☐

appraisal
[əˈpreɪzl]

n. 评估

evaluation

记忆尺

☐ ☐ ☐ ☐ ☐

efficacy
[ˈefɪkəsi]

n. 效力

effectiveness

记忆尺

☐ ☐ ☐ ☐ ☐

eliminate
[ɪˈlɪmɪneɪt]

v. 消除

get rid of

记忆尺

☐ ☐ ☐ ☐ ☐

impervious to

不受干扰的

unaffected by

记忆尺

☐ ☐ ☐ ☐ ☐

Word List 17

音频

bulk [bʌlk]	*n.* 大多数，大量 the greatest part / mass	记忆尺 ☐☐☐☐☐
convince [kənˈvɪns]	*v.* 使…确信 persuade	记忆尺 ☐☐☐☐☐
exceedingly [ɪkˈsiːdɪŋli]	*adv.* 极其 extremely / highly	记忆尺 ☐☐☐☐☐
give rise to	引起 produce	记忆尺 ☐☐☐☐☐
sensible [ˈsensəbl]	*adj.* 合情理的 reasonable	记忆尺 ☐☐☐☐☐
differ [ˈdɪfər]	*v.* 不同 vary	记忆尺 ☐☐☐☐☐
flawed [flɔːd]	*adj.* 有瑕疵的 incorrect	记忆尺 ☐☐☐☐☐
flaw [flɔː]	*n.* 弱点 fault	记忆尺 ☐☐☐☐☐
boom [buːm]	*n.* 激增 expansion	记忆尺 ☐☐☐☐☐
trivial [ˈtrɪviəl]	*adj.* 琐碎的 small	记忆尺 ☐☐☐☐☐

relevant	*adj.* 相关的	记忆尺
['reləvənt]	applicable	☐ ☐ ☐ ☐ ☐
devour	*v.* 吞噬	记忆尺
[dɪ'vauər]	eat	☐ ☐ ☐ ☐ ☐
gifted	*adj.* 有才华的	记忆尺
['ɡɪftɪd]	talented	☐ ☐ ☐ ☐ ☐
splendid	*adj.* 壮观的	记忆尺
['splendɪd]	magnificent	☐ ☐ ☐ ☐ ☐
sponsor	*v.* 赞助	记忆尺
['spɑːnsər]	support	☐ ☐ ☐ ☐ ☐
bustling	*adj.* 忙碌的，繁华的	记忆尺
['bʌslɪŋ]	busy / lively	☐ ☐ ☐ ☐ ☐
provoke	*v.* 引起	记忆尺
[prə'voʊk]	bring about	☐ ☐ ☐ ☐ ☐
transform	*v.* 改变	记忆尺
[træns'fɔːrm]	change	☐ ☐ ☐ ☐ ☐
compulsory	*adj.* 强制的	记忆尺
[kəm'pʌlsəri]	required	☐ ☐ ☐ ☐ ☐
despite	*prep.* 尽管	记忆尺
[dɪ'spaɪt]	even though	☐ ☐ ☐ ☐ ☐
escalate	*v.* 逐步升级	记忆尺
['eskəleɪt]	intensify	☐ ☐ ☐ ☐ ☐
insight into	对…的深刻理解	记忆尺
	an understanding of	☐ ☐ ☐ ☐ ☐
insight	*n.* 洞察力	记忆尺
['ɪnsaɪt]	perceptiveness	☐ ☐ ☐ ☐ ☐

| **seclude** | 🔖 *v.* 隔离 | 记忆尺 |
| [sɪˈkluːd] | 📖 isolate | ☐ ☐ ☐ ☐ ☐ |

| **sever** | 🔖 *v.* 切断 | 记忆尺 |
| [ˈsevər] | 📖 cut off | ☐ ☐ ☐ ☐ ☐ |

| **viable** | 🔖 *adj.* 能生存的 | 记忆尺 |
| [ˈvaɪəbl] | 📖 able to survive | ☐ ☐ ☐ ☐ ☐ |

| **colossal** | 🔖 *adj.* 庞大的 | 记忆尺 |
| [kəˈlɑːsl] | 📖 enormous | ☐ ☐ ☐ ☐ ☐ |

| **effort** | 🔖 *n.* 努力 | 记忆尺 |
| [ˈefərt] | 📖 attempt | ☐ ☐ ☐ ☐ ☐ |

| **prolonged** | 🔖 *adj.* 延长的 | 记忆尺 |
| [prəˈlɔːŋd] | 📖 lengthy | ☐ ☐ ☐ ☐ ☐ |

| **prolong** | 🔖 *v.* 延长 | 记忆尺 |
| [prəˈlɔːŋ] | 📖 extend | ☐ ☐ ☐ ☐ ☐ |

| **seek** | 🔖 *v.* 寻求，设法 | 记忆尺 |
| [siːk] | 📖 attempt | ☐ ☐ ☐ ☐ ☐ |

| **sequence** | 🔖 *n.* 顺序 | 记忆尺 |
| [ˈsiːkwəns] | 📖 order / series | ☐ ☐ ☐ ☐ ☐ |

| **whereas** | 🔖 *conj.* 尽管 | 记忆尺 |
| [ˌwerˈæz] | 📖 although / while | ☐ ☐ ☐ ☐ ☐ |

| **authoritative** | 🔖 *adj.* 当局的 | 记忆尺 |
| [əˈθɔːrəteɪtɪv] | 📖 official | ☐ ☐ ☐ ☐ ☐ |

| **comparative** | 🔖 *adj.* 比较而言的 | 记忆尺 |
| [kəmˈpærətɪv] | 📖 relative | ☐ ☐ ☐ ☐ ☐ |

| **innumerable** | 🔖 *adj.* 数不清的 | 记忆尺 |
| [ɪˈnuːmərəbl] | 📖 countless | ☐ ☐ ☐ ☐ ☐ |

seep [siːp]	☑ v. 渗出 ☐ flow slowly	记忆尺 ☐☐☐☐☐
arduous ['ɑːrdʒuəs]	☑ adj. 费力的 ☐ difficult	记忆尺 ☐☐☐☐☐
devise [dɪ'vaɪz]	☑ v. 发明 ☐ create	记忆尺 ☐☐☐☐☐
ensuing [ɪn'suːɪŋ]	☑ adj. 随后的 ☐ subsequent	记忆尺 ☐☐☐☐☐
pale [peɪl]	☑ v. 相形见绌 ☐ lose significance	记忆尺 ☐☐☐☐☐
graphically ['græfɪkli]	☑ adv. 生动地 ☐ vividly	记忆尺 ☐☐☐☐☐
harness ['hɑːrnɪs]	☑ v. 利用 ☐ utilize	记忆尺 ☐☐☐☐☐
humble ['hʌmbl]	☑ adj. 简陋的 ☐ modest	记忆尺 ☐☐☐☐☐
pessimistic [ˌpesɪ'mɪstɪk]	☑ adj. 悲观的 ☐ negative	记忆尺 ☐☐☐☐☐
regulate ['regjuleɪt]	☑ v. 管理 ☐ control	记忆尺 ☐☐☐☐☐
spearhead ['spɪrhed]	☑ v. 充当先锋 ☐ lead	记忆尺 ☐☐☐☐☐
albeit [ˌɔːl'biːɪt]	☑ conj. 尽管 ☐ though	记忆尺 ☐☐☐☐☐
coating ['koʊtɪŋ]	☑ n. 表皮 ☐ layer	记忆尺 ☐☐☐☐☐

deteriorate

[dɪ'tɪrɪəreɪt]

v. 恶化

get worse

记忆尺

☐ ☐ ☐ ☐ ☐

endeavor

[ɪn'devər]

n. 努力

effort

记忆尺

☐ ☐ ☐ ☐ ☐

term

[tɜːrm]

v. 把…称作

be known as / call

记忆尺

☐ ☐ ☐ ☐ ☐

conjunction

[kən'dʒʌŋkʃn]

n. 连接

combination

记忆尺

☐ ☐ ☐ ☐ ☐

erode	v. 侵蚀	记忆尺
[ɪ'roʊd]	wear down	☐☐☐☐☐
instructive	adj. 有指导意义的	记忆尺
[ɪn'strʌktɪv]	informative	☐☐☐☐☐
threaten	v. 威胁	记忆尺
['θretn]	endanger	☐☐☐☐☐
legible	adj. 容易辨认的	记忆尺
['ledʒəbl]	recognizable	☐☐☐☐☐
accustomed to	习惯于…	记忆尺
	used to	☐☐☐☐☐
assure	v. 确保	记忆尺
[ə'ʃʊr]	guarantee	☐☐☐☐☐
engrave	v. 雕刻	记忆尺
[ɪn'greɪv]	carve	☐☐☐☐☐
sovereign	n. 君主	记忆尺
['saːvrən]	master	☐☐☐☐☐
compulsorily	adv. 强制地	记忆尺
[kəm'pʌlsərəli]	by requirement	☐☐☐☐☐
desolate	adj. 荒无人烟的	记忆尺
['desələt]	deserted	☐☐☐☐☐

outdated [ˌaʊtˈdeɪtɪd]	*adj.* 过时的 old-fashioned	记忆尺 ☐ ☐ ☐ ☐ ☐
resurgence [rɪˈsɜːrdʒəns]	*n.* 复兴 comeback	记忆尺 ☐ ☐ ☐ ☐ ☐
conversely [ˈkɑːnvɜːrsli]	*adv.* 与此相反 on the contrary	记忆尺 ☐ ☐ ☐ ☐ ☐
intense [ɪnˈtens]	*adj.* 强烈的 strong / extreme	记忆尺 ☐ ☐ ☐ ☐ ☐
resume [rɪˈzuːm]	*v.* 重新开始 restart	记忆尺 ☐ ☐ ☐ ☐ ☐
pose [poʊz]	*v.* 提出 present	记忆尺 ☐ ☐ ☐ ☐ ☐
transition [trænˈzɪʃn]	*n.* 转变 change	记忆尺 ☐ ☐ ☐ ☐ ☐
apart from	除…之外 besides / except for	记忆尺 ☐ ☐ ☐ ☐ ☐
infrequent [ɪnˈfrikwənt]	*adj.* 罕见的 uncommon	记忆尺 ☐ ☐ ☐ ☐ ☐
legendary [ˈledʒənderi]	*adj.* 传奇的，著名的 famous	记忆尺 ☐ ☐ ☐ ☐ ☐
revise [rɪˈvaɪz]	*v.* 修订 change	记忆尺 ☐ ☐ ☐ ☐ ☐
unintentional [ˌʌnɪnˈtenʃənl]	*adj.* 非故意的 accidental / unplanned	记忆尺 ☐ ☐ ☐ ☐ ☐
to have been accidental	偶然的 to have occurred by chance	记忆尺 ☐ ☐ ☐ ☐ ☐

allusion [ə'luːʒn]	*n.* 暗示 reference	记忆尺 ☐ ☐ ☐ ☐ ☐
authenticity [ˌɔːθen'tɪsəti]	*n.* 真实性 genuineness	记忆尺 ☐ ☐ ☐ ☐ ☐
enigmatic [ˌenɪg'mætɪk]	*adj.* 神秘的 mysterious	记忆尺 ☐ ☐ ☐ ☐ ☐
location [loʊ'keɪʃn]	*n.* 位置 place	记忆尺 ☐ ☐ ☐ ☐ ☐
pristine ['prɪstiːn]	*adj.* 纯净的 pure	记忆尺 ☐ ☐ ☐ ☐ ☐
reluctant [rɪ'lʌktənt]	*adj.* 不情愿的 unwilling	记忆尺 ☐ ☐ ☐ ☐ ☐
tentatively **identified**	初步确定的 identified without certainty	记忆尺 ☐ ☐ ☐ ☐ ☐
ample ['æmpl]	*adj.* 丰富的 plentiful	记忆尺 ☐ ☐ ☐ ☐ ☐
contention [kən'tenʃn]	*n.* 争论 debate	记忆尺 ☐ ☐ ☐ ☐ ☐
debate [dɪ'beɪt]	*v.* 争论 argue about	记忆尺 ☐ ☐ ☐ ☐ ☐
elaboration [ɪˌlæbə'reɪʃn]	*n.* 详尽阐述 development	记忆尺 ☐ ☐ ☐ ☐ ☐
imaginative [ɪ'mædʒɪnətɪv]	*adj.* 有想象力的 creative	记忆尺 ☐ ☐ ☐ ☐ ☐
option ['ɑːpʃn]	*n.* 选择 choice	记忆尺 ☐ ☐ ☐ ☐ ☐

| **practical** | adj. 实用的 | 记忆尺 |
| ['præktɪkl] | usable | ☐☐☐☐☐ |

| **reasonable** | adj. 合情理的 | 记忆尺 |
| ['riːznəbl] | sufficient | ☐☐☐☐☐ |

| **therefore** | adv. 因此 | 记忆尺 |
| ['ðerfɔːr] | as a result | ☐☐☐☐☐ |

| **cramp** | v. 阻碍 | 记忆尺 |
| [kræmp] | confine | ☐☐☐☐☐ |

| **fringe** | n. 边缘 | 记忆尺 |
| [frɪndʒ] | border | ☐☐☐☐☐ |

| **gain** | n. 增加 | 记忆尺 |
| [geɪn] | increase | ☐☐☐☐☐ |

| **momentous** | adj. 关键的 | 记忆尺 |
| [moʊ'mentəs] | very important | ☐☐☐☐☐ |

| **prospect** | n. 预料 | 记忆尺 |
| ['prɑːspekt] | possibility | ☐☐☐☐☐ |

| **shift** | v. 转变 | 记忆尺 |
| [ʃɪft] | change | ☐☐☐☐☐ |

| **supersede** | v. 取代 | 记忆尺 |
| [ˌsuːpər'siːd] | replace | ☐☐☐☐☐ |

| **terrestrial** | adj. 陆地的 | 记忆尺 |
| [tə'restriəl] | land | ☐☐☐☐☐ |

| **accumulation** | n. 聚集 | 记忆尺 |
| [ə,kjuːmjə'leɪʃn] | deposit | ☐☐☐☐☐ |

| **circumstance** | n. 环境 | 记忆尺 |
| ['sɜːrkəmstæns] | condition | ☐☐☐☐☐ |

enjoy
[ɪnˈdʒɔɪ]

v. 享有
experience

记忆尺
☐ ☐ ☐ ☐ ☐

friction
[ˈfrɪkʃn]

n. 摩擦
conflict

记忆尺
☐ ☐ ☐ ☐ ☐

heterogeneous
[ˌhetərəˈdʒiːniəs]

adj. 各种各样的
varied

记忆尺
☐ ☐ ☐ ☐ ☐

音频

legitimately [lɪ'dʒɪtɪmətli]	*adv.* 正当地 properly	记忆尺 ☐☐☐☐☐
likewise ['laɪkwaɪz]	*adv.* 同样地 similarly	记忆尺 ☐☐☐☐☐
reveal [rɪ'viːl]	*v.* 揭示 show	记忆尺 ☐☐☐☐☐
substantiate [səb'stænʃieɪt]	*v.* 证实 confirm	记忆尺 ☐☐☐☐☐
suppress [sə'pres]	*v.* 镇压 stop by force	记忆尺 ☐☐☐☐☐
trend [trend]	*n.* 趋势 tendency	记忆尺 ☐☐☐☐☐
empirical [ɪm'pɪrɪkl]	*adj.* 凭经验的 based on observation	记忆尺 ☐☐☐☐☐
illuminate [ɪ'luːmɪneɪt]	*v.* 照明 light	记忆尺 ☐☐☐☐☐
progressive [prə'gresɪv]	*adj.* 逐步的 increasing	记忆尺 ☐☐☐☐☐
impediment [ɪm'pedɪmənt]	*n.* 阻碍 obstruction	记忆尺 ☐☐☐☐☐

inflate [ɪn'fleɪt]	v. 膨胀 enlarge	记忆尺 ☐ ☐ ☐ ☐ ☐
norm [nɔːrm]	n. 规范 rule	记忆尺 ☐ ☐ ☐ ☐ ☐
signal ['sɪgnəl]	v.（发信号）通知 communicate	记忆尺 ☐ ☐ ☐ ☐ ☐
analogous to	与…类似的 similar to	记忆尺 ☐ ☐ ☐ ☐ ☐
consensus [kən'sensəs]	n. 共识 agreement	记忆尺 ☐ ☐ ☐ ☐ ☐
ethic ['eθɪk]	n. 道德规范 a set of moral principles	记忆尺 ☐ ☐ ☐ ☐ ☐
interplay ['ɪntərpleɪ]	n. 相互作用 interaction	记忆尺 ☐ ☐ ☐ ☐ ☐
intrinsically [ɪn'trɪnzɪkli]	adv. 本质上 fundamentally	记忆尺 ☐ ☐ ☐ ☐ ☐
meager ['miːgər]	adj. 贫乏的 thin / very low	记忆尺 ☐ ☐ ☐ ☐ ☐
postulate ['pɑːstʃəleɪt]	v. 假设 hypothesize	记忆尺 ☐ ☐ ☐ ☐ ☐
repudiate [rɪ'pjuːdieɪt]	v. 拒绝 reject	记忆尺 ☐ ☐ ☐ ☐ ☐
course through	流过 run through	记忆尺 ☐ ☐ ☐ ☐ ☐

deceive	*v.* 欺骗	记忆尺
[dɪ'siːv]	mislead	☐☐☐☐☐
drastic	*adj.* 极端的	记忆尺
['dræstɪk]	extreme	☐☐☐☐☐
extended	*adj.* 延长的	记忆尺
[ɪk'stendɪd]	long	☐☐☐☐☐
afford	*v.* 供给	记忆尺
[ə'fɔːrd]	offer / provide	☐☐☐☐☐
interlock	*v.* 连结	记忆尺
[ˌɪntər'lɑːk]	link	☐☐☐☐☐
flow	*n.* 流动	记忆尺
[floʊ]	movement	☐☐☐☐☐
adept	*adj.* 熟练的	记忆尺
[ə'dept]	skillful	☐☐☐☐☐
credible	*adj.* 可信的	记忆尺
['kredəbl]	believable	☐☐☐☐☐
paradoxically	*adv.* 自相矛盾地	记忆尺
[ˌpærə'dɑːksɪkli]	surprisingly	☐☐☐☐☐
prestige	*n.* 威望	记忆尺
[pre'stiːʒ]	status	☐☐☐☐☐
verify	*v.* 证实	记忆尺
['verɪfaɪ]	establish the truth of	☐☐☐☐☐
deviate	*v.* 脱离	记忆尺
['diːvieɪt]	depart	☐☐☐☐☐
endow	*v.* 赋予	记忆尺
[ɪn'daʊ]	provide	☐☐☐☐☐

potent ['poʊtnt]	adj. 有效的 powerful	记忆尺 □□□□□
quantifiable [ˌkwɑːntɪˈfaɪəbl]	adj. 可量化的 measurable	记忆尺 □□□□□
size up	估计 evaluate	记忆尺 □□□□□
assist in	有助于 help with	记忆尺 □□□□□
depict [dɪˈpɪkt]	v. 描述 picture / portray	记忆尺 □□□□□
fracture [ˈfræktʃər]	n. 断裂 crack	记忆尺 □□□□□
immobile [ɪˈmoʊbl]	adj. 不动的 motionless	记忆尺 □□□□□
neglect [nɪˈglekt]	v. 忽略 fail to do	记忆尺 □□□□□
overshadow [ˌoʊvərˈʃædoʊ]	v. 使失色 distract from	记忆尺 □□□□□
paradox [ˈpærədɑːks]	n. 自相矛盾的话 contradiction	记忆尺 □□□□□
regard [rɪˈgɑːrd]	v. 把…视为… consider	记忆尺 □□□□□
context [ˈkɑːntekst]	n. 环境 environment	记忆尺 □□□□□
core [kɔːr]	n. 核心 center	记忆尺 □□□□□

| **impose on** | 把…强加于 | 记忆尺 |
| | place on | ☐ ☐ ☐ ☐ ☐ |

| **prediction** | *n.* 预测 | 记忆尺 |
| [prɪ'dɪkʃn] | expectation | ☐ ☐ ☐ ☐ ☐ |

音频

preposterous [prɪ'pɑːstərəs]	释 *adj.* 不合理的	记忆尺
	同 unbelievable / ridiculous	▢▢▢▢▢
innovation [ˌɪnə'veɪʃn]	释 *n.* 革新	记忆尺
	同 new development / change	▢▢▢▢▢
deliberation [dɪˌlɪbə'reɪʃn]	释 *n.* 协商	记忆尺
	同 discussion	▢▢▢▢▢
erratic [ɪ'rætɪk]	释 *adj.* 不稳定的	记忆尺
	同 unpredictable	▢▢▢▢▢
instigate ['ɪnstɪɡeɪt]	释 *v.* 煽动	记忆尺
	同 cause	▢▢▢▢▢
invoke [ɪn'voʊk]	释 *v.* 请求	记忆尺
	同 call upon	▢▢▢▢▢
status ['stætəs]	释 *n.* 重要地位	记忆尺
	同 importance	▢▢▢▢▢
champion ['tʃæmpiən]	释 *v.* 拥护	记忆尺
	同 support	▢▢▢▢▢
out of sight	释 隐藏的	记忆尺
	同 hidden	▢▢▢▢▢
overlie [ˌoʊvər'laɪ]	释 *v.* 躺（或伏）在…上面	记忆尺
	同 cover	▢▢▢▢▢

| **penchant** | *n.* 倾向 | 记忆尺 |
| ['pentʃənt] | inclination | ☐ ☐ ☐ ☐ ☐ |

| **plug** | *v.* 填塞 | 记忆尺 |
| [plʌg] | fill up | ☐ ☐ ☐ ☐ ☐ |

| **phenomenon** | *n.* 现象 | 记忆尺 |
| [fə'nɑːmɪnən] | occurrence | ☐ ☐ ☐ ☐ ☐ |

| **prone** | *adj.* 有可能的 | 记忆尺 |
| [proʊn] | likely | ☐ ☐ ☐ ☐ ☐ |

| **so much for** | 有关…就到此为止 | 记忆尺 |
| | that is enough about | ☐ ☐ ☐ ☐ ☐ |

| **aggregate** | *v.* 聚集 | 记忆尺 |
| ['ægrɪgeɪt] | combine | ☐ ☐ ☐ ☐ ☐ |

| **compression** | *n.* 压缩 | 记忆尺 |
| [kəm'preʃn] | crush | ☐ ☐ ☐ ☐ ☐ |

| **diverse** | *adj.* 各种各样的 | 记忆尺 |
| [daɪ'vɜːrs] | varied | ☐ ☐ ☐ ☐ ☐ |

| **ratio** | *n.* 比例 | 记忆尺 |
| ['reɪʃioʊ] | proportion | ☐ ☐ ☐ ☐ ☐ |

| **static** | *adj.* 静止的 | 记忆尺 |
| ['stætɪk] | unchanging | ☐ ☐ ☐ ☐ ☐ |

| **appreciate** | *v.* 理解 | 记忆尺 |
| [ə'priːʃieɪt] | understand | ☐ ☐ ☐ ☐ ☐ |

| **agency** | *n.* 力量 | 记忆尺 |
| ['eɪdʒənsi] | force | ☐ ☐ ☐ ☐ ☐ |

		记忆尺
keep pace with	和…保持同步 match the increase in	☐☐☐☐☐
logical ['lɑːdʒɪkl]	*adj.* 合乎逻辑的 reasonable	☐☐☐☐☐
mutually beneficial	互利的 helpful to one another	☐☐☐☐☐
document ['dɑːkjumənt]	*n.* 记录 record	☐☐☐☐☐
compel [kəm'pel]	*v.* 迫使 require	☐☐☐☐☐
obligation [ˌɑːblɪ'geɪʃn]	*n.* 义务 responsibility	☐☐☐☐☐
amount to	合计 total	☐☐☐☐☐
method ['meθəd]	*n.* 方法 way	☐☐☐☐☐
squander ['skwɑːndər]	*v.* 挥霍 waste	☐☐☐☐☐
accrete [ə'kriːt]	*v.* 附着 come together	☐☐☐☐☐
agitate ['ædʒɪteɪt]	*v.* 煽动 create movement in	☐☐☐☐☐
assistance [ə'sɪstəns]	*n.* 协助 help	☐☐☐☐☐

channel	v. 引导	记忆尺
['tʃænl]	direct	□ □ □ □ □

concept	n. 概念	记忆尺
['kɑːnsept]	idea	□ □ □ □ □

concur	v. 同意	记忆尺
[kən'kɜːr]	agree	□ □ □ □ □

despondent	adj. 沮丧的	记忆尺
[dɪ'spɑːndənt]	unhappy	□ □ □ □ □

expand	v. 扩张	记忆尺
[ɪk'spænd]	enlarge	□ □ □ □ □

fastidious	adj. 挑剔的	记忆尺
[fæ'stɪdiəs]	demanding	□ □ □ □ □

gather some momentum	取得进展	记忆尺
	make progress	□ □ □ □ □

gratify	v. 使满足	记忆尺
['grætɪfaɪ]	satisfy	□ □ □ □ □

illusory	adj. 错觉的	记忆尺
[ɪ'luːsəri]	misleading	□ □ □ □ □

immeasurably	adv. 极大地	记忆尺
[ɪ'meʒərəbli]	greatly	□ □ □ □ □

inclination	n. 倾向	记忆尺
[ˌɪnklɪ'neɪʃn]	tendency	□ □ □ □ □

precious	adj. 宝贵的	记忆尺
['preʃəs]	valuable	□ □ □ □ □

prestigious [preˈstɪdʒəs]	adj. 有威信的 highly regarded	记忆尺 ☐ ☐ ☐ ☐ ☐
propulsion [prəˈpʌlʃn]	n. 推进 moving forward	记忆尺 ☐ ☐ ☐ ☐ ☐
provided that	conj. 只要 as long as / if	记忆尺 ☐ ☐ ☐ ☐ ☐
rate [reɪt]	v. 评价 judge	记忆尺 ☐ ☐ ☐ ☐ ☐

练习部分

1

C The word "fragile" in the passage is closest in meaning to
A. defective
B. rarely touched
C. easily damaged
D. ill-founded

In some circumstances, the most fragile species of plants are killed off, then invasive species take over.

2

A The word "interpreted" in the passage is closest in meaning to
A. compromised
B. favored
C. surrendered
D. understood

The odd finding has been interpreted as the remains of a bath where the whole family and its guest would relax and chat.

3

D The word "match" in the passage is closest in meaning to
A. explore
B. sustain
C. surpass
D. equal

Due to global warming, glaciers have been melting, evaporating and calving (slit into smaller masses of ice) at higher rates because there is not enough snowfall to match or exceed the annual loss.

4

D The word "occasionally" in the passage is closest in meaning to
A. preferably
B. skillfully
C. frequently
D. sometimes

Occasionally, the discovery of an artifacts-rich area permits a comprehensive study of one particular historic era in that area.

CONTINUE

5 *B*

The word "perceived" in the passage is closest in meaning to
A. accredited
B. expressed
C. communicated
D. saw

Although the Copernican principle was sound, many people at the time perceived the idea as something too far from their experience and everyday life.

6 *B*

The phrase "a wealth of" in the passage is closest in meaning to
A. something prosperous
B. a source of valuables
C. deep interest in
D. an abundance of

There is a wealth of tax benefits for families with many children; in fact, the government is increasingly relieving the tax-burden on big families.

7 *A*

The phrase "susceptible to" in the passage is closest in meaning to
A. likely to be affected by
B. make a difference in
C. likely to affect
D. react to something

During the recovery period, a patient's injured limb is extremely susceptible to infections. Thus, doctors recommend absolute rest.

8 *B*

The phrase "vulnerable to" in the passage is closest in meaning to
A. nonexistent
B. dominated over
C. easily attacked by
D. outnumbered

Rodents are vulnerable to wild dogs and other vicious predators, and consequently their populations are decreasing in areas where predator populations are increasing.

9 *D*

The phrase "appealed to" in the passage is closest in meaning to
A. counted on
B. respected
C. sustained
D. attracted

Ministers from different countries appealed to European governments to request that air pollution standards be applied consistently across industries in the whole European Union.

CONTINUE

10 *D*

The word "ascended" in the passage is closest in meaning to
A. arrived at
B. dived
C. connected
D. climbed

The climbers ascended the rocky trail by snapping through branches.

11 *B*

The word "apparent" in the passage is closest in meaning to
A. considerable
B. obvious
C. handsome
D. decent

It was apparent that the artifact had been there for a long time, so the hikers notified archaeologists, who carefully excavated the relict.

12 *C*

The word "comprehensive" in the passage is closest in meaning to
A. hard-working
B. clever
C. thorough
D. harsh

Experts claim that to promote the advantages of nuclear power plants, we need a comprehensive climate policy that puts a price on carbon emissions and promotes sources of renewable energy.

13 *A*

The word "continuously" in the passage is closest in meaning to
A. for a limited amount of time
B. unlimited time
C. quite a long time
D. determined amount of time

For the next few weeks, the researchers will continuously measure water levels.

14 *B*

The word "encompasses" in the passage is closest in meaning to
A. commits
B. includes
C. enters
D. registers for

The Department of Public Safety's recent policy change encompasses a number of rules intended to prevent accidents caused by reckless drivers.

112

CONTINUE

15

D The word "ensure" in the passage is closest in meaning to
A. improve
B. raise
C. control
D. guarantee

Governmental authorities took action to ensure a food supply from alternative sources when the famine devastated local crops and killed the country's livestock.

16

C The word "faithful" in the passage is closest in meaning to
A. unpredictable
B. extensive
C. exact
D. historical

It was a faithful reproduction of one particular cup the Templars used to serve wine at their famous round table.

17

C The word "lethal" in the passage is closest in meaning to
A. beneficial
B. deadly
C. consequential
D. proactive

Heat is lethal to senior citizens, animals and small children – this isn't an issue of comfort, it's an issue of safety.

18

C The word "merely" in the passage is closest in meaning to
A. additionally
B. conversely
C. only
D. newly

And yet, the different cultures and traditions of each civilization merely represent different ways of being human.

19

B The word "segregated" in the passage is closest in meaning to
A. separated
B. left
C. quitted
D. accused

After conquering most of Europe, the ruthless emperor segregated it into different provinces to increase his imperial power across multiple domains.

CONTINUE

20

The word "speculated" in the passage is closest in meaning to
A. concluded from evidence
B. recognized
C. put forward as a possibility
D. stood for

Many people speculated on the origins and use of such a colossal structure until archeologists discovered that it was used as a burial site.

21

The word "subsequent" in the passage is closest in meaning to
A. concurrent
B. following
C. postponed
D. in order

Researchers were not preoccupied because usually, abnormal test results normalize in subsequent tests.

22

The word "tremendous" in the passage is closest in meaning to
A. temporary
B. endless
C. unexpected
D. enormous

Yet, geologists who work in different areas observe tremendous differences in local sediment composition, structure and formation, which all depend on past weather conditions and local biota.

23

The word "unintentional" in the passage is closest in meaning to
A. concurrent
B. unplanned
C. fortunate
D. appropriate

Mr. King argued that unintentional race biases permeated the society we lived in, especially the disproportional number of nonwhite prisoners who were incarcerated for petty crimes.

24

The word "unrivaled" in the passage is closest in meaning to
A. troubled
B. uneven
C. unequaled
D. unbalanced

The vessel offers researchers a unique, unrivaled opportunity to study 18th-century shipbuilding.

CONTINUE

25

The word "leftover" in the passage is closest in meaning to

A. legacy
B. remaining
C. surviving
D. spare

At the end of each business day, the coffee shop employees donate the store's leftover muffins to the soup kitchen.

26

The phrase "admiration for" in the passage is closest in meaning to

A. applause
B. honor
C. love
D. a high opinion of

Although most psychologists have admiration for Sigmund Freud, very few maintain his theories as correct.

27

The word "garment" in the passage is closest in meaning to

A. article of clothing
B. costume
C. uniform
D. ritual

The Kung bushman's garment left little to the stuffy anthropologist's imagination. In contrast, the scientist stood covered from head to foot in linen.

28

The word "obtained" in the passage is closest in meaning to

A. achieved
B. gathered
C. seized
D. purchased

After repeating the experiment several times, the chemist was confident that she had obtained enough data for publication.

29

The word "preserved" in the passage is closest in meaning to

A. frozen
B. survived
C. protected
D. sustained

The Union was preserved after four bloody years of Civil War in which brother was pitted against brother on the battlefield.

CONTINUE

30

The phrase "put up with" in the passage is closest in meaning to
A. bolster
B. enforce
C. support
D. tolerate

Few bankers were able to put up with the severe downturn in the Stock Market following the crash of 1929.

31

The word "entails" in the passage is closest in meaning to
A. encompasses
B. necessitates
C. involves
D. brings about

Archaeological excavation entails careful digging with a trowel and detailed note-taking, so that the context of the finds can be understood.

32

The word "essential" in the passage is closest in meaning to
A. crucial
B. needed
C. necessary
D. main

The biologist was unable to convince the peer reviewers that his essential hypothesis about yeast reproduction was borne out with enough experimentation.

33

The word "annual" in the passage is closest in meaning to
A. weekly
B. monthly
C. decennially
D. yearly

New York's annual New Year's Eve festival attracts over one-million partygoers who withstand freezing temperatures to stand for hours in Time Square.

34

The word "observation" in the passage is closest in meaning to
A. consideration
B. view
C. measurement
D. finding

Despite a rigorous methodology and robust sample size in his study, the sociologist's observation about the success of "Free Needle" programs was met by skepticism and contempt by those who thought such programs only promoted drug use.

CONTINUE

The word "verified" in the passage is closest in meaning to
A. authorized
B. confirmed
C. challenged
D. substituted

Eratosthenes calculated the circumference of the earth in ca. 200 BCE with only crude instruments and complex mathematics, but his findings have been verified by many scholars, ancient and modern.

The word "converged" in the passage is closest in meaning to
A. met at
B. assembled
C. mingled
D. coincided

Because of the downed traffic light, all the cars from both roads converged on the intersection, creating a hopeless deadlock.

The word "vanishing" in the passage is closest in meaning to
A. disappearing
B. dying out
C. clearing
D. becoming invisible

With global warming, the polar icecaps are vanishing at an incredible rate, resulting in a higher sea level.

The word "feature" in the passage is closest in meaning to
A. component
B. aspect
C. factor
D. detail

A prominent feature of the high Sierras is the rounded, granite mountain tops that form distinctive dome and half-dome shapes.

The word "verging" in the passage is closest in meaning to
A. ending
B. abutting
C. bordering
D. communicating

With rampant fiscal deregulation and loose loan requirements, the US's economy was verging on a recession for years prior to 2009.

CONTINUE

40

The word "admirably" in the passage is closest in meaning to
A. faultlessly
B. correctly
C. very well
D. densely

The Civil Rights leaders of the 1950s and 1960s fought admirably for the equal rights of all, and their efforts helped bring about the seminal Civil Rights Act of 1964.

41

The phrase "almost universal" in the passage is closest in meaning to
A. nearly ubiquitous
B. closely approaching
C. without exception
D. used by almost all

The presence and use of fins to help in swimming is almost universal among fish, both fresh and saltwater.

42

The word "identifiable" in the passage is closest in meaning to
A. attributable
B. recognizable
C. accountable
D. verifiable

Individuals suffering from Bubonic Plague are immediately identifiable in Medieval art by the presence of swollen glands on their necks and legs.

43

The word "attests" in the passage is closest in meaning to
A. ratifies
B. announces
C. swears
D. confirms

Although a body was never found, the glut of blood at the crime scene attests the murder of the missing man.

44

The word "inherent" in the passage is closest in meaning to
A. implicit
B. essential
C. built-in
D. congenital

Because of their inherent ability to find their home, pigeons have been used to send messages by traveling nobleman for centuries.

CONTINUE

45

The word "fluid" in the passage is closest in meaning to
A. solution
B. changing
C. liquid
D. juice

As the slug crawls across the sidewalk, he leaves behind a viscous fluid attesting to his earlier travels.

46

The word "insists" in the passage is closest in meaning to
A. states forcefully
B. demands
C. presses
D. persists

The yoga instructor always insists that she isn't a picky eater, but her elaborate coffee order suggests otherwise.

47

The word "copious" in the passage is closest in meaning to
A. extensive
B. eager
C. lavish
D. abundant

Fearful that he would not have enough subjects for his experiment, the social psychologist offered a monetary reward that lured copious volunteers—some of whom he had to turn away!

48

The word "assertion" in the passage is closest in meaning to
A. insistence
B. claim
C. prediction
D. defense

Despite an overwhelming majority of scientists and doctors asserting the contrary, some in the public still support the baseless assertion that vaccines are harmful to growing children.

49

The word "remnants" in the passage is closest in meaning to
A. detritus
B. residue
C. remains
D. excess

Not all the remnants of lost cultures that are excavated find their way to museums; most of the material is stored in anonymous storage facilities in their country of origin.

119

The word "anchors" in the passage is closest in meaning to
A. becomes active
B. holds in place
C. combines forces
D. lasts briefly

Unlike other members of the plant kingdom, lichens are actually a partnership between two plants. The framework of a lichen is usually a network of minute hairlike fungus that anchors the plant.

END

1

The phrase "compensate for" in the passage is closest in meaning to
A. work against
B. conceal a fault
C. make up for
D. spread over

The sector is already expanding towards overseas markets to compensate for reduced domestic request, due to the massive banking crisis.

2

The word "crude" in the passage is closest in meaning to
A. urgent
B. man-made
C. primitive
D. alternative

The crude reality in which Roman infants were brought up, shaped their thinking and their attitude towards life.

3

The word "culminated" in the passage is closest in meaning to
A. aimed for the top
B. reached a high point with
C. heeded expectations
D. finished

Evidence points out that a decisive stimulus behind the rise of early civilizations was the development of agriculture, which caused a series of changes and, eventually, the organization of stable communities that culminated in the rise of reigns.

4

The word "decisive" in the passage is closest in meaning to
A. possible
B. determining
C. helpful
D. limiting

When decisive experiments are unavailable, scientists may resort to forecasts, obtained by using models or computer simulations.

CONTINUE

5

The word "designation" in the passage is closest in meaning to
A. identification
B. reference
C. finding
D. association

The designation of the pink fairy armadillos as a threatened species creates new limitations on the trade of such animal, and might even limit invasive scientific research on them.

6

The word "favor" in the passage is closest in meaning to
A. prefer
B. champion
C. expose
D. explore

Researchers who favor nature over nurture as the primary determinant in human development largely ignore the role that socialization plays in developmental processes.

7

The word "imminent" in the passage is closest in meaning to
A. frequent
B. well understood
C. looking for
D. about to happen

Because climate change has been ignored and diminished for such long time, now the threat it poses is imminent.

8

The word "obsolete" in the passage is closest in meaning to
A. hazardous
B. superfluous
C. criticized
D. out of date

Such an obsolete medical procedure has not been used since the early 19th Century because it is deemed too dangerous.

9

The word "striking" in the passage is closest in meaning to
A. understandable
B. necessary
C. confining
D. noteworthy

One striking event which changed the curse of history was the proliferation of Christianity— which occurred when the once a persecuted cult, became one of the foundations of many states.

CONTINUE

10

The phrase "20 people or so" in the passage is closest in meaning to
A. not even 20 people
B. roughly 20 people
C. much more than 20 people
D. exactly 20 people

The excavation mission carried out by the Egyptian government was comprised of 20 people or so, and, due to the sensitivity of the matter, all of them were sworn to secrecy.

11

The phrase "accounts for" in the passage is closest in meaning to
A. foresees
B. explains
C. defends
D. aggravates

Drunk driving accounts for the majority of fatal incidents, especially during weekends and holidays.

12

The phrase "little short of miraculous" in the passage is closest in meaning to
A. extremely controversial
B. criticized by many because unrealistic
C. amazing because almost impossible
D. planned surprisingly well

The achievements of the team of French archeologists during the restoration of the church's frescos are little short of miraculous.

13

The phrase "expelling" in the passage is closest in meaning to
A. be left by
B. be abandoned by
C. be punished for
D. be bullied by

In light of the dire economic conditions, the European Parliament considered the possibility of expelling Greece from the European Union.

CONTINUE

14

The word "disruption" in the passage is closest in meaning to
A. verification
B. allowance
C. denouncement
D. disturbance

During the presidential candidate's speech, a woman wearing a hijab caused a disruption by openly challenging the candidate's xenophobic remarks.

15

The word "ambitious" in the passage is closest in meaning to
A. impressive but difficult to achieve
B. serving a higher purpose
C. limited by the reality of the facts
D. devoted to a cause

Unless countries develop more ambitious plans, the Earth will suffer from detrimental phenomena, including debilitating heat waves, food shortages, and fast-rising seas.

16

The word "determinants" in the passage is closest in meaning to
A. consequences
B. causes
C. skills
D. occasions

The American Cancer Association contends that tobacco use, asbestos fibers, and familial predisposition are primary determinants in disease contraction.

17

The word "devastated" in the passage is closest in meaning to
A. responded
B. conducted
C. attacked
D. destroyed

The United States coal industry has devastated over 500 mountaintops in West Virginia with the controversial mountaintop removal mining method.

18

The word "dominated" in the passage is closest in meaning to
A. remodeled
B. adapted
C. inspired
D. controlled

Unfortunately, the spurge of industry-driven economies has created an environment dominated by profit-oriented individuals who would do anything to increase their revenue.

CONTINUE

19

The word "emerges" in the passage is closest in meaning to
A. ensures
B. arises
C. argues
D. vents

In Greek mythology, the phoenix emerges from the ashes of its predecessor, which resonates with rebirth tropes across multiple cultural myths and legends.

20

The word "eventual" in the passage is closest in meaning to
A. despotic
B. final
C. universal
D. rigid

Scientists hope to gain enough know-how from Chinese program to be used for eventual long-term space missions.

21

The word "exercised" in the passage is closest in meaning to
A. petitioned
B. spread
C. registered
D. applied

Voters exercised their right to vote, and ousted the unpopular incumbent in favor of a more likable candidate.

22

The word "exhibit" in the passage is closest in meaning to
A. decide
B. resolve
C. specify
D. display

Catalan Chef Ferran Adrain chose to exhibit plasticine models of his food at Somerset House in London, in honor of his landmark restaurant El Bulli.

23

The word "exotic" in the passage is closest in meaning to
A. controversial
B. foreign
C. distant
D. indistinct

Brazilian supermodel Giselle Bundchen appeals to high fashion audiences for her exotic looks and vibrant personality.

CONTINUE ➤

24

The word "focus" in the passage is closest in meaning to
A. depend
B. fund
C. concentrate
D. publish

While many preschool programs focus primarily on cognitive gains and preparing the kids for the formal instruction they will receive in kindergarten, some are geared towards promoting social and emotional development.

25

The word "further" in the passage is closest in meaning to
A. additional
B. clean
C. recent
D. new

Interrupting or slowing down the water cycle will definitely lead to further difficulties with regards to energy production.

26

The word "hence" in the passage is closest in meaning to
A. afterward
B. thus
C. most definitely
D. in particular

The presidential election may have extreme consequences for global relations, hence several economists have decided to stay home on election day in order to watch the results as they are reported.

27

The word "imitator" in the passage is closest in meaning to
A. a person who copies someone else
B. a person who teaches someone else
C. a person who competes against someone else
D. a person who studies under someone else

Early in his professional career, Lebron James rejected accusations that he was an imitator of Michael Jordan, achieving his own records and awards with notable merit.

CONTINUE

28

The word "initially" in the passage is closest in meaning to
A. at first
B. eventually
C. lately
D. for instance

Initially, the research findings were inconclusive, and the medical technology team was discouraged at the lack of progress on their innovative equipment design.

29

The word "lateral" in the passage is closest in meaning to
A. side
B. opposite
C. visional
D. debated

Generally, these entomological projects involve taking top, bottom and lateral pictures of the specimen.

30

The word "penetrated" in the passage is closest in meaning to
A. pierced
B. scattered
C. scared
D. threw

The bullet penetrated with ease through the first layer of ice and continue into the second layer, until it reached the soil underneath.

31

The word "perfected" in the passage is closest in meaning to
A. improved
B. adopted
C. publicized
D. made profitable

Progress has been made in solar technology, and we can see that solar panels are increasingly used even by private citizens; however, the system still needs to be perfected.

32

The word "precise" in the passage is closest in meaning to
A. exact
B. predicted
C. estimated
D. required

Research suggests that public speakers' precise words are less important than their body language, tone and brevity.

CONTINUE ➡

33

The word "predominates" in the passage is closest in meaning to
A. is in the majority
B. is together
C. is increasing
D. first to appear

Along the coast, the type of tree that predominates is the cypress, not the palm.

34

The word "refined" in the passage is closest in meaning to
A. attended
B. cleaned
C. improved
D. paid attention to

Thanks to refined maps, 13th century sailors could trace their path with increased accuracy.

35

The word "rely" in the passage is closest in meaning to
A. depend
B. trust
C. approve
D. connect

The policy encourages citizens to rely more on public transportation or car-sharing and to make their houses more energy-efficient, so as to contribute to the protection of the environment.

36

The word "startled" in the passage is closest in meaning to
A. frustrated
B. confident
C. surprised
D. resisted

Residents have been startled at the dramatic increase in cost of living, including food costs, which have risen 4% since last year.

37

The word "suitable" in the passage is closest in meaning to
A. appropriate
B. certain
C. time-consuming
D. demanding

The ethics committee deemed it was not suitable for the physician to advise against a controversial treatment merely because he did not want to administer it to a dying patient.

CONTINUE ➡

38

The word "tactic" in the passage is closest in meaning to
A. rationale
B. strategy
C. objective
D. cause

This tactic of leaving traditions untouched was extremely beneficial for the central government — this way new colonies would not have perceived the Roman empire as cultural threat.

39

The phrase "take precedence over" in the passage is closest in meaning to
A. have greater importance than
B. more wildly known
C. commonly believed true
D. influential

In the European system, laws emanated by the European Parliament take precedence over national legislation.

40

The word "virtually" in the passage is closest in meaning to
A. enough
B. almost
C. well off
D. positively

Virtually all the parties were equally fit for the throne, however only the families with both fortune and connections stood a chance in the fight for the succession.

41

The word "proximity" in the passage is closest in meaning to
A. contiguity
B. distance
C. immediateness
D. closeness

Although the closest star outside the solar system to Earth at about 4.2 light years away, Alpha Centauri's relative proximity is still too distant for any astronaut to reach using modern aerospace technology.

42

The word "intense" in the passage is closest in meaning to
A. acute
B. strong
C. bitter
D. harsh

The blast from a thermonuclear bomb is so intense that its power is only matched by volcanic eruptions or the impact of large asteroids.

CONTINUE

43

The word "considerably" in the passage is closest in meaning to
A. significantly
B. rather
C. well
D. noticeably

Eventually leading to the First World War, the assassination of Archduke Franz Ferdinand had considerably greater international implications than the Black Hand conspirators could have ever imagined.

44

The word "sentimental" in the passage is closest in meaning to
A. silly
B. emotional
C. passionate
D. corny

A sentimental occasion for most awardees, the Nobel Prize seemed almost an annoyance to the recent Literature prize winner, Bob Dylan.

45

The word "assimilate" in the passage is closest in meaning to
A. comprehend
B. digest
C. absorb
D. learn

Not just a casual vacationer to the Greek islands, Janice strives to assimilate even the tiniest aspects of Hellenic culture, including the gestures, language, and predilection for ouzo.

46

The phrase "pointed out" in the passage is closest in meaning to
A. declared
B. stated
C. disguised
D. created

As a pedant studying Art History in college, the pretentious twenty-something pointed out minor aspects of the Monet's landscapes as meaningful clues to the artist's state of mind.

47

The word "contains" in the passage is closest in meaning to
A. accommodates
B. embodies
C. includes
D. incorporates

As the definitive compendium on Petrarch, the massive tome contains every poem and piece of writing by the Renaissance author.

CONTINUE

48

The word "approached" in the passage is closest in meaning to
A. walked toward
B. met
C. threatened
D. came close

Because no pitcher of the modern era has even 70% of his total wins, Cy Young's record will likely never be surpassed or even approached.

49

The word "anonymous" in the passage is closest in meaning to
A. unidentifiable
B. nameless
C. undisclosed
D. inoffensive

Fully carbonized in the eruption of Vesuvius, the papyrus's anonymous text cannot be read without the help of some unknown future technology.

50

The word "beneficial" in the passage is closest in meaning to
A. helpful
B. good
C. profitable
D. benign

Recent reports suggest that coffee consumption is far more beneficial than as just a daily stimulant; it also lowers blood pressure and provides salubrious minerals and vitamins.

END

1

The word "essential" in the passage is closest in meaning to
A. serious
B. acute
C. pedantic
D. fundamental

It is essential to one's health to balance out beneficial bacteria and disease-causing bacteria.

2

The word "feat" in the passage is closest in meaning to
A. average result
B. ambitious approach
C. courageous remark
D. remarkable achievement

Although she chose to climb with a Sherpa guide, Junko Tabei's successful attempt up Mount Everest remains an amazing feat.

3

The word "maintained" in the passage is closest in meaning to
A. requested
B. calmed
C. claimed
D. caused

The managerial team maintained that the new procedures were meant to reduce accidents and diminish the pressure on the single worker.

4

The phrase "a surge of" is closest in meaning to
A. a mixture of
B. a new approach to
C. a sudden increase in
D. going back to

Advances in solar energy technology brought a surge of investments in this field; both private companies and government departments financed a variety or start-ups, which promised to deliver cost-efficient solar panels in a timely manner.

CONTINUE ➡

The phrase "is composed of" in the passage is closest in meaning to
A. get by with
B. is needed for
C. is made up of
D. is put to best use

Water, the human body's major component, is composed of approximately 11% hydrogen and 89% oxygen.

The word "abandoned" in the passage is closest in meaning to
A. indulged in
B. reckoned
C. limited
D. left

While exploring the Amazonian forest, a group of researchers stumbled upon a series of utensils that were abandoned by an ancient tribe.

The word "abrupt" in the passage is closest in meaning to
A. moderate
B. subtle
C. predictable
D. sudden

The abrupt change in farming techniques had a profound consequence on soil fertility, so much so that farmers had to intervene with chemical fertilizers.

The word "adjacent" in the passage is closest in meaning to
A. nearby
B. available
C. adherent
D. fresh

When planning the construction of a skyscraper, both architects and engineers must take into consideration the repercussion of this building on adjacent structures.

The word "advocate" in the passage is closest in meaning to
A. discover
B. complicate
C. support
D. inquire

Those who advocate for nuclear power are focusing their efforts on keeping existing plants in use, rather than building new ones.

CONTINUE

10

The word "alternate" in the passage is closest in meaning to
A. take turns at
B. change
C. follow orders
D. occur

Doctors have been experimenting with a new treatment for malignant carcinomas. They now tend to start with a non-invasive treatment, which makes the cancer more vulnerable, and then alternate between that and a more invasive one.

11

The word "assert" in the passage is closest in meaning to
A. declare
B. resort
C. guide
D. talk about

Experts assert that the climate is indeed changing rapidly; however, both nature and humans are responsible for this change.

12

The word "chronology" in the passage is closest in meaning to
A. a detailed account of previous rulers
B. a fictional historical account
C. a list that pairs past events with dates
D. a famous biography

Although very detailed, the accounts are sometimes hard to follow; the chronology and geography are confusing.

13

The word "coincidence" in the passage is closest in meaning to
A. an alignment of two planets
B. predetermined by a supernatural power
C. a clash of opposing feelings
D. at the same time and by chance

In the case of the dinosaurs, new data have confirmed that the timing of a previously presumed coincidence was suspicious.

CONTINUE

14

The word "compelling" in the passage is closest in meaning to
A. well known
B. persuasive
C. original
D. practical

Compelling ideas were presented, which could change the way we perceive art in modern society. However, these ideas are not yet sufficient to bring about concrete change.

15

The word "conceived" in the passage is closest in meaning to
A. imagined
B. cooked
C. drewed attention
D. enjoyed

The farmlands which characterize modern agriculture are highly artificial, far from anything nature ever conceived.

16

The word "dependable" in the passage is closest in meaning to
A. constant
B. exclusive
C. reliable
D. devoted

Scientists predict that climate will become decreasingly dependable, especially due to severe weather changes across the globe.

17

The word "drastically" in the passage is closest in meaning to
A. severely
B. arguably
C. constantly
D. inalterably

The National Football League is developing new helmets and other safety equipment in an effort to drastically reduce head injuries among its players.

18

The word "elaborately" in the passage is closest in meaning to
A. of extreme value
B. with great detail
C. in its entirety
D. planned long ago

Since its unveiling in 1994 by Pope John Paul II, tourists to the Sistine Chapel have admired the elaborately executed restoration, including color matching to return its vivid scenes to their original hues.

CONTINUE

19

The word "exceed" in the passage is closet in meaning to
A. rise to
B. go beyond
C. maintain
D. reduce

Conservation and alternative energy exceed fossil fuels in cost effectiveness, and promote a healthier planet.

20

The word "formulated" in the passage is closest in meaning to
A. fermented
B. developed
C. infused
D. constructed

In their effort to eradicate poverty among citizens, New York City has formulated new minimum wage laws that will go into effect by the end of 2018.

21

The word "integrate" in the passage is closest in meaning to
A. unify
B. sustain
C. enhance
D. analyze

Many high school counselors integrate their efforts to promote higher education with the admission offices of local colleges and universities.

22

The word "intended" in the passage is closest in meaning to
A. loose
B. abandoned
C. worried
D. desired

One part of the latest economic development plan did not have the intended results, and economists were dismayed at the plan's ultimate failure.

23

The word "permanent" in the passage is closest in meaning to
A. at no time
B. forever
C. resulting
D. for sure

Although many ideas have been presented, none of them posited a permanent solution for global warming.

CONTINUE

24

The word "pioneered" in the passage is closest in meaning to
A. carried out
B. linked
C. produced
D. introduced

Mr. Tony pioneered a new revolutionary heating and cooling system that promises by using semiconductors, and the system will be more efficient and less expensive.

25

The word "potential" in the passage is closest in meaning to
A. powerful
B. possible
C. incredible
D. reliable

Medical personnel should be able to recognize and assess trauma from exposure and its potential negative health consequences.

26

The word "Presumably" in the passage is closest in meaning to
A. It is reasonable that
B. Many believe that
C. It can be argued that
D. It is narrated that

Presumably the weed is taking something from the soil; perhaps it is also contributing something to it.

27

The phrase "remarkably close" in the passage is closest in meaning to
A. almost there
B. extremely close
C. quite distant
D. connected

Astronomers predict that the "Twin comet" will fly remarkably close to the Earth.

28

The word "revered" in the passage is closest in meaning to
A. paid
B. served
C. honored
D. obeyed

Although revered by most, Alexander the Great was not immune from critics and skepticism.

CONTINUE

29

The word "rudimentary" in the passage is closest in meaning to
A. valuable
B. antique
C. mythological
D. primitive

It was during the long winter evenings, when the work had slowed down somewhat, that youngsters might be given a rudimentary education at home.

30

The word "scatter" in the passage is closest in meaning to
A. spread apart
B. exhibit
C. make known
D. smooth

This process causes dust to scatter around the star, producing an excess of infra-red radiation that is easily detected from Earth.

31

The word "supplemented" in the passage is closest in meaning to
A. promoted
B. added to
C. continued
D. counted

The new policy on reduced coal emission supplemented the already existing legislation.

32

The word "undoubtedly" in the passage is closest in meaning to
A. normally
B. actually
C. certainly
D. eventually

Given the research findings on lung cancer, it will undoubtedly become public knowledge that cigarettes are indeed lethal and people should quit smoking if they want to prolong their life.

33

The word "unprecedented" in the passage is closest in meaning to
A. unavoidable
B. unpleasant
C. unrepeatable
D. not previously experienced

An unprecedented heating of our world has caused water shortage and desertification in various regions of the Earth.

CONTINUE

The word "vacated" in the passage is closest in meaning to
A. transferred
B. migrated
C. escaped
D. abandoned

Under duress, the protester vacated the area and returned to his neighborhood to protest from afar.

The word "vicinity" in the passage is closest in meaning to
A. boundary
B. region
C. population
D. resource

All hazardous activities need to stop in the vicinity of a nuclear plant.

The word "competence" in the passage is closest in meaning to
A. qualification
B. fitness
C. savvy
D. ability

The university's IT program aspires to provide all its majors with the computer programming competence to work at any of the nation's leading tech firms.

The word "experimented" in the passage is closest in meaning to
A. competed
B. tried
C. succeeded
D. struggled

With no formal training as a mechanic, the homebody, Jeff, experimented with restoring his boat to make it a sea-worthy vessel.

The word "unprecedented" in the passage is closest in meaning to
A. bizarre
B. unlike anything in the past
C. miraculous
D. unrivaled

Christopher Columbus's seemingly unprecedented discovery of Earth's spherical shape had, in fact, been a relatively well-known among ancient Greeks and Romans.

CONTINUE

39

The word "ceaselessly" in the passage is closest in meaning to
A. unending
B. tirelessly
C. continually
D. forever

With the changing of the seasons, the Canadian geese population ceaselessly makes its biannual migration across continents.

40

The word "extract" in the passage is closest in meaning to
A. remove
B. locate
C. glean
D. distill

There is no need to visit a doctor to extract the sting of a sea urchin; the body will naturally expel the stingers in the course of time.

41

The word "bare" in the passage is closest in meaning to
A. not covered by
B. exposed
C. stripped
D. divested

Losing their brilliant coat of leaves, the bare trees of New England brace themselves to withstand the bitter cold of winter.

42

The word "intriguing" in the passage is closest in meaning to
A. alluring
B. puzzling
C. fascinating
D. stirring

Freakonomics is an intriguing read that captures the reader by demonstrating the underlying economics of everyday decisions.

43

The word "appreciably" in the passage is closest in meaning to
A. emotionally
B. somewhat
C. noticeably
D. significantly

Since the world-wide shortage in cotton began, the cost of clothing has grown appreciably without any indication of a downturn on the horizon.

CONTINUE

44

The word "fluctuation" in the passage is closest in meaning to
A. liquidity
B. variation
C. inconstancy
D. ambivalence

A common attribute of many Middle Eastern styles of singing is a rapid fluctuation in pitch during extended runs of notes.

45

The word "keen" in the passage is closest in meaning to
A. sharp
B. anxious
C. ardent
D. fierce

The edge of an obsidian blade—as little as one atom in thickness—is so keen that it remains among the best tools for eye surgery.

46

The word "secreted" in the passage is closest in meaning to
A. stowed
B. expelled
C. created
D. perspired

As a natural byproduct, a small quantity of pure gold is secreted by the combination of relatively inexpensive compounds.

47

The word "bizarre" in the passage is closest in meaning to
A. paranormal
B. strange
C. comical
D. spectacular

In a bizarre combination of light and moisture in the sky, a fiery cross, or solar halo, can appear in the sky.

48

The word "unpredictable" in the passage is closest in meaning to
A. erratic
B. uncertain
C. unreliable
D. chancy

To many, the next solar eclipse is an unpredictable event, but astronomers and scientists can tell us with extreme accuracy the time of all occurrences in the future.

CONTINUE

49

The word "subdued" in the passage is closest in meaning to
A. defeated
B. restrained
C. checked
D. controlled

In what became known as the "high water mark" of the war, the Battle of Gettysburg resulted in a subdued rebel army that never entered the North again.

50

The word "self-sufficient" in the passage is closest in meaning to
A. efficient
B. closed
C. confident
D. independent

An entirely self-sufficient vessel— one that can produce oxygen, grow food, manage waste, etc.— must be built before there can be a successful colonization of Mars.

END

1

The word "mundane" in the passage is closest in meaning to
A. material
B. ordinary
C. treasured
D. useful

Even mundane chores were difficult for the first artificial intelligence prototype.

2

The word "resolved" in the passage is closest in meaning to
A. settled
B. avoided repeating
C. untied
D. selected

In ancient times there was no such a thing as a defeat in war because wars were resolved when the parties had exhausted their resources.

3

The phrase "excluded from" in the passage is closest in meaning to
A. removed from
B. altered
C. added
D. reduced

The Arkansas Medical Cannabis Act was excluded from the November ballot when supporters failed to secure the necessary number of signatures for its inclusion.

4

The word "allegedly" in the passage is closest in meaning to
A. inevitably
B. continuously
C. supposedly
D. increasingly

The smoking ban was introduced, allegedly, to protect the health of both bartenders and costumers.

CONTINUE

5

The word "artificial" in the passage is closest in meaning to
A. attractive
B. not real
C. short-term
D. well designed

Modern medicine has permitted the creation of artificial limbs, which helps countless patients recover from traumatic losses.

6

The word "capacity" in the passage is closest in meaning to
A. variety of goods
B. distance
C. quality
D. available storage space

The Seed Bank in Svalbard has a particularly high capacity for storage of dormant seeds.

7

The word "collective" in the passage is closest in meaning to
A. outcast
B. public
C. private
D. group

During the Roman Empire (27 BC–476 AD), only aristocrats and few merchants were able to afford private burials; the rest of the population had to endure collective burials, since they were much cheaper.

8

The word "constituents" in the passage is closest in meaning to
A. causes
B. equivalents
C. components
D. goods

The shape and constituents of human artifacts have changed greatly over the course of human history, and they are essential to every archeological study because they offer an insight to the culture and lifestyle of the era.

9

The word "contracts" in the passage is closest in meaning to
A. reduces to
B. expands beyond
C. withdraws below
D. elevates above

Volcanic eruptions spark chemical changes in magma, which contracts to a dark colored ash that escapes into the atmosphere, often causing detrimental impact to human health, aviation, and critical infrastructure, including buildings and roadways.

CONTINUE

10

The word "diffuse" in the passage is closest in meaning to
A. spread
B. destruct
C. squeeze
D. allow

Infectious disease control professionals warn that airborne diseases are the most alarming, considering they diffuse at rapid speed and cannot be controlled once released in open air.

11

The word "dispersal" in the passage is closest in meaning to
A. distribution
B. understanding
C. connection
D. system

During the 2008 economic crisis, many American citizens were infuriated at the federal government's dispersal of $700 billion to U.S. banks.

12

The word "distinct" in the passage is closest in meaning to
A. short
B. simple
C. separate
D. comparable

Although they share most of their genetic material, identical twins often have distinct personalities, passions, and plans for their futures.

13

The word "durable" in the passage is closest in meaning to
A. determined
B. serious
C. passionate
D. long lasting

Even the most durable dinosaur specimens, which usually belong to male dinosaurs, have not proven to be useful in research for dimorphism.

14

The word "elevated" in the passage is closest in meaning to
A. strong
B. keen
C. dear
D. high

In mammals, especially humans, elevated levels of stress hormones adversely impact the immune system by creating a physical condition of perpetual flight versus fight sensations, causing the adrenal system to fatigue.

CONTINUE

15

The word "evolved" in the passage is closest in meaning to
A. developed
B. united
C. freed
D. excused

From 800 to 300 BCE Greek sculptors took inspiration from Egyptian and Near Eastern monumental artists, however, their art evolved into a uniquely Greek style.

16

The word "favorable" in the passage is closest in meaning to
A. powerful
B. advantageous
C. intense
D. persuasive

When Paul Pogba joined Manchester United, he gave the team a favorable boost among the Premier League clubs.

17

The word "fortunately" in the passage is closest in meaning to
A. heroically
B. cautiously
C. luckily
D. clumsily

Race car driver Martin Donnelly fortunately survived a Formula One crash in Spain, when he was thrown from the vehicle before his Lotus 102 disintegrated into a concrete barrier.

18

The word "gradual" in the passage is closest in meaning to
A. crucial
B. original
C. helpful
D. slow

Some economists suggest that the decline among global economies was gradual, which is why many families did not experience the negative effects sooner.

19

The word "hasten" in the passage is closest in meaning to
A. hurry
B. worry
C. apologize
D. impede

In her efforts to hasten research findings, Theranos founder Elizabeth Holmes committed one of the most embarrassing medical fallacies in the history of healthcare technology.

CONTINUE

The word "hierarchical" in the passage is closest in meaning to
A. having several levels of authority
B. dependent on military support
C. based on merit
D. nondemocratic

The Mediterranean society shifted from an agriculture-based, hierarchical society to a war-driven dictatorship.

The word "ideally" in the passage is closest in meaning to
A. absolutely
B. meticulously
C. definitely
D. perfectly

The research findings of the Zika virus study would need to be replicated, ideally in other laboratories and on more test subjects, before being confirmed.

The word "inconclusive" in the passage is closest in meaning to
A. not decisive
B. unimportant
C. not valid
D. misleading

Despite the inconclusive results, the project was refunded the next year.

The word "initiated" in the passage is closest in meaning to
A. looked after
B. exposed
C. started
D. pursued

The recently-elected university Chancellor initiated new policies that halted hazing practices among fraternities and sororities known for extreme pre-membership rituals.

The word "installing" in the passage is closest in meaning to
A. adjusting
B. growing
C. putting in place
D. aiming

Cities and villages throughout the empire adopted Roman habits, thus installing Roman architecture and other traditional symbols of their newly adopted culture.

CONTINUE

25

The word "intact" in the passage is closest in meaning to
A. developing
B. primitive
C. severe
D. undamaged

For unknown reasons, many of such utensils were disposed of and they were later found, often intact, in the Western region of the excavation area.

26

The word "promoted" in the passage is closest in meaning to
A. repeated
B. altered
C. encouraged
D. staged

The new technology and the introduction of the assembly line promoted the development of other industries, such as that of the automobile.

27

The word "reinforce" in the passage is closest in meaning to
A. offer
B. prolong
C. strengthen
D. widen

This study's results reinforce Alexander Friedmann's theory, and justify earlier findings as statistically significant research.

28

The word "seldom" in the passage is closest in meaning to
A. not often
B. on occasion
C. in time
D. weekly

Seldom did the judge ever rule in favor of the defendant, but the present case was lacking evidence that the defendant was guilty of a crime.

29

The word "specified" in the passage is closest in meaning to
A. inferred
B. stated
C. rejected
D. demanded

The type of treatment that the patients will receive has not been specified since doctors are unsure which patients will receive a placebo and which will receive a new drug for testing.

CONTINUE

30

The word "substantially" in the
passage is closest in meaning to
A. mannerly
B. traditionally
C. significantly
D. naturally

Education and family values can
substantially influence one's
attitude and character.

31

The word "superficially" in the
passage is closest in meaning to
A. in the opinion of experts
B. without further delay
C. when done properly
D. without deeper analysis

Superficially, the two test subjects
produced the same results;
however, a deeper analysis
revealed the differences in cell
composition.

32

The word "unanticipated" in the
passage is closest in meaning to
A. without regrets
B. wished for
C. not expected
D. wrongful

The fast development of
renewable technologies—such
as solar panels, wind turbines,
hydroelectric plants and many
others—had some unanticipated
outcomes.

33

The word "properties" in the
passage is closest in meaning to
A. characteristics
B. lands
C. abilities
D. hallmarks

Iron was initially favored over
bronze, not because of its
durability or strength properties,
but because tin, an essential
component of bronze, was difficult
to obtain.

34

The word "allied" in the passage is
closest in meaning to
A. joined
B. connected
C. related
D. bound

The subject matter, hypotheses,
and results were not just allied
in the two papers, but whole
sections of prose were ripped off
from the other.

CONTINUE

The word "compilation" in the passage is closest in meaning to
A. assembling
B. collection
C. unifying
D. digest

For some, a scrapbook is not just a compilation of significant objections, but a long document of lifetime's greatest memories.

The word "unethical" in the passage is closest in meaning to
A. improper
B. illegal
C. unfair
D. dirty

Although not strictly against company policy, it is considered unethical within the climate of the office to "call in sick" in order to extend a personal vacation.

The word "succeeding" in the passage is closest in meaning to
A. accomplished
B. gained
C. replacing
D. following

The succeeding president canceled many of the big-budget items of his predecessor, such as costly research programs and travel grants.

The word "persuasive" in the passage is closest in meaning to
A. cogent
B. valid
C. convincing
D. potent

The parents' alliance failed to make persuasive arguments to the schoolboard in support of a proposed classroom ban on evolution and the science textbooks remained unchanged.

The word "corroborate" in the passage is closest in meaning to
A. endorse
B. substantiate
C. confirm
D. justify

Unable to corroborate the results of the first yeast-growth experiment in subsequent tests, the biologists were forced to resign their hypothesis and move on to a new experiment.

CONTINUE

40

The phrase "related to" in the passage is closest in meaning to
A. in proportion to
B. a family of
C. similar to
D. identical with

With the 1:20,000 scale provided in the map's legend, the real length of the trail was related to the small drawing on the map.

41

The word "distracted" in the passage is closest in meaning to
A. made distraught
B. preoccupied
C. abstracted
D. troubled

On his way to the coop, the chicken is distracted by an unfamiliar stimulus and he fails to reach his nest.

42

The word "mutual" in the passage is closest in meaning to
A. communal
B. collective
C. associated
D. shared

Sharing a mutual distrust, the candidates for state governor verbally attacked each other at both the debates and in private meetings.

43

The word "booming" in the passage is closest in meaning to
A. rapidly growing
B. prosperous
C. roaring
D. profitable

Population sizes in cities are booming with millennials increasingly choosing urban life over suburban.

44

The word "intrusive" in the passage is closest in meaning to
A. nosy
B. meddlesome
C. unwelcome
D. forward

Although mold is a sure sign that food has gone bad, other intrusive bacteria can be wreaking havoc in food that otherwise looks pristine.

CONTINUE ▶

45

The word "barring" in the passage is closest in meaning to
A. except for
B. blocking
C. despite
D. avoiding

The tennis match will be played as scheduled, barring any inclement weather or act of god.

46

The word "classic" in the passage is closest in meaning to
A. simple
B. standard
C. vintage
D. typical

When his car broke down on the way to the airport, the man swore that it was a classic example of his bad luck.

47

The word "fabricate" in the passage is closest in meaning to
A. assemble
B. contrive
C. produce
D. invent

3D printers are able to fabricate identical versions of single items with nearly zero error; their high cost, at the moment, is the only factor preventing their widespread adoption.

48

The word "ringed" in the passage is closest in meaning to
A. ring-shaped
B. encircled
C. girded
D. coned

The janitor's keychain was a ringed piece of metal that was sufficiently sturdy and large to hold his full array of keys for the entire lab.

49

The word "cycles" in the passage is closest in meaning to
A. commonplace objects
B. gradual increases
C. patterns of events that repeat themselves
D. largest categories

As the Earth developed, the concentrations of the pollutants were altered by various chemical reactions; they became components in biogeochemical cycles.

CONTINUE

50

The word "customarily" in the passage is closest in meaning to
A. naturally
B. necessarily
C. commonly
D. certainly

In effect, as molten glass cools, it progressively stiffens until rigid, but does so without setting up a network of interlocking crystals customarily associated with that process.

END

词汇练习
List 7 05

1

The word "critical" in the passage is closest in meaning to
A. debatable
B. essential
C. argumentative
D. methodological

Excellent vision is critical for Navy Seals who execute highly secretive military operations in locations around the world.

2

The word "continuous" in the passage is closest in meaning to
A. unpredictable
B. sharp
C. dangerous
D. uninterrupted

Because the evolutionary theory, presented by Darwin, is actually still incomplete, it requires continuous adjustment and debate over its weakest points.

3

The word "exploit" in the passage is closest in meaning to
A. divide
B. understand
C. utilize
D. transmit

For decades, western oil companies have pursued possibilities to exploit the former Soviet Union's immense oil reserves, and the end of the Cold War brought about this opportunity.

4

The word "obvious" in the passage is closest in meaning to
A. visible
B. argumentative
C. research-worthy
D. explicable

The infant's short neck, small head, and flattened facial profile made it obvious to doctors that she had Down syndrome.

CONTINUE

The phrase "coupled with" in the passage is closest in meaning to
A. caused by
B. stirred up
C. affected by
D. combined with

Alzheimer's disease, coupled with dementia, is extremely detrimental to people's health and well-being.

The phrase "peculiar to" in the passage is closest in meaning to
A. damaging to
B. unique to
C. rare in
D. strange for

Some languages are peculiar to only one particular area of the region.

The phrase "sensitive to" in the passage is closest in meaning to
A. affected by
B. surprised at
C. justified by
D. determined

The ethnographer was sensitive to his research subjects' plight, and after the data was collected, he vowed to fight for their rights to freedom from imperial oppression.

The word "absolutely" in the passage is closest in meaning to
A. definitely
B. familiarly
C. uncommonly
D. similarly

Considering quantum mechanics led to the inventions of the laser, electron microscope, and magnetic resonance imaging (MRI), it is absolutely possible that medical science would not be as advanced as it is today without quantum theory.

The word "advantageous" in the passage is closest in meaning to
A. favorable
B. accommodating
C. demanding
D. challenging

As a political philosopher, it is advantageous that Michel Foucault studied Machiavelli's *The Prince* while a student at University.

CONTINUE

10

The word "adversely" in the passage is closest in meaning to
A. certainly
B. brilliantly
C. negatively
D. publically

The architect adversely affected her own career when she publically denounced the work of Alejandro Aravena, this year's recipient of the prestigious Pritzker Prize.

11

The word "constructed" in the passage is closest in meaning to
A. elevated
B. graphed
C. created
D. envisioned

Takero Shimazaki Architects constructed the 2016 award winning refurbishment design Curzon Bloomsbury in London.

12

The word "eradicate" in the passage is closest in meaning to
A. decrease
B. increase
C. eliminate
D. strengthen

The United Nations outlined their plan to eradicate extreme poverty by 2020, a bold move toward reducing child mortality rates and global hunger.

13

The word "aggregations" in the passage is closest in meaning to
A. parties
B. accumulations
C. factions
D. companies

Scientists are working to determine whether comets are truly solid bodies or whether they are aggregations of smaller portions of dark matter, held together by the force of gravity.

14

The word "allow" in the passage is closest in meaning to
A. result in
B. make possible
C. succeed
D. spread

In principle, quantum mechanics would certainly allow Schrödinger, or his cat, to enter a state of quantum superposition.

CONTINUE

15

The phrase "are entitled to" in the passage is closest in meaning to

A. are unreasonable
B. behave badly
C. fight to obtain
D. are given the right to

Although they are not really legally entitled to marry, many are the couple who decide to live together and act as they were married.

16

The word "assumed" in the passage is closest in meaning to

A. accomplished
B. controlled
C. took on
D. influenced

Anna Wintour assumed her role at *Vogue* in 1988, and she continues to run the magazine as editor-in-chief to this day.

17

The word "attributed" in the passage is closest in meaning to

A. ascribed
B. left
C. limited
D. contradicted

Scientists sustain that, while some record heat can be attributed to climate change, normal weather variations also contribute to high temperatures.

18

The word "autonomy" in the passage is closest in meaning to

A. independence
B. influence
C. ability to make a living
D. ability to provide for one's family

Major rebel and opposition groups refused to cast their vote on the law, which proposed that a particular region would have more autonomy than the others.

19

The word "besides" in the passage is closest in meaning to

A. in addition to
B. more important than
C. in spite of
D. together with

Nowadays, messaging apps must show that they can do many other tasks besides messaging.

CONTINUE

20

The word "characteristic" in the passage is closest in meaning to
A. typical
B. familiar
C. chosen
D. fortunate

Low muscle tone, slightly flattened facial profile, and an upward slant to both eyes are characteristic of an infant born with Down syndrome.

21

The word "cluster" in the passage is closet in meaning to
A. form
B. group
C. move
D. rise

The data derived from the study tend to cluster around 6th Century BCE, which suggests that this is the approximate age of the fist civilizations around the Mediterranean Sea.

22

The word "compact" in the passage is closest in meaning to
A. difficult
B. sanguine
C. simple
D. hard

The compact surface could be the result of ice grains crystallizing under solar irradiance.

23

The word "comprises" in the passage is closest in meaning to
A. consists of
B. brings about
C. is similar to
D. takes care of

The question proposed gets at the core of what comprises human knowledge: How do we actually know something to be true?

24

The word "congestion" in the passage is closest in meaning to
A. overcrowding
B. incident
C. value
D. interest

The government should consider investing in improvements for traffic congestion, air quality, pedestrian conditions, noise, and light pollution.

CONTINUE

25

The word "congregating" in the passage is closest in meaning to
A. beginning
B. gathering
C. running
D. expecting

Factory relocation is a phenomenon that seems to have taken momentum; the trend is that of congregating new factories in relatively poor and less educated counties.

26

The word "consequence" in the passage is closest in meaning to
A. benefit
B. privilege
C. result
D. error

According to social scientists at Yale-New Haven Teachers Institute, extreme poverty is one consequence of rapid population growth.

27

The word "continually" in the passage is closest in meaning to
A. normally
B. abundantly
C. regularly
D. profusely

There exists a cluster of nerve cells near the optic nerve that continually regulates sleep-wake cycles, and may cause extreme distress to normative sleep patterns if the cluster becomes damages.

28

The word "distortion" in the passage is closest in meaning to
A. irregularity
B. gap
C. singularity
D. difference

Members of the research team have noticed a distortion among themselves in the way each records and interprets data, causing the Institutional Research Board to temporarily halt research pending an investigation into the team's research ethics.

29

The word "explicit" in the passage is closest in meaning to
A. demonstrative
B. educational
C. clearly stated
D. argumentative

Anita Archer, Washington's top educational consultant, argues that explicit instruction is the most effective indicator of whether or not a pedagogical design is appropriate for college classrooms.

CONTINUE

30

The word "facilitate" in the passage is closest in meaning to

A. erase
B. ease
C. calm
D. manage

Although of chemical origin, fertilizers greatly facilitate the growth of plants by providing them with the necessary supplements of nitrogen, phosphate and potassium.

31

The word "furnished" in the passage is closest in meaning to

A. equipped
B. melded
C. articulated
D. designed

As his first speech writer after taking office, Jon Favreau furnished Barak Obama with many of the President's most memorable quotations during his first term.

32

The word "implement" in the passage is closest in meaning to

A. reduce the cost of
B. put into effect
C. give consideration to
D. postpone

During the 1990s, farmers in the United States were instructed to implement soil preservation plans because of continuous erosion in much of the Midwest.

33

The word "implication" in the passage is closest in meaning to

A. relation
B. prestige
C. cause
D. significance

Society at large is still unaware of the implication of such bold labor and pensions reforms. It is likely that sudden changes to social security policies will bring about social unrest.

34

The word "justifiable" in the passage is closest in meaning to

A. reasonable
B. debatable
C. certain
D. argumentative

Her violent actions were certainly justifiable given the fact that an intruder broke into her home and threatened to kidnap her children.

CONTINUE

The word "lucrative" in the passage is closest in meaning to
A. strong
B. didactic
C. convincing
D. profitable

Such products can perpetrate racism in society, so, although the market is lucrative, we must consider the moral implication of distributing the product.

The word "preceded" in the passage is closest in meaning to
A. occurred after
B. occurred before
C. surprised
D. eliminated

The opening ceremonies preceded the first game, and provided fans with a spectacular display of local culture, including music and dance.

The word "preoccupations" in the passage is closest in meaning to
A. necessities
B. concerns
C. struggles
D. unpredictability

In ancient times, individuals lived simpler lives, had simpler needs and preoccupations— mainly they were concerned with having adequate food, shelter and clothing.

The word "prevailing" in the passage is closest in meaning to
A. intense
B. convincing
C. passionate
D. dramatic

In ancient cultures, before the advent of Christianity, the prevailing belief was that the Sun and the Moon were gods.

The word "repulsed" in the passage is closest in meaning to
A. drove back
B. dominated
C. argued
D. occupied

The Cherokee warriors successfully repulsed their attackers, and maintained complete control of their native lands.

CONTINUE

The word "retained" in the passage is closest in meaning to
A. inherited
B. preserved
C. gathered
D. called

Throughout most of the 20th century, American Telephone and Telegraph retained a monopoly over the use of telecommunication in the United States.

The word "sparsely" in the passage is closest in meaning to
A. thinly distributed
B. hospitably
C. cordially
D. randomly

The sparsely populated city was a reminder that although rural communities are neighborly, they are not as dense as suburban areas.

The word "suspicion" in the passage is closest in meaning to
A. distrust
B. disgust
C. corruption
D. misplacement

There was an increasing suspicion for the candidate, who constituents rarely trusted due to his bravado and crass candor.

The word "temporary" in the passage is closest in meaning to
A. concise
B. short-term
C. firm
D. well-made

A temporary solution was found to the immigration issue; but the problem still remains unsolved in the long term.

The word "transparent" in the passage is closest in meaning to
A. can be clearly examined
B. can be seen through
C. flawless
D. extraordinary

The transparent substance was the result of many years of efforts and experiments.

CONTINUE

45

The word "unceasingly" in the passage is closest in meaning to
A. continually
B. debatably
C. magnificently
D. disturbingly

The laborers were forced to work unceasingly, and not given regular breaks or granted time off for lunch.

46

The word "vigorously" in the passage is closest in meaning to
A. kindly and gently
B. practically
C. strongly and healthily
D. attentively

Given the right atmospheric condition, such species will grow vigorously and produce large numbers of fruits.

47

The word "witnessed" in the passage is closest in meaning to
A. experienced
B. debated
C. violated
D. overcame

Concentration camp survivors witnessed unspeakable atrocities, globally considered as one of the most tragic realities in human history.

48

The word "discontent" in the passage is closest in meaning to
A. regret
B. unhappy
C. restless
D. uneasy

The undergraduate advisor was utterly discontent upon learning that his student had failed to begin even the first chapter of his thesis.

49

The word "strenuous" in the passage is closest in meaning to
A. demanding
B. arduous
C. exhausting
D. uphill

Although not physically strenuous, the constant mental demands in academia are enough to bring low even the most confident and strong person.

CONTINUE

50

The word "acute" in the passage is closest in meaning to
A. sharp
B. keen
C. severe
D. smart

The hurricane was an acute weather event that brought far more havoc on the city than anyone had planned.

END

1

The word "derive" in the passage is closest in meaning to
A. maintain
B. expel
C. obtain
D. enroll

Newton was able to derive from his first principle (an object will remain in uniform motion in a straight line unless acted upon) the laws of planetary motion that had been discovered earlier by Kepler.

2

The word "fleeing" in the passage is closest in meaning to
A. running to
B. running away from
C. flying over
D. overseeing

Global migratory movements have increased due to the number of people fleeing their homelands in search of better living conditions elsewhere in the world.

3

The word "fleeting" in the passage is closest in meaning to
A. bright
B. rich
C. brief
D. abundant

Although catching a glimpse of the fleeting Comet McNaught was difficult, those who witnessed it in 2007 were astounded by its spectacular lights display, which lit the entire nighttime sky.

4

The word "nevertheless" in the passage is closest in meaning to
A. anyway
B. however
C. until now
D. as yet

Mechanics have worked at the engine for weeks now, nevertheless, the fundamental problem of overheating remains.

CONTINUE ➤

The word "restricted" in the passage is closest in meaning to
A. improved
B. succeeded
C. limited
D. continued

When the child was diagnosed with type 1 diabetes, his mother immediately restricted the boy's consumption of sugar.

The phrase "a foundation in" in the passage is closest in meaning to
A. the essence of
B. regards
C. a basis in
D. a consequence of

In many Western cultures, forgiveness has a foundation in the Christian belief that we should love and accept one another, as God does.

The phrase "in profile" in the passage is closest in meaning to
A. facial recognition
B. copycat design
C. viewed from the side
D. artistic rendering

In profile, her doppelganger was a nearly identical silhouette of forehead, nose, and chin.

The phrase "with regard for" in the passage is closest in meaning to
A. with concern for
B. adhering to
C. seeking to protect
D. demonstrating exceptionalism

She continued to work for human rights, especially with regard for the elderly populations, which she deemed most vulnerable in a society that perpetuated ageism.

The word "appreciation" in the passage is closest in meaning to
A. innocence
B. recognition
C. wisdom
D. forgiveness

There is one way in which the sciences of stress and depression are closely aligned: the growing appreciation of their complexity.

CONTINUE

10

The word "burgeoning" in the passage is closest in meaning to
A. increasingly expanding
B. rapidly decreasing
C. awkwardly adapting
D. confidently dissipating

Social scientists report that the beginning of the 21st Century is experiencing a burgeoning population trend in urban areas across the world.

11

The word "check" in the passage is closest in meaning to
A. encouragement
B. concealment
C. provoker
D. limit

One important natural check is a restriction on the number of suitable habitats for different species.

12

The word "confirmed" in the passage is closest in meaning to
A. believed
B. taught
C. proved
D. begged

It has been repeatedly confirmed that there is an increase in glacial melting rates in the Northern Hemisphere.

13

The word "controversial" in the passage is closest in meaning to
A. limited
B. compelling
C. irrelevant
D. debatable

Some have proposed a controversial, yet effective solution to global warming: government should ensure that no subsidies, incentives, or commitments are made to new coal-fired plants unless they produce zero emissions.

14

The word "deciphered" in the passage is closest in meaning to
A. cancelled
B. alarmed
C. interpreted
D. figured out

The Egyptian hieroglyphics were not deciphered until the discovery of the Rosetta Stone, in 1799.

CONTINUE

The word "diminishing" in the passage is closest in meaning to
A. reducing
B. affecting
C. deflecting
D. determining

German economist Johann Heinrich von Thünen was one of the first experts to explore the economic laws of diminishing returns, thus assuring his place in history books.

The word "dismissed" in the passage is closest in meaning to
A. broke away
B. offered
C. recycled
D. rejected

The governor dismissed the idea that climate change would concern future generations, arguing that the issue would be resolved by the current generation in power.

The word "divert" in the passage is closest in meaning to
A. explain
B. redirect
C. eliminate
D. cause

School psychologists in Texas claim that the best way to divert a student's attention when she is misbehaving is to put her in charge of a simple group task.

The word "enduring" in the passage is closest in meaning to
A. lasting
B. terminal
C. extreme
D. unalterable

J. K. Rowling has enjoyed the enduring effects that her *Harry Potter* series has had on children's literacy worldwide.

The word "excessive" in the passage is closet in meaning to
A. too much
B. not enough
C. daily
D. urgent

According to researchers at Indiana University, excessive shopping is a sign of an addiction, as shoppers become addicted to how their brains respond when they are buying.

CONTINUE

20

The word "fluctuations" in the passage is closest in meaning to
A. developments
B. variations
C. contrasts
D. origins

There are great fluctuations in the statistics on teen pregnancy in the United States, which largely depends on each state's policies on school-based sexual education and access to birth control without parental consent.

21

The word "fulfill" in the passage is closest in meaning to
A. perform
B. counter
C. acknowledge
D. justify

The actor could not fulfill the terms of his contract, and withdrew from the film.

22

The word "function" in the passage is closest in meaning to
A. center
B. practice
C. composition
D. purpose

The function of white blood cells includes protecting the body against infectious diseases in order to maintain physical health.

23

The word "impede" in the passage is closest in meaning to
A. restrict
B. impose
C. remove
D. dismiss

In spite of their fierce determination, the soldiers at the Alamo could not impede Santa Anna's Mexican army, and Texas lost all of its warriors in the battle at San Antonio.

24

The word "induces" in the passage is closest in meaning to
A. stimulates
B. resolves
C. saves
D. emancipates

The man contends that meditation induces the mind for increased concentration, intentional living, and peaceful images that optimize bodily functioning.

169

25

The word "inevitable" in the passage is closest in meaning to
A. unprecedented
B. undesirable
C. unavoidable
D. unpredictable

While oil consumption is necessary for the automobile industry, its exploitation will result in an inevitable depletion of all reserves unless more is done to decrease global use.

26

The word "mask" in the passage is closest in meaning to
A. reveal
B. hide
C. embellish
D. claim

It was difficult for the candidate to mask his disdain for his opponent, often referring to the other candidate as "unfit" and "inadequate" for public office.

27

The word "modest" in the passage is closest in meaning to
A. reasonable
B. debatable
C. uncertain
D. definite

The accountant provided her client with a modest estimate of loss following the stock market's abrupt decline.

28

The word "motive" in the passage is closest in meaning to
A. solution
B. idea
C. reason
D. justification

Her motive for seeking public office was uncertain and led to confusion among the staff who were tasked with writing her campaign speeches.

29

The word "ornaments" in the passage is closest in meaning to
A. miniatures
B. decorations
C. toys
D. imitations

The females of the species have ornaments too, but they are not as elaborate as their male counterparts.

CONTINUE

30

The word "paralleled" in the passage is closest in meaning to
A. argued
B. linked
C. matched
D. supported

The development and success of shipbuilding in the Netherlands was never paralleled, that is why, in a short period of time the Dutch obtained a high international status.

31

The word "peak" in the passage is closest in meaning to
A. the highest point
B. idea
C. availability
D. beginning

Clean air demand reached a peak during winter months, when the city became uninhabitable for people with asthma and other respiratory conditions.

32

The word "persistently" in the passage is closest in meaning to
A. constantly
B. doubtfully
C. convincingly
D. amazingly

He persistently asked her to marry him, until she eventually succumbed to his wishes and said yes.

33

The word "prerequisite" in the passage is closest in meaning to
A. precaution
B. preparation
C. requirement
D. accomplishment

Ancient wisdom traditions have long held that gratitude is a prerequisite for fulfillment.

34

The word "proliferation" in the passage is closest in meaning to
A. request
B. conquest
C. increase
D. understanding

It was not until the end of the Imperial Era that the proliferation of Christianity occurred and, by the reign of Theodosius I, Nicene Christianity was recognized as the only state religion.

171

CONTINUE

35

The word "recommended" in the passage is closest in meaning to
A. supported
B. discouraged
C. denied
D. persuaded

The outgoing executive recommended her company's vice president as a successor to the position.

36

The word "rigid" in the passage is closest in meaning to
A. fixed
B. unfair
C. just
D. safe

The professor had rigid rules that were inflexible, and students knew they had no hope of her making any acceptations to the no-late-work policy.

37

The word "sabotage" in the passage is closest in meaning to
A. regret
B. change
C. intentionally damage
D. modify

In an effort to sabotage the election results, hackers broke into tabulation systems, but were caught before any real harm occurred.

38

The word "sleek" in the passage is closest in meaning to
A. smooth
B. expensive
C. deadly
D. certain

The new Ford Bronco is designed for a sleek ride, offering drivers safe and hassle-free experiences on the road.

39

The word "sophisticated" in the passage is closest in meaning to
A. tangled
B. complex
C. multiple
D. problematical

The particle accelerator has undergone very sophisticated adaptations in order to increase efficiency and stability.

CONTINUE

The word "sought" in the passage is closest in meaning to
A. tried to obtain
B. denied
C. rebuked
D. studied

He sought answers to life's most complex curiosities, and in doing so, became a world renown philosopher and theologian.

The word "spectacular" in the passage is closest in meaning to
A. important
B. imaginary
C. remarkable
D. major

Stonehenge is a spectacular prehistoric monument because of its size and grandeur, which dates back to 3100 BC.

The word "stamina" in the passage is closest in meaning to
A. patience
B. flexibility
C. endurance
D. understanding

Certain diets and physical exercise will help improve one's stamina, flexibility and strength.

The word "straightforward" in the passage is closest in meaning to
A. powerful
B. trustworthy
C. simple
D. obvious

Although the plan is quite straightforward, its application may incur in several difficulties.

The word "subtly" in the passage is closest in meaning to
A. annoyingly
B. politely
C. slightly
D. angrily

She subtly shifted her opinions from staunch conservativism to moderate politics, making her a much more pleasant conversation partner at dinner.

CONTINUE

The word "sustain" in the passage is closest in meaning to
A. maintain
B. observe
C. gain
D. guard

It was because of the new middle class that the aristocracy could sustain their expensive lifestyle.

The word "systematically" in the passage is closest in meaning to
A. abruptly
B. randomly
C. methodically
D. forcefully

The social scientist systematically divided his research subjects into categories of race, class, gender, and religion.

The word "uniformly" in the passage is closest in meaning to
A. completely
B. clearly
C. properly
D. partly

Farmers, mainly in developed countries, tend to grow crops uniformly across large plantations.

The word "worshippers" in the passage is closest in meaning to
A. who visit the temples
B. who praise deities
C. who argue with their spouses
D. who understand gender inequity

Hindu worshippers segregate themselves at the door of the temple, and women go into one entrance while men enter another.

CONTINUE

The word "underlying" in the passage is closest in meaning to
A. hidden
B. bottom
C. veiled
D. basic

It is impossible to read advanced Latin texts without a clear understanding of the underlying grammatical concepts that comprise the language.

The word "accommodating" in the passage is closest in meaning to
A. adapting
B. fitting
C. allowing
D. modifying

The restaurant prides itself on inclusivity by accommodating all aids or other devices that a patron might need to enjoy his or her time there.

1

The phrase "in essence" in the passage is closest in meaning to
A. actually
B. basically
C. anyway
D. moreover

In essence, the continental model offered a viable alternative to the already instable political environment of the time.

2

The word "advent" in the passage is closest in meaning to
A. arrival
B. development
C. expansion
D. situation

The advent of mobile phones has had a profound impact on society at large, which triggered many changes in people's daily habits and way of thinking.

3

The phrase "attest to" in the passage is closest in meaning to
A. guarantee
B. construct
C. happen
D. confirm

Presumably, the inhabitants of a remote region in South America, probably only a few thousand people, grew their own crops to trade for a variety of manufactured artifacts. The latest archeological discoveries attest to trade relations over a wide region.

4

The word "configuration" in the passage is closest in meaning to
A. preparation
B. foreground
C. arrangement
D. bargain

Phrenologists were convinced that the configuration of a person's skull could reveal much about that person's future and character.

CONTINUE

5

The word "fragments" in the passage is closest in meaning to
A. campaigns
B. trends
C. motions
D. pieces

In a most extreme case, experts reconstructed the entire genome using DNA fragments from a single cell.

6

The word "generates" in the passage is closest in meaning to
A. weakens
B. releases
C. produces
D. presents

First tried on the screen of a smartphone, placing a pyramid shaped object over a source of light generates a 3D image.

7

The word "prevalent" in the passage is closest in meaning to
A. widespread
B. endemic
C. singular
D. convincing

In Equatorial Guinea agriculture is the main economic activity, and the prevalent food crop is cassava.

8

The phrase "as opposed to" in the passage is closest in meaning to
A. when copied by
B. in contrast to
C. because of
D. in likeness of

What are the differences in life styles of the Northern European as opposed to the Southerner?

9

The phrase "back up" in the passage is closest in meaning to
A. counterattack
B. deny
C. support
D. withhold

To this day it is not certain whether the government did or did not completely back up the Manhattan project.

177

CONTINUE

10

The phrase "in principle" in the passage is closest in meaning to
A. practically
B. eventually
C. after all
D. theoretically

Leaders from the G8 have agreed, in principle, to an agreement on climate change and reduction of hazardous emissions.

11

The phrase "ruled out" in the passage is closest in meaning to
A. elected
B. forced
C. excluded
D. welcomed

Upon winning the election, he quickly ruled out any former opponents who spoke ill of him or his family from being nominated to his advisory committee.

12

The word "adapting" in the passage is closest in meaning to
A. thriving
B. motivating
C. withdrawing
D. adjusting

Veterans from the First World War had many problems adapting to civilian life, and many of them craved a return to military service.

13

The word "baffled" in the passage is closest in meaning to
A. contradicted
B. explained
C. puzzled
D. completed

The new Artificial Intelligence machine could solve problems in just a few minutes that had baffled mathematicians for centuries.

14

The word "skeptical" in the passage is closest in meaning to
A. critical
B. frightened
C. doubtful
D. confident

When George Lemaître noted, in 1927, that our universe could have originated from a single point–The Big Bang Theory–many supporters of the Steady State Universe were skeptical about his idea.

CONTINUE

15

The word "ardent" in the passage is closest in meaning to
A. sullen
B. undeniable
C. enthusiastic
D. profitable

The ardent support for Martin Luther King Jr.'s ideas brought about many changes to the American society and culture at large.

16

The phrase "associated with" in the passage is closest in meaning to
A. determined
B. signified
C. gathered together
D. connected to

Certain components in food have been associated with health benefits, however, they cannot be yet classified as a macro or micro nutrient.

17

The word "components" in the passage is closest in meaning to
A. materials
B. pieces
C. shapes
D. digits

Components and even entire products can be tested in their digital form, often using virtual reality.

18

The word "conducive" in the passage is closest in meaning to
A. reasonable
B. powerful
C. overwhelming
D. favorable

On an atomic level one might ask, why are certain elements more conducive to electricity than others?

19

The word "confined" in the passage is closest in meaning to
A. juxtaposed
B. carried out
C. restricted
D. disseminated

The epidemic of bluetongue was confined to the Southern regions of the Mediterranean area.

CONTINUE

20

The word "constraint" in the passage is closest in meaning to
A. limit
B. bureaucracy
C. cause
D. reality

Through improvement in energy storage, we will eventually break the constraint that power must be produced at the same rate that it is consumed.

21

The word "consumption" in the passage is closest in meaning to
A. question
B. meal
C. disease
D. utilization

This year, for the first time, the government plan includes a goal to limit the country's total energy consumption.

22

The word "discarded" in the passage is closest in meaning to
A. abandoned
B. modified
C. replaced
D. justified

Throughout Western civilization, there have been numerous scientific theories that were supported under political authorities, and once political power shifted, the theories were widely discarded.

23

The word "distinctive" in the passage is closest in meaning to
A. recognizable
B. debatable
C. convincing
D. infallible

According to the paleontology team at the American Museum of Natural History, distinctive marks on the dinosaur bones suggested the animal lived during the Bronze Age.

24

The word "dramatic" in the passage is closest in meaning to
A. partial
B. complex
C. common
D. striking

A dramatic climate change must have happened, one that completely subverted the previous environmental conditions of Sub-Saharan Africa.

CONTINUE

25

The word "dramatically" in the passage is closest in meaning to
A. distinctly
B. greatly
C. obviously
D. directly

When the European diet expanded to include potatoes, farmers' conditions dramatically improved; not only were they able to produce much more food, they also gained protection against the catastrophe of a grain crop failure caused by famine.

26

The word "enable" in the passage is closest in meaning to
A. prepare
B. need
C. allow
D. distribute

Identifying the cause of pancreatic cancer will enable medical researchers to revise their treatment testing as they work toward finding a cure.

27

The word "exceptional" in the passage is closest in meaning to
A. extraordinary
B. famous
C. legendary
D. vast

Great Britain held an exceptional reputation in the 19th Century as a builder, owner and operator of the shipping industries, including manufacturing and trading vessels.

28

The word "generally" in the passage is closest in meaning to
A. additionally
B. preferably
C. usually
D. casually

The theory of evolution, now a widely accepted scientific theory, was generally considered bizarre only few decades ago.

29

The word "impressive" in the passage is closest in meaning to
A. beautiful
B. aghast
C. controversial
D. striking

The combined beauty and intelligence of famed human rights lawyer Amal Clooney contributes to her impressive status as an international celebrity.

CONTINUE

30

The word "invariably" in the
passage is closest in meaning to
A. unfortunately
B. convincingly
C. always
D. frustratingly

No matter what researchers
tried, the results were invariably
the same, and they abandoned
the study altogether when they
realized its findings were not
statistically significant.

31

The word "irritating" in the passage
is closest in meaning to
A. alarming
B. annoying
C. awkward
D. complex

A higher concentration of salt in
salt water can be irritating for the
human eyes.

32

The word "lone" in the passage is
closest in meaning to
A. primary
B. single
C. best
D. worst

He quickly emerged as the
lone candidate from a field of
disappointing applicants.

33

The word "painstaking" in the
passage is closest in meaning to
A. with great effort
B. unquestioning
C. authoritative
D. laborious

It was a painstaking task, which
required precision, great skills and
a deep knowledge of physics, as
well as mathematics.

34

The word "periodically" in the
passage is closest in meaning to
A. never
B. continuously
C. sometimes
D. at regular intervals

The experiment was repeated
periodically, every couple of
months, for two years.

CONTINUE

35

The word "perplexed" in the passage is closest in meaning to
A. challenged
B. avoided
C. puzzled
D. deflected

The question had perplexed astronomers and philosophers for decades, until the first woman in the field, Hippatia, discovered the answer to this phenomenon.

36

The word "pervasive" in the passage is closest in meaning to
A. innovative
B. talented
C. eventual
D. widespread

Human activities such as pollution and overpopulation are leaving a pervasive and long-lasting mark on Earth.

37

The word "proponent" in the passage is closest in meaning to
A. lawyer
B. supporter
C. professional
D. consultant

The Republican candidate was a proponent of the new law on low-carbon emissions.

38

The word "prosperous" in the passage is closest in meaning to
A. famous
B. wealthy
C. powerful
D. noble

A prosperous society benefits from incredible riches, both economically and socially.

39

The word "quest" in the passage is closest in meaning to
A. search
B. challenge
C. query
D. embarkation

The quest aimed to locate her missing son, who had been lost in the Kentucky National Forest for over six hours.

CONTINUE

The word "readily" in the passage is closest in meaning to
A. honestly
B. increasingly
C. mostly
D. quickly

Businessmen wanted to maximize their profits, which they could do readily by introducing the assembly line process.

The word "renewed" in the passage is closest in meaning to
A. reused
B. recycled
C. restored
D. saved

University administrators remain skeptical that the newly announced academic center will reflect a renewed commitment to climate research.

The word "resembled" in the passage is closest in meaning to
A. copied
B. imagined
C. looked like
D. denounced

Although the painting closely resembled a Van Gogh, accurate testing revealed that it was a fake.

The word "scanty" in the passage is closest in meaning to
A. few
B. thorough
C. silly
D. detailed

Keeping scanty records negatively impacts the work of many companies when they cannot demonstrate proof of responsible and ethical business practices.

The word "scrutiny" in the passage is closest in meaning to
A. interest in
B. deep knowledge
C. superficial analysis
D. close observation

Many factories have come under scrutiny for using harmful chemicals and releasing them in the environment.

CONTINUE

The word "slightest" in the passage is closest in meaning to
A. smallest
B. most easy
C. least stable
D. emptied

Even the slightest mistake in data collection would jeopardize the whole study, causing a major setback for cancer research.

The word "surely" in the passage is closest in meaning to
A. certainly
B. commonly
C. possibly
D. simply

There is surely some truth to these accusations, but it has not been confirmed yet.

The word "swift" in the passage is closest in meaning to
A. extravagant
B. wild
C. impure
D. quick

A swift rate of change in developing markets was driven by a strong desire for higher and better education and financial stability.

The word "tend" in the passage is closest in meaning to
A. search for
B. accompany
C. select
D. take care of

In many cultures throughout the world, children are expected to tend their old parents.

CONTINUE

The phrase "the aftermath of a founder event" in the passage is closest in meaning to
A. the situation that causes a founder event
B. the future of a company
C. the impact of the foundation of a company
D. the situation that results from a founder event

In the aftermath of a founder event, the new species could colonize a place which its members previously uninhabited.

The word "widespread" in the passage is closest in meaning to
A. shared
B. common
C. low
D. vulgar

The period from 400,000 to 200,000 Before Present, when the use of controlled fire became widespread, marks the transition from the Lower to the Middle Paleolithic.

END

1

The word "erase" in the passage is closest in meaning to
A. move
B. eliminate
C. embellish
D. replace

The boastful politician claimed his plan would erase all municipality debt by the second year of his term.

2

The word "hitherto" in the passage is closest in meaning to
A. sooner than
B. above
C. before the very eyes of
D. up till then

The discovery of such rare fossils offered a unique opportunity to glimpse the origins of the species—hitherto paleontologists had not experienced such an opportunity.

3

The word "indicator" in the passage is closest in meaning to
A. effect
B. standard
C. sign
D. limit

Rising temperatures are the most common indicator of global warming, but there are other, subtler signs, that can be observed as well.

4

The word "investigated" in the passage is closest in meaning to
A. instigated
B. narrowed
C. caused
D. looked into

When scientists investigated the diet of this remote tribe in Africa, they found that it was free from any sort of chemical agent.

CONTINUE

5

The word "moreover" in the passage is closest in meaning to
A. so far
B. already
C. in addition
D. nonetheless

Moreover, many estimates do not account for factors such as catastrophic changes and tipping points.

6

The phrase "a case in point" in the passage is closest in meaning to
A. a good example
B. a model
C. standard
D. an inspirational case

In an extremely competitive business environment, strong motivation and commitment drive the success of numerous start-ups; Uber is a case in point.

7

The phrase "found wanting" in the passage is closest in meaning to
A. looked forward to
B. widely accepted
C. judged inadequate
D. finished off

Brazilian laws against political corruption were found wanting, which resulted in radical changes following the impeachment of President Dilma Rousseff.

8

The word "accumulation" in the passage is closest in meaning to
A. make-up
B. gathering
C. extent
D. increasing

Sedimentary rocks are types of rock that are formed by the accumulation of debris and other materials on the Earth's surface.

9

The word "adequate" in the passage is closest in meaning to
A. suitable
B. rich
C. fulfilling
D. correct

An adequate intake of protein guarantees a vast array of functions within living organisms, including DNA replication, responding to stimuli, and transporting molecules from one location to another.

CONTINUE

The word "admitted" in the passage is closest in meaning to
A. recalled
B. accepted the truth of
C. approved
D. gave recognition to

After the defeat of the Nazis in the Second World War, Germany admitted its faults and has been trying to make amends ever since.

The word "anxiety" in the passage is closest in meaning to
A. need
B. worry
C. pressure
D. force

Both meditation and outdoor exercise have proven beneficial in the treatment of anxiety, depression, and other psychological disorders.

The word "assess" in the passage is closest in meaning to
A. adapt
B. think of
C. evaluate
D. esteem

Researchers are struggling to assess risks related to the treatment of the Zika virus, partly because there is little research on the virus itself.

The word "barred" in the passage is closest in meaning to
A. invited
B. joined
C. excluded
D. compelled

Scientists have recognized the risks of the chemicals barred by national regulations; however, the Parliament hasn't given officials the authority to act on their knowledge.

The word "commonplace" in the passage is closest in meaning to
A. famous
B. concrete
C. ordinary
D. temporal

Economists and social researchers agreed that tax evaders were commonplace well before the late economic crisis, and that small enterprises were majorly affected by this phenomenon.

CONTINUE

15

The word "compatible" in the passage is closest in meaning to
A. consistent
B. concurrent
C. connected
D. fixed

After years of strenuous research, the results were frustrating; the atmosphere on Mars was not completely averse to life in general, yet it was not seemingly compatible with human life in particular.

16

The word "conducted" in the passage is closest in meaning to
A. brought
B. surpassed
C. staged
D. carried out

The study was conducted using sample data taken from about 300,000 people all over Europe.

17

The word "confined" in the passage is closest in meaning to
A. related
B. limited
C. postponed
D. helped

Before the advent of modern medicine, patients with infectious diseases were rarely treated in hospitals, because the knowledge on the subject was still confined.

18

The word "courteous" in the passage is closest in meaning to
A. clever
B. polite
C. grand
D. fashionable

Because cellphones are so popular, users should be thoughtful, courteous, and respectful to the people around them.

19

The word "duration" in the passage is closest in meaning to
A. batch
B. section
C. length
D. era

Physicians claim that it is possible to use sleep duration as a measure of general health and wellbeing for most cardiology patients.

CONTINUE ➡

20

The word "edible" in the passage is closest in meaning to
A. fit to be eaten
B. not dangerous
C. not threatening
D. used quickly

Advocates for reducing hunger among children living in North Texas claim that discarding edible products because of packaging expiration dates contribute unnecessarily to food waste.

21

The word "embrace" in the passage is closest in meaning to
A. use up
B. soften
C. adopt
D. engage

The United States and Somalia were the only two UN member countries who refused to embrace the Convention on the Rights of the Child.

22

The word "era" in the passage is closest in meaning to
A. stop
B. lesson
C. period
D. space

The twenty-first century is an era of unrestrained industrialization, in which people seldom challenge the right to make money at whatever cost.

23

The word "evenly" in the passage is closest in meaning to
A. as it happens
B. surprisingly
C. smoothly
D. equally

Evenly spaced hydrogen molecules disrupt when salt is dissolved in water.

24

The word "founding" in the passage is closest in meaning to
A. practice
B. government
C. venture
D. establishment

The founding of a democratic constitution was a difficult and long process for the Democratic Republic of the Congo in 2006.

191

CONTINUE

25

The word "harsh" in the passage is closest in meaning to
A. tight
B. severe
C. simple
D. redundant

The topology of the Mojave Desert in North America is as harsh as its climate.

26

The word "highlights" in the passage is closest in meaning to
A. agrees
B. sympathizes
C. emphasizes
D. offers

Ta-Nehisi Coates's *Between the World and Me*, highlights the institutional racism experienced by many African-American men living in the United States.

27

The word "ignore" in the passage is closest in meaning to
A. throw away
B. know something thoroughly
C. pay no attention to
D. run away

Corporations that ignore ecological, social and economic norms and the global values expressed by the international conventions show a lack of respect and integrity.

28

The word "inadvertently" in the passage is closest in meaning to
A. generally
B. unintentionally
C. predominantly
D. hypothetically

Chinese alchemists, who were trying to discover the elixir of immortality, inadvertently created the gunpowder.

29

The word "incentives" in the passage is closet in meaning to
A. authorities
B. obligations
C. reflections
D. motivations

Some States have instituted a series of measures to address global warming—like the incentives for diesel or hybrid vehicles.

CONTINUE

30

The word "margins" in the passage is closest in meaning to
A. contrasts
B. pauses
C. limits
D. interiors

The explorer was famous for traveling to the outermost margins of foreign lands, risking his life in search of undiscovered plant and insect species.

31

The word "massive" in the passage is closest in meaning to
A. exceptional
B. absolute
C. high ranking
D. very large

The massive stone foundations near the temple, the function of which is not definitively known by modern scholars, are proposed to have been the supporting platform of the Colossus.

32

The word "nominal" in the passage is closest in meaning to
A. giving someone power and then taking it away
B. to be named person in charge because most competent
C. to aspire to power, but never get it
D. named someone as the person in charge but did not give her/him power

She was the nominal leader, however everyone in the company knew that the real power remained with her predecessor.

33

The word "pragmatic" in the passage is closest in meaning to
A. effective
B. sensitive
C. practical
D. creative

Underdeveloped nations often take a more pragmatic approach towards policy-making, ignoring the moral part of it.

CONTINUE

34

The word "profound" in the passage is closest in meaning to
A. interesting
B. increasing
C. far-reaching
D. influential

The arrival and growth of Christianity in the Mediterranean Sea had a profound impact on the region and civilizations living there at the time, and also, indirectly, on the parts of Europe controlled by the Roman Empire.

35

The word "proposed" in the passage is closest in meaning to
A. narrated the legend
B. offered the theory
C. debated a theory
D. analyzed

The first man who proposed that the planets were material objects, much similar to our Earth, was Kepler.

36

The word "recognized" in the passage is closest in meaning to
A. accepted
B. commented on
C. recommended
D. adopted

After almost half a century from the battle, the new leadership recognized their nation's faults and asked the enemy for forgiveness.

37

The word "remote" in the passage is closest in meaning to
A. obscure
B. isolated
C. hostile
D. infertile

Remote islands were scarcely inhabited, moreover they presented limited species diversity.

38

The word "result" in the passage is closest in meaning to
A. option
B. knowledge
C. meaning
D. consequence

The final result affected the western nations negatively, as political leaders were forced to admit economic defeat.

194

CONTINUE

39

The word "shallow" in the passage is closest in meaning to
A. having little length
B. in a very brief time
C. continuative
D. having little depth

Shallow waters are conducive to shark attacks, as the predators are able to swim in close proximity to their victims.

40

The word "simultaneously" in the passage is closest in meaning to
A. continuously
B. separately
C. one after the other
D. at the same time

Air pollution, for example, simultaneously damages both the surrounding environment and human health.

41

The word "spurt" in the passage is closest in meaning to
A. quickly end
B. sporadically change
C. suddenly increase
D. temporarily start

The biggest volcano in Europe– Mount Etna, began to spurt lava, which caused geologists to warn area residents about potential danger.

42

The word "stimulated" in the passage is closest in meaning to
A. funded
B. structured
C. challenged
D. encouraged

The high position of artists in society stimulated creativity and innovation, which led to new techniques and time-efficient design methods.

43

The word "substantial" in the passage is closest in meaning to
A. average
B. smaller
C. considerable
D. surprising

To better coordinate individual and community efforts, substantial investments and international commitment are necessary.

CONTINUE

44

The word "sufficient" in the passage is closest in meaning to
A. acceptable
B. abundant
C. enough
D. welcome

To be part of the aristocracy, being wealthy was not sufficient, one also needed to have royal lineage.

45

The phrase "the course of change" in the passage is closest in meaning to
A. the path towards development
B. the reasons behind the change
C. the way the change developed
D. the factors which influenced the change

Stoics are able to adapt to the course of change with indifference, and accept both the positive and negative outcomes of development.

46

The word "trace" in the passage is closest in meaning to
A. action
B. proof
C. evidence
D. symbol

There is no trace of such species in all of the sites examined by the archeologists so far, and so the research team has decided to declare that in fact, the species never existed in the region.

47

The word "trait" in the passage is closest in meaning to
A. story
B. cause
C. skill
D. feature

Resilience could be a necessary trait given the unfriendly environment.

CONTINUE

48

The word "unique" in the passage is closest in meaning to

A. unfamiliar
B. precious
C. one-of-a-kind
D. mysterious

Unique in its shape and magnificence, the structure ranks among the earliest human building projects and it's one of the most impressive ones.

49

The word "appreciated" is closest in meaning to

A. experienced
B. understood
C. explored
D. increased

Glass fibers were little more than a novelty until the 1930s, when their thermal and electrical insulating properties were appreciated and methods for producing continuous filaments were developed.

50

The word "candidate" in the passage is closest in meaning to

A. solution
B. truth
C. original condition
D. a thing suited to be chosen for something specified

The Hellas Basin, which measures some 3,000 kilometers across and has a floor that lies nearly 9 kilometers below the basin's rim, is another candidate for an ancient Martian sea.

END

1

The word "ingenious" in the passage is closest in meaning to
A. inventive
B. famous
C. academic
D. precise

A further, ingenious experiment will allow the NASA team to observe the edges of a black hole.

2

The word "inspecting" in the passage is closest in meaning to
A. examining
B. trailing
C. noting
D. indicating

Controls must be carried out, for instance, by implementing a compulsory monitoring system, comparing results from different test subjects and by inspecting data surveillance mechanisms.

3

The word "methodically" in the passage is closest in meaning to
A. aggressively
B. promptly
C. secretly
D. systematically

After collecting the specimens, the archeologists arranged them methodically by date and location.

4

The word "monotonous" in the passage is closest in meaning to
A. unchanging
B. eternal
C. fluctuant
D. daily

Despite what many people believe, the climate in the Artic is anything but monotonous; its variability causes extreme changes in temperatures and viability for human life.

CONTINUE

5

The word "optimal" in the passage is closest in meaning to
A. most favorable
B. most popular
C. pleasing
D. original

The new development plan allows for the optimal development of the city's economy and infrastructure, which will benefit its residents for generations to come.

6

The phrase "relative to" in the passage is closest in meaning to
A. complete
B. comparable to
C. based on
D. modified by

The government will adjust taxation relative to income, so as to relieve the burden of the poor.

7

The word "stationary" in the passage is closest in meaning to
A. common
B. fixed
C. ancient
D. conservative

A stationary source of lights or sound emits a set of spherical waves.

8

The word "triggered" in the passage is closest in meaning to
A. pulled
B. initiated
C. ended up
D. pressured

Breathing air with a high concentration of pollen triggered an allergic reaction.

9

The phrase "are drawn to" in the passage is closest in meaning to
A. have special attentions for
B. are close to
C. are attached to
D. are obliged to

Psychologists have argued that we are drawn to horror stories and movies because they trigger one of our most basic instincts—fear.

CONTINUE

10

The phrase "maintenance of" in the passage is closest in meaning to
A. developing
B. supporting
C. linking
D. stimulating

New archeological research has found that ritualistic sacrifices played a pivotal role in the maintenance of hierarchical ancient societies.

11

The word "accelerates" in the passage is closest in meaning to
A. puts out
B. speeds up
C. slows down
D. turns around

In case of fire, a high concentration of oxygen accelerates the development of the fire; thus, it is erroneous to believe that wind helps prevent the spread of flames.

12

The word "considerable" is closest in meaning to
A. of enormous weight
B. a large amount of
C. relatively small
D. very close together

Economic development is not without considerable cost to the surrounding environment.

13

The word "notion" in the passage is closest in meaning to
A. idea
B. regulation
C. degree
D. tradition

In fact, the very notion that Mars is a livable planet is still questionable considering there is no concrete proof that Mars ever sustained life.

14

The word "accordingly" in the passage is closest in meaning to
A. correspondingly
B. regularly
C. repeatedly
D. genuinely

Upon hearing of the iceberg, the captain of the Titanic shouted out his orders for the ship's course to be changed accordingly.

CONTINUE

15

The word "authority" in the passage is closest in meaning to
A. servant
B. expert
C. extremist
D. helper

Psychologists have proven that the sense of camaraderie makes people more susceptible to peer pressure, thus more obedient to authority figures.

16

The word "conspicuous" in the passage is closest in meaning to
A. normal
B. noticeable
C. different
D. colorful

Color patterns can be conspicuous under certain lights, while they go unnoticed in other circumstances.

17

The word "conventional" in the passage is closest in meaning to
A. standard
B. eccentric
C. forced
D. moderate

There are a few minor problems with the conventional approach to the study of dark matter.

18

The word "detect" in the passage is closest in meaning to
A. identify
B. describe
C. study
D. organize

So far, astronomers have identified more than 2,000 exoplanets around other stars, mostly using indirect methods which detect changes in distant stars.

19

The word "discrepancy" in the passage is closest in meaning to
A. inconsistency
B. condemnation
C. obstruction
D. antipathy

Even the smallest discrepancy could compromise the outcome of the ambitious project of the CERN physicists.

CONTINUE

20

The word "duplicate" in the
passage is closest in meaning to
A. print
B. provoke
C. copy
D. stimulate

Many technology companies have
decided to duplicate Apple's effort
to attract consumers by offering
high-end customer service, which
increases customer satisfaction
and brand loyalty.

21

The word "elusive" in the passage
is closest in meaning to
A. hard to imagine
B. hard to identify
C. misunderstood
D. controversial

The causes of various autoimmune
diseases are relatively elusive
since many of them, including
lupus, Raynaud's syndrome,
and fibromyalgia, all have similar
symptomology.

22

The word "eminent" in the passage
is closest in meaning to
A. traditional
B. distinguished
C. vulnerable
D. satisfactory

The eminent paleontologist,
Professor Benton from Bristol
University, agreed with the findings
on the mysteries of the Permian
extinction.

23

The word "enormous" in the
passage is closest in meaning to
A. vast
B. deserted
C. absolute
D. main

Astronomers have recently
discovered a new breed of
enormous spiral galaxies—
significantly larger than the Milky
Way.

24

The word "excreted" in the
passage is closest in meaning to
A. reported
B. released
C. cleared
D. rescued

The drug works by binding to
excess iron and removing it from
certain cells in the body, such as
liver cells, before being excreted.

CONTINUE

The word "extract" in the passage is closest in meaning to
A. remove
B. resent
C. reiterate
D. recite

There are multiple ways to extract salt: solar evaporation, rock salt mining and solution mining.

The word "flourishing" in the passage is closest in meaning to
A. gaining
B. appearing
C. reaching
D. prospering

History proves that the Mediterranean Sea's habitat was conducive to human life, as we can observe by the flourishing of several civilizations—from the Egyptians to the Romans.

The word "hazardous" in the passage is closest in meaning to
A. exciting
B. compromised
C. dangerous
D. controversial

The presence of dangerous chemicals makes the production process hazardous for workers and other personnel involved in the project, as well as being dangerous for the environment.

The word "impractical" in the passage is closest in meaning to
A. traditional
B. legendary
C. unrealistic
D. unbearable

Ancient armors were extremely impractical, most people could not even stand while wearing them, let alone swing a sword.

The word "integral" in the passage is closest in meaning to
A. concentrated
B. qualified
C. essential
D. leading

The use of modern materials and trendy fabrics is an integral part of award-winning interior design.

CONTINUE

30

The word "isolated" in the passage is closest in meaning to
A. productive
B. separate
C. cooperative
D. self-sufficient

Even though Western medicine treats it in isolated systems, the human body is actually a multi-faceted and interconnected organism.

31

The word "launched" in the passage is closest in meaning to
A. paid for
B. started
C. asked
D. agreed on

The President announced with incredible resolve that a military operation was recently launched to rescue the prisoners from war camps.

32

The word "magnitude" in the passage is closest in meaning to
A. size
B. category
C. theory
D. orbit

So far, War World I and II are the conflicts with the biggest magnitude, both in terms of scope and casualties.

33

The word "mean" in the passage is closest in meaning to
A. average
B. ordinary
C. malevolent
D. poor

Participants in the pharmaceutical research study had a mean age of 25 years.

34

The word "mimic" in the passage is closest in meaning to
A. recycle
B. reproduce
C. request
D. criticize

Computational software programs can mimic with accurate precision winds that are effected by skyscrapers to determine their impact on the surrounding structures when they bend at the edges of tall buildings.

CONTINUE

The word "overwhelmed" in the passage is closest in meaning to
A. been too large for
B. consumed
C. added to
D. recycled

Exorbitant funding for federal defense programs have overwhelmed the national budget, and caused extensive cuts for social programs that aid the poor.

The word "particular" in the passage is closest in meaning to
A. specific
B. related
C. significant
D. limited

A particular example of biodiversity is the Amazon rainforest, home to over 40,000 different plant species.

The word "persuasively" in the passage is closest in meaning to
A. consistently
B. convincingly
C. persistently
D. intelligently

In time, scientists proved persuasively that such an ice-free corridor did not exist until about 12,000 million years ago, when the continental ice began its final retreat.

The word "proper" in the passage is closest in meaning to
A. appropriate
B. external
C. recurrent
D. easy

The laboratory did not have the proper equipment to deal with such dangerous chemicals.

The word "relative" in the passage is closest in meaning to
A. compared to
B. bigger than
C. moved by
D. adequate

Alchemists believed that gold could be obtained by changing the relative proportion of fire and earth in copper.

CONTINUE

40

The word "relatively" in the passage is closest in meaning to
A. comparatively
B. incredibly
C. significantly
D. dangerously

Humans appeared relatively late in history—the first Homo Sapiens has been dated to only 2.5 million years ago.

41

The word "replicated" in the passage is closest in meaning to
A. formed
B. faked
C. copied
D. displayed

The scientist claimed that the study could not be replicated in other cultures because the conditions necessary for conducting each experiment were particularized to one geographical location.

42

The word "severe" in the passage is closest in meaning to
A. simple
B. intense
C. cold
D. solid

The problem is that under climate change, the heat waves are more frequent and severe—even though ocean temperature has only increased modestly.

43

The word "severity" in the passage is closest in meaning to
A. width
B. harshness
C. unexpectedness
D. completeness

The severity of the terroristic threat calls for immediate action.

44

The word "significant" in the passage is closest in meaning to
A. sufficient
B. considerable
C. increasing
D. tiny

The finding had significant importance for later experiments on particle acceleration.

CONTINUE

The word "stagnated" in the
passage is closest in meaning to
A. dominated
B. lack of growth
C. depended on others
D. descended

Since trade stagnated, the city of
Venice could not thrive anymore
without financial gain from foreign
imports and exports.

The word "surplus" in the passage
is closest in meaning to
A. additional equipment
B. superfluous goods
C. excellent material
D. extra goods

The surplus produced by
agriculture in the United States
has fostered a culture of
abundance and scarce recognition
for poverty.

The word "sustained" in the
passage is closest in meaning to
A. limitless
B. proactive
C. uninterrupted
D. unaltered

Rapid time zone changes in
otherwise sustained circadian
rhythm can bring about excessive
sleepiness and lack of alertness.

The word "tasks" in the passage is
closest in meaning to
A. beliefs
B. ideas
C. jobs
D. goals

Artificial Intelligence still relies on
a variety of different programs to
complete its tasks.

CONTINUE

49

The phrase "a lowest effective temperature" in the passage is closest in meaning to
A. the lowest temperature which supports life
B. the lowest temperature at which distillation can be accomplished
C. the lowest temperature at which solidification occurs
D. the lowest temperature at which chemical reactions are possible

With a lowest effective temperature of -7℃, salt is a relatively slow and ineffective solution for ice melt.

50

The word "typically" in the passage is closest in meaning to
A. predictably
B. expectantly
C. commonly
D. acceptably

Planets do not typically orbit in a perfectly flat circle.

1

The phrase "in profusion" in the passage is closest in meaning to
A. profoundly
B. abundantly
C. sparsely
D. brilliantly

Sunflowers grow in profusion in the backyard.

2

The word "convey" in the passage is closest in meaning to
A. transmit
B. postpone
C. travel
D. scream

The message many politicians convey is, beyond dispute, inappropriate.

3

The word "criteria" in the passage is closest in meaning to
A. standards
B. findings
C. ideas
D. methods

Mathematicians have applied these criteria to a similar problem, proving that the matrix method was truly effective.

4

The word "exerted" in the passage is closest in meaning to
A. put forth
B. misused
C. demanded
D. accepted

Subtle changes in diet could have exerted major evolutionary changes, which lead to the reshaping of the species' skull.

CONTINUE ➤

5

The word "intermittent" in the
passage is closest in meaning to
A. experiencing a sudden disruption
B. with frequent errors
C. quick starting
D. starting and stoping often

Doctors recommend to insert
intermittent fasting into your eating
habits.

6

The word "scarce" in the passage
is closest in meaning to
A. short in supply
B. highly dangerous
C. more expensive
D. less productive

Arable land was scarce, thus the
government had to make sure
to protect farmlands from urban
spread.

7

The phrase "akin to" in the
passage is closest in meaning to
A. considered like
B. similar to
C. characteristic of
D. consequent to

The literary characters in Jane
Austin's works are akin to her real
life moral character.

8

The phrase "at intervals" in the
passage is closest in meaning to
A. periodically
B. particularly
C. uncommonly
D. randomly

A team of doctors and nurses
recorded patients' cognitive skills,
such as language and memory
skills, before and at intervals after
the operations.

CONTINUE

The phrase "more permeable" in the passage is closest in meaning to
A. having more places where crossing could occur
B. having more space for confrontation
C. more open to other ideas
D. aware of the surroundings

A soil with good structure will be more permeable than a soil of the same texture that has poor structure.

The word "annihilate" in the passage is closest in meaning to
A. conquer
B. use
C. separate
D. settle

Now, technological advances in medicine mean that humans will soon be able to permanently annihilate their fear of illness and pain.

The word "comparable" in the passage is closest in meaning to
A. funny
B. similar
C. interesting
D. occasional

Due to limited funds for adaptation and revision, it is very important to have a comparable system of surveillance for all coastal regions.

The word "altogether" in the passage is closest in meaning to
A. fairly
B. mainly
C. fully
D. somewhat

The researchers involved in the cancer treatment project say that the discovery is a minor setback that does not preclude the idea altogether.

CONTINUE

13

The word "ambiguous" in the passage is closest in meaning to
A. out of focus
B. foggy
C. untold
D. unclear

Earlier examples of ambiguous images are constrained to shape effects—many were the people that confused a vase for two faces or vice versa.

14

The word "approximate" in the passage is closest in meaning to
A. put together
B. assemble
C. resemble
D. look like

As technology improves, the nature of mechanical interactions, such as phone calls, voice messages and other means, will increasingly approximate actual face-to-face meetings.

15

The word "astonishment" in the passage is closest in meaning to
A. disturbance
B. gift
C. surprise
D. start

The wider scientific community expressed astonishment and skepticism when it was presented with the imploding universe theory.

16

The word "augments" in the passage is closest in meaning to
A. sums up
B. provides
C. adds to
D. speeds up

Exercise also, and perhaps most resonantly, augments adult immune system capability, which is the ability to produce new antibodies.

17

The word "breakthroughs" in the passage is closest in meaning to
A. developments
B. problems
C. accidents
D. conglomerations

The immense library hosts 50 million books covering every scientific topic, from obscure physics experiments published centuries ago to the latest breakthroughs in biotechnology.

CONTINUE

18

The word "combination" in the passage is closest in meaning to
A. performance
B. concert
C. mix
D. benefit

The combination of descending land and rising sea levels caused by global warming means we can expect that Venice and other small islands in the Pacific Ocean will soon be inundated.

19

The word "complex" in the passage is closest in meaning to
A. delicate
B. elaborate
C. special
D. public

Social relationships are the drive of our humaneness; what helps us navigate the complex web of social interactions.

20

The word "complexity" in the passage is closest in meaning to
A. sophistication
B. adaptation
C. development
D. variation

According to researchers, biochemical breakthroughs will reduce the complexity of identifying genetic abnormalities in a fetus, reducing in turn the risk of future diseases.

21

The word "consulted" in the passage is closest in meaning to
A. traveled
B. thought
C. asked
D. raised

We consulted a group of VR experts in order to better understand the potential of virtual reality in different fields, for instance, psychology.

22

The word "contradictory" in the passage is closest in meaning to
A. conclusive
B. absolute
C. absurd
D. conflicting

There are seemingly contradictory results to our research on the Zika virus, maybe due to gaps in our knowledge.

CONTINUE

23

The phrase "corresponded to" in the passage is closest in meaning to
A. devoted to
B. matched
C. set off
D. showed

Two-thirds of the participants were able to complete the task in the faintest light, which corresponded to a moonless summer night.

24

The word "countering" in the passage is closest in meaning to
A. attending to
B. criticizing
C. combating
D. taking hold of

Another way of countering drug consumption is to have periodical health checks in schools and other institutions; this way people are incentivized to stay clean.

25

The word "cumulative" in the passage is closest in meaning to
A. formal
B. systematic
C. unorganized
D. combined

According to experts, the soil of a few large plantations of tobacco have sustained a "cumulative and well-nigh permanent poisoning."

26

The word "deliberately" in the passage is closest in meaning to
A. friendly
B. quickly
C. purposely
D. abruptly

Poisonous agents are often used to guarantee potable water; in fact, some are deliberately applied to bodies of water to destroy plants, insects, or unwanted fishes.

27

The word "episodes" in the passage is closest in meaning to
A. occurrences
B. locations
C. consequences
D. combinations

Epilepsy, which is the fourth most common neurological disorder in the United States, causes episodes of unpredictable seizures which can result in irreversible brain damage if severe.

CONTINUE

28

The word "equivalent" in the passage is closest in meaning to
A. different
B. stable
C. just
D. comparable

The study concludes that, when it comes to these two genes, the stem cells and artificial stem cells are functionally equivalent.

29

The word "extreme" in the passage is closest in meaning to
A. bold
B. progressive
C. organic
D. great

Recent medical findings in the field of stem cell research are of extreme interest for those seeking cures to paralysis and Alzheimer's disease.

30

The word "implied" in the passage is closest in meaning to
A. defended
B. suggested
C. demonstrated
D. analyzed

Although the judge did not directly accuse the defendant of wrongdoing, her harsh case introduction implied that she fully agreed with the prosecution's opening statements.

31

The phrase "in retrospect" in the passage is closest in meaning to
A. looking back
B. against
C. in exchange for
D. finally

In retrospect, it was very peculiar that a man with such strong religious conviction would develop a theory that completely denied the churches' claims.

32

The word "invited" in the passage is closest in meaning to
A. encouraged
B. provoked
C. developed
D. started

Still, women are not often invited to sit on scientific advisory boards or to guide scientific research departments.

215

CONTINUE

33

The word "manifestation" in the passage is closest in meaning to
A. abstraction
B. talent
C. expression
D. purpose

As a sign of good faith and a manifestation of gratitude, the kings would send gifts and money to their respective counterparts.

34

The word "obscure" in the passage is closest in meaning to
A. little known
B. observable
C. direct
D. unattractive

The obscure symbol belongs to an ancient cult whose members tattooed the symbols on their forearms as a sign of their fidelity to the sun god.

35

The word "ongoing" in the passage is closest in meaning to
A. uncertain
B. full-speed
C. important
D. continuing

Ongoing investigations on the matter have discovered that the team responsible for the first round of testing had tampered with the equipment.

36

The word "plentiful" in the passage is closest in the meaning to
A. popular
B. wonderful
C. numerous
D. complicated

The supply of oil from the Northern region of the country is not plentiful anymore, resulting in a shortage of resources for the entire nation.

37

The word "predominant" in the passage is closest in meaning to
A. intense
B. principal
C. severe
D. total

The archaeological evidence points out that, in Mesopotamia, the Sumer was the civilization that arose as a predominant force.

CONTINUE

The word "prolific" in the passage is closest in meaning to
A. most discussed
B. very convincing
C. extremely practical
D. highly productive

The new technology confirmed that, in the most remote galaxies, new stars are created at a prolific rate.

The word "prompted" in the passage is closest in meaning to
A. stimulated
B. devoted
C. dissolved
D. asserted

The war prompted a spike in spice prices, because it had become very arduous to procure them.

The word "recall" in the passage is closest in meaning to
A. assert
B. create
C. develop
D. remember

The survivors of the battle of Iwo Jima recall how surprised Japanese soldiers who surrendered were that "the enemy" received them with compassion and generosity.

The word "remarkable" in the passage is closest in meaning to
A. mystical
B. mundane
C. extraordinary
D. exciting

By using a cosmic distance ladder, astronomers can calculate the distance of an object in space with remarkable precision.

The word "routinely" in the passage is closest in meaning to
A. efficiently
B. regularly
C. quickly
D. affordably

The phenomenon of supernova is now routinely observed in various galaxies.

217

CONTINUE

43

The word "sculpted" in the
passage is closet in meaning to
A. quarried
B. anticipated
C. shaped
D. developed

Michel sculpted a monumental
statue out of a stone that was
roughed out a basic shape.

44

The word "steadily" in the passage
is closest in meaning to
A. constantly
B. at an unvarying rate
C. quickly
D. sporadically

Annual rainfall has been steadily
decreasing as the climate changes
and drought grips the region.

45

The word "suspected" in the
passage is closest in meaning to
A. dreamt of
B. doubted
C. criticized
D. opposed

Some people suspected that the
monument had not been made
by primitive men, without proper
equipment.

46

The word "tangible" in the passage
is closest in meaning to
A. physical
B. relevant
C. significant
D. helpful

The strategy has not produced
tangible benefits; thus, the
laboratory has been urged to
change their approach in order
to increase measurable and
observable results.

47

The word "norms" in the passage
is closest in meaning to
A. commons
B. acceptances
C. supports
D. yields

Before equality can truly become
part of our communities, societal
norms at large, not only the norms
of the workplace, must change.

CONTINUE

The phrase "upon reflection" in the passage is closest in meaning to
A. based on
B. after consideration
C. in fact
D. as a rule

Upon reflection, the emperor decided not to retaliate in order to avoid the possibility of further insubordination.

The word "converted" in the passage is closest in meaning to
A. added
B. changed
C. recovered
D. reduced

However, rather than generating electricity, the new facility would produce fuel, which could be converted to gasoline.

The word "mobilize" in the passage is closest in meaning to
A. put into action
B. record
C. protect
D. yield

While the world has begun to mobilize in the fight against the virus, many fear the effort is coming too late.

END

1

The word "erect" in the passage is closest in meaning to
A. design
B. construct
C. safeguard
D. decorate

Because the environment was hostile to settlers, they could not use the entire plot, and were forced to erect the village on a margin of the grassland.

2

The word "feasible" in the passage is closest in meaning to
A. practical
B. customary
C. acceptable
D. prudent

Modern architects are planning feasible strategies to convert old, abandoned buildings in modern functional areas.

3

The word "frigid" in the passage is closest in meaning to
A. moving
B. giant
C. authentic
D. cold

New discoveries suggest that, despite the frigid temperatures, Mars could be able to host water on its surface.

4

The word "henceforth" in the passage is closest in meaning to
A. instead of this
B. in addition
C. from this time on
D. actually

Venice proved to be a more powerful adversary, and while at first relatively equal, the Genoese fleet was soon eliminated at the mouth of the lagoon; henceforth, Venice became the leading sea city.

CONTINUE

5

The word "incited" in the passage is closest in meaning to
A. permitted
B. stimulated
C. forced
D. helped

That observation suggests that it was the presence of other possible mates that incited the peacock to make its mating dance more and more elaborate.

6

The word "obliged" in the passage is closest in meaning to
A. forced
B. allowed
C. expected
D. convinced

Because of the dangerous chemicals that can dissipate into the waterways, the town council was obliged to impose restrictions to washing freshly dyed clothes in the river.

7

The word "relentless" in the passage is closest in meaning to
A. tiresome
B. endless
C. obscure
D. unceasing

Incredible scientific discoveries in recent years arose from researchers' relentless pursuit of answers about the world works.

8

The word "subdue" in the passage is closest in meaning to
A. remove
B. fight
C. defeat
D. dare

The tradition is that pretender to the throne fight one another, those who are not prepared for war might find it advantageous to step away from rivals who they cannot subdue.

9

The word "synthesized" in the passage is closest in meaning to
A. joined
B. integrated
C. reported
D. supported

Before the advent of modern chemicals, pharmacists synthesized natural products with useful properties and created effective remedies.

CONTINUE

10

The word "tied" in the passage is closest in meaning to
A. connected
B. changed
C. needed
D. developed

Sustainability is fundamentally tied to development and economic growth.

11

The phrase "be deficient in" in the passage is closest in meaning to
A. desire more than one needs
B. not have enough
C. make up for
D. recover from a loss

The vegetarian diet will most likely be deficient in vitamins and proteins. In fact, according to experts, Vitamin B12 is rarely present in a vegetarian diet.

12

The phrase "several simultaneous developments" in the passage is closest in meaning to
A. inconclusive developments
B. developments that reinforced each other
C. developments that occurred at the same time
D. developments that followed one another in a sequence

The interaction of several simultaneous developments strongly impacted the society of the time—cooperative guilds were created and trade started to flourish.

13

The word "adhesive" in the passage is closest in meaning to
A. vicious
B. sticky
C. moldy
D. liquids

The deposition of a fossil in adhesive Substances assists in fossil preservation.

CONTINUE ➡

14

The word "ceased" in the passage is closest in meaning to
A. slowed down
B. speeded up
C. stopped
D. followed

The danger of venomous snakes' bites recently started making its way back into the news when journalists discovered that the main pharmaceutical companies in the world had ceased developing antidotes.

15

The word "chaotic" in the passage is closest in meaning to
A. disorganized
B. dirty
C. vague
D. forgetful

Scientists are trying to determine whether the hotter temperatures and chaotic weather turns produced by climate change are responsible for higher rates of violence.

16

The word "cite" in the passage is closest in meaning to
A. suspect
B. believe
C. compare
D. mention

Analysts often cite a prior study, which suggests that long-lasting temperature fluctuations affect people's belief in global warming.

17

The word "coalesced" in the passage is closest in meaning to
A. joined
B. got sick
C. analyzed
D. discussed

Two separate research groups soon coalesced around one conclusion—that the Einstein's theory of relativity had various applications in the field of astronomy.

18

The word "constant" in the passage is closest in meaning to
A. continual
B. endless
C. brief
D. loyal

It will take constant effort to ensure the correct functioning of the sophisticated particle accelerator and prevent incidents.

CONTINUE

19

The word "curious" in the passage is closest in meaning to
A. brilliant
B. clear
C. strange
D. magnificent

Due to their flexible dorsal shell and silky fur, the pink fairy armadillo of central Argentina is one of the world's most curious creatures.

20

The word "domestic" in the passage is closest in meaning to
A. spiritual
B. household
C. remote
D. controversial

In 2010, New York became the first state to pass employment laws for those employed in domestic settings, halting decades of labor abuse among elite employers in the nation's wealthiest cities.

21

The word "embodies" in the passage is closest in meaning to
A. extends
B. initiates
C. promotes
D. incorporates

Princess Kate Middleton embodies many of the graceful mannerisms of her husband's late mother, Princess Diana of Wales.

22

The word "emit" in the passage is closest in meaning to
A. release
B. speak
C. trust
D. use

Large social panel plantations can be built quickly and easily expanded, and do not emit carbon dioxide or other pollutant.

23

The word "engaged" in the passage is closest in meaning to
A. hired
B. encouraged
C. praised
D. simplified

Donatella Versace engaged the new designer immediately following his successful internship with her fashion company.

CONTINUE

24

The word "excavated" in the passage is closest in meaning to
A. dug from the ground
B. concentrated in solid form
C. deposited
D. collected

Coal mining was a traditional activity in rural West Virginia, and many factories excavated surrounding mines for decades.

25

The word "extensive" in the passage is closest in meaning to
A. confirmed
B. established
C. ordinary
D. widespread

Large elliptical galaxies usually have an extensive system of globular clusters—a collection of stars that orbits around the galaxy.

26

The word "foster" in the passage is closest in meaning to
A. increase
B. commence
C. determine
D. encourage

It is essential to foster a greater level of integration between agriculture and urban development plans.

27

The word "fuel" in the passage is closest in meaning to
A. provide energy for
B. determine the route of
C. hold
D. break up

Hot climates can dry out the underbrush and ground litter could fuel a spontaneous fire.

28

The word "fundamental" in the passage is closest in meaning to
A. famous
B. basic
C. innovative
D. original

The old assembling machines are responsible for many of the fundamental functions, thus they cannot be replaced yet.

225

CONTINUE

29

The word "incredible" in the passage is closest in meaning to
A. wildly disproved
B. absurd
C. controversial
D. impossible to believe

It seems incredible that humans were able to travel to space and build devices that orbit around Earth with only limited technology.

30

The word "justify" in the passage is closest in meaning to
A. include within the social system
B. provide a rational basis for
C. employ
D. discourage

For the first time, there was enough request for professional photography to justify the existence of full-time photographer.

31

The word "mandate" in the passage is closest in meaning to
A. contribute to
B. produce
C. constrict
D. require

These provisions mandate all the coal burning companies adhere to the new standards of production of toxic-release chemicals, such as arsenic, lead, mercury, and copper.

32

The phrase "needless to say" in the passage is closest in meaning to
A. obviously
B. possibly
C. eventually
D. finally

Needless to say, in ancient times hygiene standards and medical practices were not advanced, which explains so many deaths from the common cold and other treatable conditions.

33

The word "obligate" in the passage is closest in meaning to
A. accuse
B. persecute
C. oppress
D. require

The new emissions laws obligate factories in the northwest to reduce their toxic output by at least 7%.

CONTINUE

34

The word "outweigh" in the passage is closest in meaning to
A. exceed
B. disregard
C. minimize
D. disguise

In this circumstance, the advantages of moving to a more expensive area of town outweigh the downsides.

35

The word "particularly" in the passage is closest in meaning to
A. usually
B. obviously
C. especially
D. recently

Providing water for farming is sometimes easier than providing drinkable water, particularly when there is high demand for clean water and little opportunity to build purification plants.

36

The word "pertinent" in the passage is closest in meaning to
A. extraordinary
B. relevant
C. intelligent
D. notorious

This question of why young people abandon their native lands is particularly pertinent for developed countries, where there is no apparent need to leave in search of "better" opportunities.

37

The word "ponders" in the passage is closest in meaning to
A. explains
B. argues over
C. thinks about
D. discovers

Adam Smith ponders the many reasons that a society, at a given time, is more influential and powerful than others.

38

The word "preserved" in the passage is closest in meaning to
A. limited
B. revealed
C. maintained
D. produced

There are thousands of delicate insect fossils, some of them even with their coloration preserved.

227

CONTINUE

39

The word "principally" in the passage is closet in meaning to
A. clearly
B. apparently
C. mainly
D. originally

Sea-level rise as a consequence of global warming is principally caused by the thermal expansion of the oceans, not the melting of ice-caps.

40

The word "rapports" in the passage is closest in meaning to
A. excitements
B. equilibriums
C. bonds
D. fascinations

Because of the many conspiracies and the games of power, it was very difficult to create trustworthy rapports in ancient Rome.

41

The word "edge" in the passage is closest in meaning to
A. rim
B. force
C. setback
D. advantage

Timberline trees have some edge over deciduous trees in the extreme environments.

42

The word "regimes" in the passage is closest in meaning to
A. cities
B. buildings
C. governments
D. factories

In the 15th and 16th Centuries, European regimes started hiring artists to celebrate their nations' power and wealth.

43

The word "remnant" in the passage is closest in meaning to
A. remainder
B. resident
C. reproductive
D. reserved

Remnant biotas (animals and plants) are still adjusting to the effects of fragmentation and the effects associated with the loss of past and current habitat.

CONTINUE

44

The word "replenish" in the passage is closest in meaning to
A. incorporate
B. restore
C. contain
D. obtain

If the earth's inhabitants use up most of the fresh water, it will be difficult to replenish it in a timely manner.

45

The word "scale" in the passage is closest in meaning to
A. method
B. bias
C. peace
D. size

The scale of the economic growth prompted the government to promote free market ideas, including capitalism and consumerism.

46

The word "signify" in the passage is closest in meaning to
A. mold
B. indicate
C. initiate
D. require

In that time, white smoke came to signify that the cardinal assembly had chosen a new Pope. This tradition continues to this day.

47

The word "suspended" in the passage is closest in meaning to
A. dissolved
B. floated
C. ignored
D. released

Suspended from the vaulted ceiling was a wooden sledge that Robert Peary and Matthew Henson used in their 1909 North Pole expedition.

48

The word "thrilled" in the passage in closest in meaning to
A. aimed
B. weakened
C. meant
D. excited

Experts are thrilled by the new advancement in the field of AI.

CONTINUE

49

The word "ultimately" in the passage is closest in meaning to
A. probably
B. promptly
C. eventually
D. frequently

Funds have been allocated for a project that promises to ultimately solve the issue of global warming.

50

The word "vitality" in the passage is closest in meaning to
A. style
B. energy
C. cause
D. quality

Slavery had depleted classical civilization of its vitality.

END

1

The phrase "with no warning" in the passage is closest in meaning to
A. without any indication beforehand
B. without any further due
C. without proper protections
D. regardless of the circumstances

With no warning Mount Vesuvius erupted, causing the destruction of the city of Pompeii.

2

The word "consumed" in the passage is closest in meaning to
A. used up
B. threw away
C. drank up
D. tucked in

The meteorite is believed to have caused, besides the extinction of most species of dinosaurs, widespread fires that consumed large portions of forests and grassland.

3

The word "exposed" in the passage is closest in meaning to
A. unprotected
B. remarkable
C. unfinished
D. unexecuted

Several dinosaur specimens were found in the desert where they had been exposed to various atmospheric agents, which had compromised the fossils' integrity.

4

The word "find" in the passage is closest in meaning to
A. hold
B. prevail
C. locate
D. fail

After years of strenuous research, the team was able to find the exact location of the hidden chamber in the tomb of Tutankhamun.

CONTINUE

The word "plagued" in the passage is closest in meaning to
A. was discussed in
B. was found in
C. separated
D. caused trouble for

Famine plagued populations across Europe for thousands of years, including the major food shortage which happened in the 14th Century.

The word "pursuing" in the passage is closest in meaning to
A. revising
B. assembling
C. training
D. practicing

Environmentalists also say that pursuing new sources of gas–a fossil fuel or organic oil–is not compatible with efforts to tackle climate change.

The phrase "contributes to" in the passage is closest in meaning to
A. learns from
B. eases off
C. takes advantage of
D. adds to

Like other pollutant agents, almost all CO_2 produced by factories is released into the atmosphere, where it contributes to climate change.

The word "activated" in the passage is closest in meaning to
A. drove
B. transformed
C. managed
D. switched on

Once the CERN generator was finished and had been activated, scientists expected the machine to simulate the conditions of the Big Bang.

CONTINUE

The word "ambiguities" in the passage is closest in meaning to
A. statements that do not follow logic
B. statements that are not well documented
C. words or statements that can be interpreted in more than one way
D. statements that can contradict the available data

Before any nations or private organizations begin exploring and exploiting settlements, ambiguities in international law regarding space exploration and settlements should be resolved.

The word "commodity" in the passage is closest in meaning to
A. product
B. waste
C. consequence
D. residue

Declining commodity prices have had only a short-term impact on the renewable energy and raw element industries.

The word "concentration" in the passage is closest in meaning to
A. application
B. affiliation
C. dense grouping
D. passion

Much praise was given to the American military operation during the Second World War, especially regarding the liberation of two concentration camps.

The word "continued" in the passage is closest in meaning to
A. ongoing
B. common
C. outdated
D. progressive

Continued public interest, effective regulations, and advanced scientific research are essential to effectively safeguard many endangered species.

CONTINUE

13

The word "contradicted" in the passage is closest in meaning to
A. limited
B. combined
C. conflicted
D. stood for

The University of Michigan published an article in 2015 saying that no subsequent study had contradicted their findings on social change patterns.

14

The word "current" in the passage is closest in meaning to
A. hypothetical
B. basic
C. alternative
D. present

After the origination of the theory of plate tectonics, estimates of current geological plate motions continue to be used broadly for geological, geophysical, and geodetic studies.

15

The word "deficiency" in the passage is closest in meaning to
A. issue
B. illness
C. shortage
D. irregularity

Fast heart rate or sensation of abnormal heartbeat are commonly associated with iron deficiency, also called anemia.

16

The word "delicately" in the passage is closest in meaning to
A. succinctly
B. fairly
C. finely
D. greatly

One branch of gastronomy explores the art of serving delicately prepared dishes that join food and culture in appetizing meals.

17

The word "denser" in the passage is closest in meaning to
A. thicker
B. more crowded
C. more interesting
D. more active

Agricultural cultures are more skilled than hunting ones, and have, as a result, denser populations; while the more skilled agricultural cultures have a denser population than the less skilled agricultural races.

CONTINUE

18

The word "detached" in the passage is closest in meaning to
A. separated
B. raised
C. loosened
D. produced

Virtual reality allows the player to be in a completely isolated environment, detached from the real world.

19

The phrase "devoid of" in the passage is closest in meaning to
A. limited by
B. lack of
C. bored by
D. distant from

Supporters contend the Black Lives Matter movement is devoid of any racism against white privilege, while opponents accuse the movement's leaders of militant actions that result in irreversible social damage.

20

The word "distributed" in the passage is closest in meaning to
A. represented
B. measured
C. spread
D. managed

Because air pollution is now distributed across the continent of North America, it is difficult to consider solutions that focus on local air quality alone.

21

The word "experimental" in the passage is closest in meaning to
A. favorable
B. trial
C. confident
D. difficult

A new experimental therapy propose to use Virtual Reality to expose people with mental disorders to extreme situations, helping them cope with their conditions.

22

The word "hostile" in the passage is closest in meaning to
A. uncaring
B. poisonous
C. unfavorable
D. cold

Supporters of republican Donald Trump took a hostile perspective of his democratic opponent, and even resorted to violence against anyone who spoke in favor of Trump's opponent.

CONTINUE

23

The word "indefinitely" in the passage is closest in meaning to
A. without limits
B. constantly
C. fixed in time
D. immutably

To the dismay of many feminists, Pope Francis recently decreed that women's denial to the priesthood would last indefinitely for the Catholic Church.

24

The word "indigenous" in the passage is closest in meaning to
A. model
B. genuine
C. creative
D. native

During colonization, indigenous species of animals and plants were gradually killed off by more aggressive European species.

25

The word "indispensable" in the passage is closest in meaning to
A. negative
B. theoretical
C. essential
D. risky

Although they were not part of the traditional diet, potatoes became indispensable for the European cuisine.

26

The word "invertebrate" in the passage is closest in meaning to
A. inferior
B. spineless
C. disabled
D. delicate

Arthropods are invertebrate animals with segmented bodies and jointed limbs, such as insects and spiders.

27

The word "irreversible" in the passage is closest in meaning to
A. universal
B. stained
C. permanent
D. old

The worst possible aspect of climate change is that it will be irreversible and irrevocable.

CONTINUE

The word "manipulated" in the passage is closest in meaning to
A. delegated
B. handled
C. felt
D. examined

She manipulated her candidacy brilliantly, eventually exposing her opposition as a corrupt and unscrupulous politician not suitable for public office.

The word "minute" in the passage is closest in meaning to
A. light
B. mundane
C. tiny
D. simple

It is possible that minute quantities of liquid water are present in pores and capillaries in the soil.

The word "monumental" in the passage is closest in meaning to
A. absolute
B. persuasive
C. well-known
D. great and significant

Officials have agreed upon a monumental plan to counteract climate change, which will be carried out in the next few years.

The word "namely" in the passage is closest in meaning to
A. in addition
B. on the other hand
C. obviously
D. that is to say

In certain areas, namely the underdeveloped rural counties, there is a lack of specialized medical personnel.

The word "novel" in the passage is closest in meaning to
A. ordinary
B. isolated
C. historical
D. new

Unfortunately, nobody has yet come up with a novel idea to solve the carbon emission issue; and although, experts are working on it constantly they have not reached a conclusive plan.

CONTINUE ➡

33

The word "perpetual" in the
passage is closest in meaning to
A. numerous
B. unlimited
C. innumerable
D. .constant

The third Newton law states that
an object in perpetual movement
will always maintain its state.

34

The word "perspectives" in the
passage is closest in meaning to
A. forms
B. figures
C. viewpoints
D. settings

People from different backgrounds
and different cultures have
different perspectives on many
issues–even the most basic ones.

35

The word "portrayed", in the
passage is closest in meaning to
A. sustained
B. represented
C. defended
D. established

Some witnesses stated that the
situation was significantly worse
than it had been portrayed, which
forced investigators to reexamine
the crime scene.

36

The word "rapid" in the passage is
closest in meaning to
A. fast
B. changing
C. erratic
D. sudden

There was a glitch in the program,
which was fixed in no time thanks
to the rapid intervention of IT
specialists.

37

The word "reflect" in the passage
is closest in meaning to
A. perform
B. show
C. learn
D. explore

The philosophers of the time–
Lucretius, Cicero, Seneca and
many others–reflect the influence
of Greek culture on the Roman
empire.

CONTINUE

38

The word "residues" in the passage is closest in meaning to
A. reminders
B. components
C. parts
D. remains

Many have raised concerns over the chemical residues of pesticides, which could be hazardous for food safety and, consequently, human health.

39

The word "retard" in the passage is closest in meaning to
A. limit
B. slow
C. control
D. oppose

To properly retard the proliferation of microbes, it is important to maintain a constant room temperature and humidity.

40

The word "retrieved" in the passage is closest in meaning to
A. found
B. recovered
C. recalled
D. hatched

The search and rescue teams did not halt their efforts until every body had been retrieved from the tornado site.

41

The word "sedimentation" in the passage is closest in meaning to
A. payment
B. deposit
C. advance
D. coating

The patterns of sedimentation show which terrains were still glaciated during that era.

42

The phrase "subjected to" in the passage is closest in meaning to
A. experienced
B. contended
C. argued
D. participated

As a species, humans have been subjected to environmental pressures which have caused our evolution from Hominidae to Homo sapiens.

CONTINUE

43

The word "subsistence" in the passage is closest in meaning to
A. resources
B. skill
C. survival
D. completion

Climate change affects everyone, from the wealthiest of nations to those that struggle most with subsistence economies.

44

The phrase "susceptible to" in the passage is closest in meaning to
A. open and honest
B. easy to adopt
C. likely to be affected by
D. likely to spread out

But even these policies may still be met by increases in mortality as aging populations are increasingly susceptible to the problems associated with pollution.

45

The word "traditional" in the passage is closest in meaning to
A. conventional
B. influential
C. truthful
D. backward

Climate change threatens traditional and cultural practices, such as fishing or hunting.

46

The word "traumatic" in the passage is closest in meaning to
A. highly stressful
B. highly contagious
C. extremely dangerous
D. worrisome

Abandoning their houses and a familiar environment, to embark in a long and dangerous journey to a foreign country was probably traumatic.

47

The word "unpromising" in the passage is closest in meaning to
A. unfavorable
B. underdeveloped
C. distant
D. expensive

Because the experiment was deemed unpromising, the results were not widely disseminated among the international scientific community.

CONTINUE

48

The word "ingested" in the passage is closest in meaning to
A. ate
B. absorbed
C. devoured
D. drank

The skinny young lady seemed to take no pleasure in food; she simply ingested her meals for the sake of basic nourishment.

49

The word "discrete" in the passage is closest in meaning to
A. various
B. separate
C. distinct
D. disconnected

Working under a microscope, the biologist injected discrete batches of unicellular organisms each with a unique slurry of genetic material.

50

The word "diverged" in the passage is closest in meaning to
A. veered
B. separated
C. radiated
D. bent

Homo Sapiens diverged from a complex branch of human and apelike species several hundred thousand years ago in the African continent.

END

1

The word "adjoined" in the passage is closest in meaning to
A. relied on
B. adjusted
C. adapted
D. bordered

It was not uncommon for poor families, during the Industrial Revolution, to live in small rooms adjoined to the factories where they worked.

2

The word "decorated" in the passage is closest in meaning to
A. recognized
B. camouflaged
C. rewarded
D. treated

As a display of their status, and because of their materialistic nature, rich Romans decorated their walls with precious art, their home with luxurious artifacts, and their person, or their spouses, with expensive jewelry.

3

The word "initiative" in the passage is closest in meaning to
A. revolution
B. energy
C. suit
D. action

The most effective initiative to combat climate change are Environmental Protection Agency regulations against air pollution in cities where manufacturing plants are the biggest culprits.

4

The phrase "originate from" in the passage is closest in meaning to
A. give birth to
B. is caused by
C. under unfortunate circumstances
D. come into existence from

Recent data suggests that Minoans (the earliest Bronze Age European civilization) did not originate from Africa, as previously believed, but from Europe.

CONTINUE ➡

5

The word "posterity" in the passage is closest in meaning to
A. further generation
B. legend
C. tradition
D. future

Several Roman writers, historians and philosophers made it their mission to record the events of the time for posterity due to their concerns for leaving a mark on history.

6

The word "pronouncements" in the passage is closest in meaning to
A. statements
B. advice
C. theories
D. examinations

Apocalyptic pronouncements from scientists and entrepreneurs have driven the surge in interest.

7

The phrase "at random" in the passage is closest in meaning to
A. luckily
B. unfortunately
C. by chance
D. by destiny

He chose his victims at random, and subsequently shot people of varying gender, ethnicity and age.

8

The word "rekindle" in the passage is closest in meaning to
A. report
B. renew
C. reiterate
D. reward

The new discovery of dwarf planets Pluto and Eris, will force scientists to rekindle the debate over what constitutes a planet.

9

The phrase "to some degree" in the passage is closest in meaning to
A. under certain conditions
B. little by little
C. in some places
D. all at once

To some degree, the new laws were not nearly as oppressive as the old ones since new legislation meant that more people enjoyed access to public transportation, parks, and community center.

CONTINUE

10

The phrase "a glimpse into" in the passage is closest in meaning to
A. the proof that
B. new information regarding
C. a brief view of
D. the whole picture

A glimpse into a very old stratum of Hellenic religion is afforded us by the records of Dodona, who is the oldest Greek oracle, possibly dating back to the second millennium BCE.

11

The phrase "beautifully preserved" in the passage is closest in meaning to
A. barely used
B. with no damage
C. somewhat new
D. protected

York is a thriving town with a certain Victorian atmosphere, all of whose buildings are beautifully preserved and still in use.

12

The phrase "insensitive to" in the passage is closest in meaning to
A. excused from
B. obvious
C. not affected by
D. spared from

The new aggressive species is insensitive to the harsh condition and can thrive where the other weaker plant died.

13

The phrase "now and then" in the passage is closest in meaning to
A. frequently
B. occasionally
C. sooner or later
D. first and last

Now and then, research studies experience glitches in their designs that prohibit statistically significant findings and reduce the studies' reliability.

14

The word "plausible" in the passage is closest in meaning to
A. preferable
B. practical
C. reasonable
D. beneficial

Another supposedly plausible theory—that the universe is expanding at a steady rate and will eventually disperse—is also wrong.

CONTINUE

The word "approached" in the passage is closest in meaning to
A. neared
B. imitated
C. traveled along
D. left

As the divers approached, they saw that the seafloor was covered in fragile staghorn corals.

The word "beneficial" in the passage is closest in meaning to
A. brilliant
B. daunting
C. advantageous
D. sharp

Any physical activity is considered beneficial to a person's health, for example, walking around the house stimulates blood circulation, thus preventing formation of vascular blockages.

The word "considered" in the passage is closest in meaning to
A. argued
B. believed
C. recorded
D. guided

It is considered paramount to make periodic examinations of the blood of nurses and doctors, who are frequently exposed to contagious diseases.

The word "counterparts" in the passage is closest in meaning to
A. additions
B. inventions
C. parts
D. equivalents

When it comes to memorizing and recording events, pen and paper are actually more efficient than their mechanical counterparts.

The word "damaged" in the passage is closest in meaning to
A. attracted
B. contravened
C. mutilated
D. invaded

Much of the arable land was damaged by the most recent earthquake.

CONTINUE

20

The word "enhance" in the passage is closest in meaning to
A. increase
B. deteriorate
C. fade
D. fabricate

Many other processes may enhance the chemical composition of a molecule; thus improving its chances for proliferation.

21

The word "entirely" in the passage is closest in meaning to
A. fairly
B. completely
C. reasonably
D. satisfactorily

Although many political pundits predicted Hillary Clinton would win the general election, the latest incident involving her email fiasco has made it entirely possible she will lose to Donald Trump.

22

The word "evade" in the passage is closest in meaning to
A. run to
B. confront
C. escape
D. tremble

It appears that the virus can rapidly mutate and adapt to evade the immune system response.

23

The word "execute" in the passage is closest in meaning to
A. accomplish
B. consume
C. end
D. refine

Once lawmakers understood challenges to the plan, they devised a strategic approach to diversity, and established relationships with other laboratories to execute it.

24

The word "formidable" in the passage is closest in meaning to
A. impressive
B. curious
C. mysterious
D. cosmic

Artificial intelligence technology now faces a formidable challenge, that of matching human psychology.

CONTINUE

25

The word "habits" in the passage is closest in meaning to

A. odd routines
B. usual behaviors
C. peculiar characteristics
D. long-standing traditions

Plants with such aggressive eating habits will survive in poor soil conditions, because they always find new sources of nitrogen and other nutrients.

26

The word "infusion" in the passage is closest in meaning to

A. result
B. combination
C. immersion
D. absorption

Columbia University's infusion of medicine, literature, and society resulted in a new course that explores the cultural and social dimensions of disease.

27

The word "key" in the passage is closest in meaning to

A. early
B. crucial
C. noticeable
D. recurrent

Among the key reasons behind the economic development there were an increase in efficiency and the expansion of the export sector.

28

The word "many-segmented" in the passage is closest in meaning to

A. not on speaking terms
B. separated at birth
C. kept in different compartment
D. divided into many parts

Scientists recently found a fossil belonging to a many-segmented slug that was about 30 million years old.

29

The word "notably" in the passage is closest in meaning to

A. properly
B. incidentally
C. particularly
D. clearly

The discovery could have many applications, notably in the fields of biochemistry and medicine.

CONTINUE

30

The word "outlying" in the passage is closest in meaning to
A. moving away for the center
B. asymmetric
C. not perfectly centered
D. far from the center

Although they city is developed and rich, its outlying villages are still affected by poverty and poor living conditions.

31

The word "overall" in the passage is closest in meaning to
A. considered as a whole
B. to some degree
C. possibly
D. clearly

Climate change will lead to a less healthy diet composition in addition to making food less available overall.

32

The word "persuaded" in the passage is closest in meaning to
A. spread out
B. warned against
C. responded to
D. talked into

However, how can we be expected to act on climate change, when the person who persuaded us to act does not take action themselves?

33

The word "premises" in the passage is closest in meaning to
A. beliefs
B. assumptions
C. obligations
D. stimulation

The premises of the first health care system were that most individuals had to have access to primary care.

34

The phrase "prior to" in the passage is closest in meaning to
A. besides
B. before
C. however
D. regardless

Prior to the settlement of Europeans to what is now North America, Vikings visited the land.

CONTINUE ➤

35

The phrase "reach consensus on" in the passage is closest in meaning to
A. debate
B. agree on
C. beg to
D. be inclined towards

Modern demographic research shows, even if experts did not reach consensus on the reasons for their deaths, that the rate of infant mortality was extremely high in ancient Rome.

36

The word "redundancies" in the passage is closest in meaning to
A. duplication
B. diversities
C. requirements
D. flexibility

Greater attention to waste disposal systems and recycling processes could reduce redundancies, as well as protect the environment.

37

The word "repeated" in the passage is closest in meaning to
A. recurred
B. quoted
C. followed
D. noted

The scientists repeated these experiments on different subjects, but the research study results did not change, increasing the findings' reliability and validity.

38

The word "reproduce" in the passage is closest in meaning to
A. raise
B. propagate
C. accumulate
D. collect

Mostly these limitations were in place so that the new molecule could not reproduce itself and eventually would have been destroyed.

39

The word "respective" in the passage is closest in meaning to
A. punctual
B. separate
C. precise
D. consistent

Respective studies have come to the same results concerning the acceleration on particles in a simulator.

CONTINUE

40

The phrase "set in motion" in the passage is closest in meaning to
A. start
B. provide
C. jump
D. rush

The event which set in motion the First War World was the assassination of Archduke Franz Ferdinand of Austria and his wife, Sophie, Duchess of Hohenberg, on 28 June 1914.

41

The word "successive" in the passage is closest in meaning to
A. ensuring
B. following
C. supporting
D. resulting

But it has become ever more obvious—as successive reports have pointed out—that the costs outweigh the benefits.

42

The word "terminated" in the passage is closest in meaning to
A. concealed
B. dissolved
C. conquered
D. ended

Although the program was originally designed to continue for twelve months, it was terminated early due to the end of the war.

43

The word "underlying" in the passage is closest in meaning to
A. most important
B. on the one hand
C. regarding
D. basic

They have assumed that this overall cooling effect has partially masked the climate's underlying sensitivity to rising carbon dioxide levels.

44

The word "uniform" in the passage is closest in meaning to
A. honorable
B. worthy
C. standard
D. official

An independent analytical evaluation was needed to set a uniform standard for carbon dating of archeological discoveries.

CONTINUE

45

The word "virtue" in the passage is closest in meaning to
A. fare
B. design
C. desirable quality
D. physical characteristic

Empathy was not considered a desirable virtue, as many people believed that it only made a man weak.

46

The phrase "to some extent" in the passage is closest in meaning to
A. regardless
B. within limitations
C. beyond limitations
D. not quite

To some extent, all societies have experienced both immigration and emigration waves, and have been able to progress beyond initial challenges and concerns.

47

The word "acquired" in the passage is closest in meaning to
A. collected
B. achieved
C. bought
D. obtained

After the death of her aunt, Janice acquired a hideous collection of plastic statues; to her surprise, an appraiser later valued her new art collection at over $100,000 apiece.

48

The phrase "indicative of" in the passage is closest in meaning to
A. an abstraction of
B. disproved by
C. proving
D. suggesting

A student's poor performance is not always indicative of his/her intelligence, but can result from a learning disability or contentious home life.

49

The word "intensive" in the passage is closest in meaning to
A. demanding
B. deep
C. strong
D. thorough

The union's intensive calls for improved compensation was met with the offer of a comprehensive benefits package and substantial pay raise.

CONTINUE ➡

50

The word "identical" is closest in meaning to in the passage
A. equally fast
B. near
C. the same
D. invisible

No two comets ever look identical, but they have basic features in common, one of the most obvious of which is a coma.

1

The phrase "coping with" in the passage is closest in meaning to
A. absorbing
B. finding
C. starting
D. managing

The governments of many Western countries are currently coping with a disastrous economic crisis.

2

The word "deterring" in the passage is closest in meaning to
A. stopping
B. continuing
C. absorbing
D. exterminating

A comprehensive and international policy against carbon emission aims at deterring factories from moving to another location in order to avoid legal consequences of illegal environmental practices.

3

The word "domains" in the passage is closest in meaning to
A. fields of experience
B. locations
C. passions
D. services

Maria Montessori was considered a brilliant physician, although her global influence extended into the domains of early childhood development and education.

4

The word "heightened" in the passage is closest in meaning to
A. increased
B. publicized
C. advocated
D. preferred

When the drug was made approved for children, it heightened the risk of children with psychiatric disorders to develop complications from liver and kidney toxicity.

CONTINUE

The word "inventive" in the passage is closest in meaning to
A. professional
B. creative
C. academic
D. accurate

Historians highlight that the cleanliness immediately noticed by visitors to Roman cities would not have been possible without their inventive methods of irrigation and distribution.

The word "mortality" in the passage is closest in meaning to
A. limitation
B. death
C. fear
D. desire

Cramped housing and poor sanitation lead to epidemics and high mortality.

The word "observe" in the passage is closest in meaning to
A. experiment
B. spy
C. monitor
D. announce

The ethnographer lived in the village among its natives in order to observe and record their daily rituals and relationship behavior patterns.

The word "perishable" in the passage is closest in meaning to
A. likely to decay
B. often damaged
C. long-lasting
D. sensitive

Among different types of delicate food, fish is the most perishable one.

The word "prohibits" in the passage is closet in meaning to
A. prevents
B. speeds up
C. affects
D. persuades

The Hippocratic Oath prohibits doctors from harming patients.

CONTINUE

10

The word "project" in the passage is closest in meaning to
A. advert
B. include
C. estimate
D. conclude

Researchers' project that HIV will become a curable disease before the end of the 21st century.

11

The word "radical" in the passage is closest in meaning to
A. drastic
B. dramatic
C. meticulous
D. religious

Martin Luther King, Jr. argued that to obtain radical changes in society, people needed to truly believe in the idea of racial equality.

12

The word "roughly" in the passage is closest in meaning to
A. on average
B. more than
C. exactly
D. approximately

The atmosphere on Venus is very thick, roughly 90 times more massive than Earth's atmosphere.

13

The word "valid" in the passage is closest in meaning to
A. reasonable
B. sensible
C. respectable
D. economical

Without a valid plan, the different departments will not be able to coordinate their effort against the imminent health threat.

14

The phrase "burdensome work rhythm" in the passage is closest in meaning to
A. fixed work schedule
B. random working times
C. light work responsibilities
D. frequent work rhythm

The less burdensome work rhythm led many farmers to fill out their calendars with intermittent work as clockmakers, shoemakers, carpenters, and weavers.

CONTINUE

15

The phrase "deflect sounds" in the passage is closest in meaning to
A. decrease the noise
B. turn up the volume
C. change the direction of the sounds
D. interpret the melody

Symphony musicians use specially-designed acoustical materials for performance halls that can deflect sounds through the reception and transmission of their music.

16

The phrase "no wonder" in the passage is closest in meaning to
A. unsurprisingly
B. incomprehensibly
C. as is well-known
D. unfortunately

No wonder the project did not obtained the desired results—the team was understaffed and their funds were low.

17

The phrase "on balance" in the passage is closest in meaning to
A. nonetheless
B. overall
C. thus
D. periodically

On balance, the negotiations at the climate conference went smoothly—every party recognized the need to take immediate actions.

18

The word "abundant" in the passage is closest in meaning to
A. plentiful
B. copious
C. scant
D. important

There is abundant evidence to declare that the specimen found by the French archeologists did, indeed, belong to the Cetacean Period.

19

The word "adverse" in the passage is closest in meaning to
A. absurd
B. tasteful
C. harmful
D. bias

Over-the-counter medications do not have significant adverse side effects; nevertheless, patients should avoid to over-medicate.

CONTINUE

20

The word "assorted" in the passage is closest in meaning to

A. common
B. various
C. several
D. similar

China is now the world's largest electronics manufacturer, with almost two-thirds of the national exports deriving from smart phone parts, semiconductor chips, and other assorted components.

21

The word "catastrophic" in the passage is closest in meaning to

A. amusing
B. strange
C. disastrous
D. extraordinary

Political analysts sustain that Americans are less likely to perceive climate change as potentially catastrophic if it improves weather in the short-term.

22

The word "collectively" in the passage is closest in meaning to

A. exclusively
B. mutually
C. jointly
D. lively

All the women on this list have collectively received almost every honor available within the scientific community.

23

The word "compound" in the passage is closest in meaning to

A. add to
B. provoke
C. cause
D. ask for

Difficulties in expression can compound and prompt foreign students to drop out of college.

24

The word "contour" in the passage is closest in meaning to

A. outline
B. condition
C. pattern
D. appearance

Only using an extremely sophisticated and powerful microscope can one observe the shape and contour of the smallest molecule.

257

CONTINUE

25

The word "define" in the passage is closest in meaning to
A. analyze
B. respect
C. regard
D. identify

Is it possible to accurately define the scientific processes which lead to the development of modern medicine?

26

The word "detrimental" in the passage is closest in meaning to
A. harmful
B. significant
C. unexpected
D. blurry

Environmental researchers argue that widespread and dismissive attitudes towards climate change have detrimental effects on humans, non-humans, and wildlife.

27

The word "disguise" in the passage is closest in meaning to
A. relinquish
B. hide
C. promote
D. discard

Cephalopods, marine animals with bilateral body symmetry, use unique characteristics to disguise themselves from predators and signal others of their presence.

28

The word "enveloping" in the passage is closest in meaning to
A. darkening
B. surrounding
C. adjoining
D. associating

Air pollution has been enveloping a crescent number of cities, especially in developing countries.

29

The word "evident" in the passage is closest in meaning to
A. impulsive
B. uncritical
C. obvious
D. binding

The same pattern of symptoms was evident in the previous group of patients tested.

CONTINUE

The word "exhausting" in the passage is closest in meaning to
A. using up
B. abandoning
C. avoiding
D. hiding

By exhausting Guatemala of its natural resources, the United States effectively deprived it of international bargaining power.

The word "exhausting" in the passage is closest in meaning to
A. thoroughly researched
B. heart breaking
C. extremely tiring
D. fully developed

Exhausting physical exercise has proven effective since it helps the body expel toxins and other, potentially dangerous, chemical agents.

The word "flexible" in the passage is closest in meaning to
A. connected
B. even
C. bendable
D. delicate

American gymnast Simone Biles is known for her flexible body, which allows her to achieve amazing heights in tumbling passes on the performance floor.

The word "indiscriminate" in the passage is closest in meaning to
A. various
B. random
C. unclear
D. apathetic

Although his actions seemed indiscriminate, Governor Chris Christie was actually intentional in his continued support of Republican nominee Donald Trump, suggesting Christie was positioning himself for Vice Presidency.

The word "intricate" in the passage is closest in meaning to
A. complex
B. mixed
C. complementary
D. unethical

Critics assailed the intricate energy policy as unrealistic to implement due to its rigorous standards for immediate and broad-sweeping changes to factory emissions.

CONTINUE

35

The word "mechanism" in the passage is closest in meaning to
A. means
B. consequence
C. need
D. benefit

The paper identifies a specific mechanism that the scientists believe could help cause such an abrupt climate shift.

36

The word "meticulously" in the passage is closest in meaning to
A. carefully
B. quickly
C. intentionally
D. indiscriminately

After years of research and travel around the country, Mr. Smith compiled a map of the British countryside so meticulously that, to the present day, can still be used.

37

The word "modified" in the passage is closet in meaning to
A. obtained
B. changed
C. returned
D. absorbed

Wind currents in cities can be modified by the presence of buildings or other structures because their presence increases air friction.

38

The word "moral" in the passage is closest in meaning to
A. lesson
B. status
C. agenda
D. capacity

The moral of the story is that one cannot trust the legal system completely, because it is not perfect and leaves a lot of room for human errors.

39

The word "oversee" in the passage is closest in meaning to
A. acknowledge
B. include
C. deliver
D. supervise

Environmental activists have created a group whose main purpose is to oversee the pesticide application in the state of Hawaii.

CONTINUE

40

The word "portable" in the passage is closet in meaning to
A. valuable
B. practical
C. moveable
D. saleable

A portable generator would provide enough energy to sustain your equipment for several hours, and prove beneficial should you need to relocate.

41

The word "propagating" in the passage is closest in meaning to
A. pursuing
B. imposing
C. multiplying
D. encouraging

The scientists' team was trying to find ways to cure the disease or prevent the virus from propagating.

42

The word "reliance" in the passage is closest in meaning to
A. obsession
B. accountability
C. dependence
D. attachment

Increased reliance on natural gas has been cited as one cause of improvement in clean energy initiatives.

43

The word "resistance" in the passage is closest in meaning to
A. hesitation
B. inclination
C. opposition
D. doubt

Resistance movements during World War II occurred in every country involved with the War by a variety of means: non-cooperation, disinformation, propaganda, hiding fugitives and even carrying out small armed missions.

44

The word "secure" in the passage is closest in meaning to
A. get
B. close in
C. stop up
D. catch up

Romans, besides being extremely good warriors, used any means necessary to secure their victory.

CONTINUE

45

The word "supplant" in the passage is closest in meaning to
A. restore
B. depart
C. occur
D. replace

Recently the spokesperson stated that artificial intelligence will serve researchers, not supplant them.

46

The word "surpasses" in the passage is closest in meaning to
A. exceeds
B. influences
C. balances
D. differs from

The food consumption of a city greatly surpasses that of the countryside.

47

The word "vast" in the passage is closest in meaning to
A. enormous
B. significant
C. convincing
D. secondary

The vast area would had been difficult to control, if it was not for the help of local officials who swore loyalty to the crown and pledged to act with the interest of the empire at heart.

48

The word "viability" in the passage is closest in meaning to
A. ability to exist
B. capability to coexist
C. vulnerability
D. obligation

Power dynamics within the reign threatened the viability of trade and resulted in decreased export profitability.

49

The word "discern" in the passage is closest in meaning to
A. identify
B. anticipate
C. perceive
D. discriminate

In the thick mist, the police officer was able to make out the outline of individual cars, but could not discern their make or model.

CONTINUE

50

The word "strutted" in the passage is closest in meaning to

A. pranced
B. supported
C. swaggered
D. was confident

Appearing to float in mid-air, the magician's hat was, in actuality, strutted by thin fishing wire.

END

1

The word "conceded" in the passage is closest in meaning to
A. gifted
B. accepted
C. resigned
D. needed

The President conceded that the reform plan was mostly in response to outside pressure on the matter of immigration trends.

2

The word "dormant" in the passage is closest in meaning to
A. inactive
B. secret
C. weak
D. remote

Committed to seed diversification in the event of global crises, the Svalbard Global Seed Vault warehouses more than 840,000 samples of dormant seeds suitable for planting and harvest.

3

The word "maximum" in the passage is closest in meaning to
A. famous
B. the greatest size
C. too big
D. the best moment

The non-profit organization is not currently functioning at maximum capacity, and so its Board of Directors has decided to increase community-based programming to better align the organization with its mission.

4

The word "negligible" in the passage is closest in meaning to
A. younger
B. impractical
C. irresponsible
D. minor

Although it looked like a negligible mistake, the error caused the whole experiment to fall apart.

CONTINUE

5

The word "asset" in the passage is closest in meaning to
A. praise
B. advantage
C. credibility
D. belief

Dedicated, skilled workforce would be an asset to a major city.

6

The word "astonishing" in the passage is closest in meaning to
A. ideal
B. predictable
C. false
D. incredible

What is astonishing is not that Italian manufacturing was affected by critical phenomena such as a decrease in sales and production, but that the crisis appeared only relatively late during the 2008 economic crisis.

7

The word "bombard" in the passage is closest in meaning to
A. scream
B. rob
C. assail
D. confuse

Even today, regardless of the much improved hygiene conditions, germs and other microbes continually bombard our immune system.

8

The word "commence" in the passage is closest in meaning to
A. control
B. engineer
C. negotiate
D. begin

Before production can commence, the plant must be prepared by cleaning out any residue that the previous production cycle might have left.

9

The word "converge" in the passage is closest in meaning to
A. help out
B. participate in
C. tie up
D. move closer

When two plates with oceanic crust converge, they typically create an island arc as one plate is subducted below the other.

CONTINUE

10

The word "critically" in the passage is closest in meaning to
A. fundamentally
B. partially
C. frequently
D. subsequently

Whether people can relate to others depends critically on their EQ, which is the capacity to recognize their and other people's emotions, distinguish among different feelings, and use emotional information to guide thinking and behavior.

11

The word "cushion" in the passage is closest in meaning to
A. control
B. protect
C. rest
D. hide

Weather-based insurances are now used by the majority of farmers because they offer a crucial cushion to protect them against financial bankruptcy in case of crop failure.

12

The word "doctrine" in the passage is closest in meaning to
A. lecture
B. academy
C. principle
D. ideology

Hillary Clinton's arguments that strengthening women's rights should be considered a healthy component of national security has been named the Hillary doctrine since she left her position as Secretary of State.

13

The word "drawback" in the passage is closest in meaning to
A. business
B. disadvantage
C. problem
D. solution

One obvious drawback to an Ivy League education is the exorbitant tuition and fees expected of all students.

14

The word "drive" in the passage is closest in meaning to
A. incentive
B. justification
C. occasion
D. case

The main drive to the climate change protests is the idea that shifting to renewable energy and capping any growth of fossil fuels will make a great difference.

CONTINUE

The word "firmly" in the passage is closest in meaning to
A. forcefully
B. securely
C. enthusiastically
D. eagerly

Serena Williams firmly established her reputation as one of the greatest athletes of all time when she won the U.S. Open a record seven times.

The word "freestanding" in the passage is closest in meaning to
A. separate
B. unwanted
C. deserted
D. capable

Freestanding kitchen appliances are relatively easy to install, and rarely require expert assistance from plumbers or electricians.

The phrase "have priority" in the passage is closest in meaning to
A. take advantage of
B. have advantages
C. ask for special treatment
D. be influential

Although the technology is very promising, nuclear plants are still dangerous facilities and, many investigators recognize that safety should have priority over other concerns—production quota, speed and so on.

The word "hint" in the passage is closest in meaning to
A. question
B. clue
C. doubt
D. theme

After winning the Nobel Prize for Literature, Bob Dylan went weeks without any hint of whether he would publically acknowledge the award, or his controversial win.

The word "homogeneous" in the passage is closest in meaning to
A. traditional
B. uniform
C. peculiar
D. divergent

The biggest complaint of Ivy League education is its formation of homogeneous scholars who are unable to think beyond the limited knowledge they attained from narrow-minded experts in philosophy and theology.

CONTINUE

20

The word "impetus" in the passage is closest in meaning to
A. crisis
B. stimulus
C. ultimatum
D. order

The impetus behind Latino emigration to the United States and Canada is largely the two countries' stable economies and plentiful jobs for people who are not native English-speakers.

21

The word "inhospitable" in the passage is closest in meaning to
A. realistic
B. artic
C. raw
D. not suitable

Scientists agree that the Southern Pole climate is an area inhospitable for humans.

22

The word "intercourses" in the passage is closest in meaning to
A. dialogues
B. exchanges
C. contests
D. assemblies

Our everyday social intercourses do not include touching the other person; in fact, our encounters often preserve a distance guaranteed by the formal recognition of the other individual as a human being.

23

The word "just" in the passage is closest in meaning to
A. real
B. complete
C. fair
D. variable

A just agreement on all the unresolved issues can be achieved with direct negotiations, and must involve the end of attacks, the restoration of peace and the return of citizens to their homes.

24

The word "mature" in the passage is closest in meaning to
A. develop
B. concentrate
C. help
D. use

During puberty, girls' bodies mature sooner than boys, often creating awkward social situations for preteens in middle grades.

CONTINUE

25

The word "merged" in the passage is closest in meaning to
A. occupied
B. combined
C. reduced
D. took

Astronomers think that El Gordo is so big because it formed when two galaxies collided and merged.

26

The word "miniature" in the passage is closest in meaning to
A. discrete
B. irrelevant
C. small
D. fake

These so called "eyes" are actually miniature cameras connected to an on-board computer that is programmed to steer the drone away from surrounding objects.

27

The word "objective" in the passage is closest in meaning to
A. unbiased
B. remote
C. formal
D. official

Although they want their research findings to be successful, experts in the field realize a systematic analysis requires the ability to interpret the outcomes in an objective way.

28

The phrase "obsession with" in the passage is closest in meaning to
A. interest in
B. fixation on
C. manipulation of
D. influence on

The current obsession with being thin is harming girls' health.

29

The word "ostentatious" in the passage is closest in meaning to
A. offensive
B. showy
C. constructed
D. bland

Ostentatious display of wealth was very common among political and religious leaders, however, in recent years this custom has changed due to the increasing numbers of poverty among most citizens.

CONTINUE

30

The word "outbreak" in the passage is closest in meaning to
A. sudden increase
B. acceleration
C. large motion
D. great gesture

Local residents were advised to avoid raw meat, so as to contain the outbreak of salmonella.

31

The word "pinpoint" in the passage is closest in meaning to
A. identify precisely
B. have a deep understanding of
C. clearly state
D. acknowledge

New technology allows astronomers to pinpoint any location in space using a system of satellites.

32

The word "prominent" in the passage is closest in meaning to
A. eminent
B. tangible
C. open
D. inevitable

Adam Smith was a prominent figure in both the fields of economic and international relations.

33

The word "relics" in the passage is closest in meaning to
A. difference
B. valuables
C. residues
D. remains

Certain rocks, usually of odd shapes, are the relics of much bigger mountains that have been eroded by atmospheric agents.

34

The word "resilient" in the passage is closest in meaning to
A. fast
B. easy to recover
C. practical
D. easy to find

Invasive plants help the ecosystem by making it more diverse and resilient to disaster.

CONTINUE

35

The word "ritual" in the passage is closest in meaning to
A. uninfluential
B. superficial
C. ceremonial
D. practical

The ritual sacrifice was performed by priests in the presence of the King and the whole court.

36

The word "ruptured" in the passage is closest in meaning to
A. escaped
B. broke
C. avoided
D. restricted

Engineers have been walking across the city's perimeter to discover exactly where the pipeline ruptured, spilling water into the downtown streets.

37

The word "scores" in the passage is closest in meaning to
A. prerequisites
B. large numbers
C. data
D. vital information

Invertebrate species that used to populate the sea were eliminated in scores by the increase in water salinity caused by global warming.

38

The word "sequentially" in the passage is closest in meaning to
A. without order
B. one after another
C. in great numbers
D. continuously

Progression through the different stages of recovery occurs sequentially and cumulatively.

39

The word "simulated" in the passage is closest in meaning to
A. artificial
B. ready-made
C. common
D. counterfeited

In manned spaceflight, simulated gravity may be a solution to the adverse effects caused by prolonged weightlessness.

CONTINUE

40

The word "spheres" in the passage is closest in meaning to
A. areas
B. groups
C. orders
D. colonies

The Greek wits were projected in other spheres—philosophy, poetry, astronomy, and literature.

41

The word "stable" in the passage is closest in meaning to
A. constant
B. hands-on
C. active
D. trustworthy

The southern provinces of the empire guaranteed a stable supply of provisions, which were essential to the capital.

42

The word "strategies" in the passage is closest in meaning to
A. options
B. plans
C. causes
D. actions

The meeting urged more research on strategies to counteract climate change.

43

The word "trapped" in the passage is closest in meaning to
A. hided
B. ruined
C. caught
D. found

There were great fears for the safety of thousands of civilians who remained trapped inside the city.

44

The word "turbulent" in the passage is closest in meaning to
A. violent
B. dark
C. confusing
D. mixed

Turbulent waters caused many ships to sink, which, in turn, caused a great loss to the city's artisans who had their goods in those ships.

CONTINUE

The word "unexpectedly" in the passage is closest in meaning to
A. unmatched
B. undecidedly
C. surprisingly
D. absolutely

Ice levels could decline slightly if weather patterns shift unexpectedly, according to the report.

The word "vital" in the passage is closest in meaning to
A. crucial
B. busy
C. bright
D. passionate

In order to better grasp ancient Roman society, it is vital to examine its poetry, literature and art because they shed light on how the Roman elite perceive the world and how society was organized.

The word "accompanies" in the passage is closest in meaning to
A. leads
B. occurs along with
C. dates
D. guides

Nothing accompanies a baseball game better than sunny weather, a hot dog, and a home team victory.

The word "precipitates" in the passage is closest in meaning to
A. brings about
B. deposits
C. combines
D. withdraws

An increase in population density often precipitates a round of emigration.

The word "timid" in the passage is closest in meaning to
A. modified
B. fearful
C. welcomed
D. demanded

Reformers felt timid because the privately owned utility companies would charge exorbitant rates for these essential services and deliver them only to people who could afford them.

CONTINUE

The word "adopted" is closest in meaning to in the passage
A. started to use
B. rose through
C. collected
D. adapted

When one animal attacks another, it engages in the most obvious example of aggressive behavior. Psychologists have adopted several approaches to understanding aggressive behavior in people.

END

1

The phrase "mutually exclusive" in the passage is closest in meaning to
A. if one of the theories is unproven, all the others must be unproven
B. if one of the theories is convincing, the other one has no use
C. if one of the theories is true, then all the others must be false
D. if one of the theories is false, all the others must be true

Many medical researchers use mutually exclusive methods to test their findings, hoping to identify one proven treatment for the disease they are studying.

2

The word "enlist" in the passage is closest in meaning to
A. assist
B. require
C. sketch
D. recruit

The ruling against the medical research institute requires that the company must enlist independent experts to examine the accuracy of their findings.

3

The word "giant" in the passage is closet in meaning to
A. huge
B. expected
C. complex
D. immediate

The giant tectonic plates that form Earth's outer layer are constantly moving.

CONTINUE ➡

The phrase "in the same breath" in the passage is closest in meaning to
A. immediately
B. at first
C. basically
D. primarily

The leadership reassured the international community with regards of its capabilities to handle the crisis, but in the same breath, asked for financial assistance.

The word "luminous" in the passage is closest in meaning to
A. dense
B. bright
C. deep
D. active

The most luminous supernova was discovered in an unconventional galaxy, quite distant from our Milky Way.

The word "regrettably" in the passage is closest in meaning to
A. unfortunately
B. surprisingly
C. possibly
D. extremely

Regrettably, the experiment did not obtain the desired results, and instead disproved the scientists' theory.

The word "signature" in the passage is closest in meaning to
A. main consequence
B. end result
C. identifying mark
D. by-product

Every government has its own signature solution to the problem of how to prevent global warming.

The phrase "impervious to" in the passage is closest in meaning to
A. hardened by
B. transformed by
C. predicted by
D. unaffected by

Some researcher erroneously posited that, due to their enormous size, oceans are impervious to changes in habitat and temperature.

CONTINUE

9

The phrase "tolerant of" in the passage is closest in meaning to
A. untouched by
B. strongly affected by
C. protected from
D. able to withstand

In the beginning, Roman emperors were not tolerant of Christian priests and had them put to death.

10

The word "boosted" in the passage is closest in meaning to
A. affected
B. established
C. raised
D. maintained

The scientists then boosted the animals' immune response by injecting them with small pieces of synthetic venom antibodies synthesized in Escherichia coli bacteria.

11

The word "abolished" in the passage is closest in meaning to
A. eliminated
B. taken
C. recycled
D. moved

In 1865, with the 13th Amendment of the Constitution, slavery was officially abolished in the United States.

12

The word "abound" in the passage is closest in meaning to
A. are interesting
B. are valuable
C. are numerous
D. are reassuring

In areas where scorpions abound, the spider population is generally kept under control.

13

The word "alliances" in the passage is closest in meaning to
A. negotiations
B. communications
C. partnerships
D. conflicts

The process of evolution favored the development of cognitive strategies that allowed many species to form and sustain cooperative alliances—individuals or groups that associate with one another for mutual benefits.

277

CONTINUE

14

The word "ancestors" in the passage is closest in meaning to
A. relatives from an earlier generation
B. people who particularly influenced the society
C. role models from ancient times
D. people who once made an important discovery

As our ancestors began to live in larger and more complex social structures, the quality of relationships became crucial to survival.

15

The word "appraisals" in the passage is closest in meaning to
A. encouragements
B. improvements
C. evaluations
D. applications

Scientists' appraisals of introverted and extroverted behavioral patterns were more or less consistent.

16

The word "attain" in the passage is closet in meaning to
A. achieve
B. show
C. overcome
D. reflect

Although drone technology has improved greatly in the past decade, most of these machines can still only attain limited altitudes and fly short distances.

17

The word "consistently" in the passage is closest in meaning to
A. typically
B. predictably
C. increasingly
D. trustworthily

For the tax policy to have significant impact on the nation's economy, it has to be implemented consistently throughout all the states.

CONTINUE

18

The word "crisis" in the passage is closest in meaning to
A. fear
B. disturbance
C. critical situation
D. deprivation

After the devastating earthquake the government had little choice but to recognize that the nation was in crisis.

19

The word "decline" in the passage is closest in meaning to
A. forgetting
B. rapidly expanding
C. abstaining
D. weakening

New data allege that dinosaurs were in decline even before the asteroid struck Earth and destroyed their habitat.

20

The word "diversification" in the passage is closest in meaning to
A. emergence of many varieties
B. extinction of specific species
C. reoccurrence of certain events
D. gathering of diverse species

The diversification of corn is a result of food science's latest trend toward genetically modified foods, regardless of consumer concern or popular science opinions.

21

The word "diversify" in the passage is closest in meaning to
A. sink
B. vary
C. diminish
D. boost

In Nigeria, the National Youth Service Organization and the Energy Commission have announced a partnership to diversify energy resources in the country, aiming for improved socio-political development and economic growth.

22

The word "dwell" in the passage is closest in meaning to
A. lead
B. originate
C. evolve
D. live

Despite harsh climate and living conditions, Aboriginal peoples continue to dwell in the Australian bush lands, hunting and gathering their foods.

CONTINUE

23

The word "efficacy" in the passage is closest in meaning to
A. effectiveness
B. advantage
C. motivation
D. commodity

The medical institute is recruiting possible candidates to test the efficacy of a new flu vaccine, and they predict that more than 20,000 people would want to participate in their research study.

24

The word "eliminate" in the passage is closest in meaning to
A. get rid of
B. avoid
C. minimize
D. absorb

Some environmental scientists argue that it is time for the Western world to eliminate all non-essential use of fossil fuel, and intentionally redirect attention toward renewable energies.

25

The word "embellish" in the passage is closest in meaning to
A. make more attractive
B. provide support for
C. duplicate
D. prepare

Although grounded theory researchers tend to embellish their findings, this qualitative research method is still useful for exploring particular human phenomena such as homelessness and hunger.

26

The word "encounter" in the passage is closest in meaning to
A. meet
B. form
C. elude
D. avoid

Arts and culture nonprofit organizations encounter numerous funding challenges as a result of the 2008 recession.

27

The word "exceptionally" in the passage is closest in meaning to
A. obviously
B. unusually
C. comparatively
D. occasionally

An exceptionally bright galaxy was recently discovered, and scientists have already confirmed that it shines brighter than our sun.

CONTINUE

28

The word "foremost" in the passage is closest in meaning to
A. latest
B. largest
C. most important
D. best understood

Foremost among space environments explored is Jupiter's moon Europa, which scientists suspect holds an internal ocean that could harbor life.

29

The word "fouled" in the passage is closest in meaning to
A. wrecked
B. polluted
C. harmed
D. influenced

The oil spill fouled miles of coastline.

30

The word "jointly" in the passage is closest in meaning to
A. together
B. therefore
C. rightfully
D. then

The newly created children's rights organization is jointly funded by a private charitable foundation and the United States' government.

31

The word "lavishly" in the passage is closest in meaning to
A. exclusively
B. additionally
C. inappropriately
D. richly

The company took a risk and lavishly supported a team of young researchers who promised to deliver an efficient and innovative air purification system for an exorbitant fee.

32

The word "managed" in the passage is closest in meaning to
A. been able
B. been forced to
C. arrived
D. raised

An experimental laboratory claims to have managed to restore the memories of different mice affected by Alzheimer disease.

CONTINUE

33

The word "marked" in the passage is closest in meaning to
A. detached
B. considerable
C. close
D. circumstantial

We might expect that ancient Roman art would be rudimental given the lack of appropriate machines to help develop materials, but the production from that Era displays a marked degree of sophistication.

34

The word "nonetheless" in the passage is closet in meaning to
A. simply
B. in a way
C. in addition
D. however

Nonetheless, religious dogmas did not influence political decisions anymore and several elected politicians denied the importance of the religious values for the society.

35

The word "perpetuates" in the passage is closest in meaning to
A. continues
B. reproduces
C. notices
D. spreads

The salary gap between men and women, which now amounts to almost 20%, perpetuates the stereotype that women do not belong in the work environment.

36

The word "persist" in the passage is closest in meaning to
A. ameliorate
B. continue
C. weaken
D. evolve

Problems caused by extreme poverty, shortage of water and poor sanitation still persist in many regions of Africa.

37

The word "persistent" in the passage is closest in meaning to
A. capable
B. powerful
C. influential
D. enduring

Persistent stress can provoke a variety of health conditions that negatively impact overall health and wellbeing.

CONTINUE

38

The word "prime" in the passage is closest in meaning to
A. low-lying
B. easily accessible
C. left over
D. high-quality

Doctors are calling for more controls over the side effects of ketamine before it becomes a prime treatment for terminal cancer.

39

The word "rebound" in the passage is closest in meaning to
A. cycle
B. status
C. recovery
D. development

The world population rebound from the black plague was not realized until the late 17th century.

40

The word "renowned" in the passage is closest in meaning to
A. talented
B. famous
C. early
D. revolutionary

Etrurians are widely recognized as one of Europe's first cultures, and are renowned for their pottery, metal-work and sumptuous burial ritual.

41

The word "sacred" in the passage is closet in meaning to
A. holy
B. traditional
C. natural
D. secret

Rome, the so called "Eternal City", is also considered sacred, largely because of the historical religious influence on art and architecture.

42

The word "scenarios" in the passage is closest in meaning to
A. effects
B. problems
C. oppositions
D. situations

The researcher clearly understood the scenarios for funding, and opted to raise money for the cancer treatment study through grant writing.

CONTINUE

The word "slope" in the passage is closest in meaning to
A. distortion
B. incline
C. path
D. bias

To guarantee proper drainage the slope should be sufficient enough for sewage to flow from its original source to the deposit site.

The word "strictly" in the passage is closest in meaning to
A. exclusively
B. mainly
C. initially
D. falsely

Because he was selective of who he trusted in his company, he strictly spoke with the executive council, and relied on his assistant to deal with all other company employees.

The word "stunning" in the passage is closest in meaning to
A. popular
B. universal
C. impressive
D. ongoing

Stonehenge was one of the most stunning archeological discoveries and its creation and function are, to this day, still a mystery.

The word "trappings" in the passage is closest in meaning to
A. sections
B. elements
C. ingredients
D. decorations

The constitution rests in a sober room, with cement walls and no unnecessary trappings.

The word "underwent" in the passage is closest in meaning to
A. experienced
B. allowed
C. prevented
D. reacted

Although the political leadership underwent a series of changes, the strength and stability of the Empire remained untouched.

CONTINUE

48

The word "undisputed" in the
passage is closest in meaning to
A. paramount
B. acknowledged
C. grateful
D. appreciated

Darwin's theory is now undisputed,
yet, just a few years ago, many
in the scientific world still did not
believe in evolution.

49

The word "vastly" in the passage
is closest in meaning to
A. obviously
B. incredibly
C. greatly
D. likely

Politics and science operate in
vastly different fields, yet they
often influence one another.

50

The word "halted" in the sentence
is closest in meaning to
A. stopped
B. froze
C. had letup
D. laid off

The university immediately halted
the experiment when it learned
that human subjects were
involved, but the proper advisory
committee had not been consulted
in advance.

END

1

The word "despite" in the passage is closest in meaning to
A. because of
B. nonetheless
C. even though
D. in the wake of

Despite receiving an adequate input of seeds, a construction site from which the soil has been tempered with or removed to expose coarse land, may remain free of vegetation.

2

The word "deterioration" in the passage is closest in meaning to
A. dissipation
B. stabilization
C. improvement
D. getting worse

Ehlers-Danlols syndrome is a heritable connective tissue disorder causing progressive deterioration of collagens, which affect joints, heart valves, organ walls, and arterial walls.

3

The word "devoured" in the passage is closest in meaning to
A. assimilated
B. damaged
C. purported
D. ate

Clean eating has devoured the traditional diet, however psychologists warn that its negative effects include eating disorders, malnourishment, and pathological obsessions.

4

The word "efforts" in the passage is closest in meaning to
A. results
B. powers
C. attempts
D. stresses

Efforts to control mint invasion, which spread through underground runners, have included the application of chemical herbicides, covering plants with dark plastic sheets, and scheduled burning to promote new growth.

CONTINUE

5

The word "exceedingly" in the passage is closest in meaning to
A. surprisingly
B. relatively
C. faithfully
D. extremely

In the southern United States, high school football culture is exceedingly competitive, and many local schools end classes early so that all students can travel to away games held in rival teams' cities.

6

The word "harnessed" in the passage is closest in meaning to
A. obtained
B. absorbed
C. recruited
D. utilized

Wind was one of the first alternative energies to be harnessed as a substitute for animal and human labor.

7

The word "insight" in the passage is closest in meaning to
A. perceptiveness
B. clarity
C. research
D. intelligence

Swiss psychologist Jean Piaget was known for his unique insight into children's behavior, which led to his pioneering theories on child development.

8

The word "pessimistic" in the passage is closest in meaning to
A. negative
B. final
C. tragic
D. hazardous

If an energy researcher had to write a report on the lasting effects of nonrenewable energy consumption, he would sketch a very pessimistic picture.

9

The word "provoked" in the passage is closest in meaning to
A. brought about
B. expanded
C. developed
D. inaugurated

Outside threats, mainly from wild animals or other savages, provoked the first steps towards the creation of cooperative communities on large scale.

CONTINUE

10

The word "regulated" in the passage is closest in meaning to
A. established
B. controlled
C. ran
D. suppressed

In the 1960s, many were the government that recognized that population growth was an issue, and it needed to be regulated.

11

The word "viable" in the passage is closest in meaning to
A. strong-minded
B. able to survive
C. unable to adapt
D. practical

The bank of Svalbard stores thousands of viable seeds of exotic, as well as common, species; to be used in case of emergencies.

12

The phrase "gave rise to" in the passage is closest in meaning to
A. outlived
B. associated with
C. produced
D. competed with

Late rains gave rise to concerns about harvest prospects and food security in Somalia and other African countries.

13

The word "albeit" in the passage is closest in meaning to
A. though
B. hence
C. nevertheless
D. in spite of

Imprisonment, albeit in various forms and lengths, continues to be used as the primary penalty and most trusted remedy for many crimes.

14

The word "arduous" in the passage is closest in meaning to
A. difficult
B. necessary
C. different
D. shared

In the past, civilizations sustained the arduous task of building entire cities from the ground up by piling up one brick after another.

CONTINUE

The word "authoritative" in the
passage is closest in meaning to
A. ceremonial
B. diffident
C. unprecedented
D. official

Various codes are compatible with
both newer and older devices,
so long as there is only one
authoritative layout.

The word "boom" in the passage
is closest in meaning to
A. crash
B. echo
C. conquest
D. expansion

The economic boom that involved
the West in the post-Second
World War, had few unique
characteristics; especially with
regards to finance and banking.

The word "bulk" in the passage is
closest in meaning to
A. strength
B. effort
C. usage
D. mass

The Amazon rainforest is split
among different nations in South
America, but the bulk of it lies in
Brazil.

The word "bustling" in the passage
is closest in meaning to
A. complicated
B. troublesome
C. busy
D. overpopulated

The new road networks shifted
the direction of trade during the
Roman Empire. In fact, most
goods were shipped north of the
Mediterranean Sea to the bustling
port of Venice.

The word "coating" in the passage
is closest in meaning to
A. quilt
B. skin
C. layer
D. tunic

These secondary salts would
rapidly encrust the heating
chambers of the evaporators
with a rock-hard coating, thereby
drastically reducing the plant's
performance.

CONTINUE

20

The word "colossal" in the passage is closest in meaning to
A. enormous
B. extinct
C. ancient
D. heavy

The meteorite that fell on the Earth and wiped out most of the dinosaurs may have been the first colossal case of bad timing.

21

The word "comparative" in the passage is closest in meaning to
A. absolute
B. familiar
C. relative
D. debatable

Children use games to explore the surrounding environment in comparative safety. This is because they are usually surrounded by adults who can intervene promptly.

22

The word "compulsory" in the passage is closest in meaning to
A. required
B. corrected
C. taken for granted
D. avoided

Compulsory military service was abolished in the aftermath of the Vietnam War.

23

The word "conjunction" in the passage is closest in meaning to
A. creation
B. concert
C. combination
D. synergy

Thus, both the favorable economic conditions and the relatively low control stimulate the process, which, in fact, seems to derive by the conjunction of the two factors.

24

The word "convince" in the passage is closest in meaning to
A. persuade
B. worry
C. inform
D. please

To convince sceptics of the successfulness of the recovery program, it was necessary to provide an effective practical example of how the initiative worked.

CONTINUE

25

The word "devised" in the passage is closest in meaning to

A. created
B. instituted
C. appointed
D. started

Architectural structures are largely devised in relation to available material and expected purpose, regardless of culture or geographical location.

26

The word "differ" in the passage is closest in meaning to

A. increase
B. need
C. vary
D. lower

Several economists in Latin American countries differ from those in North America on the socio-political benefits of capitalism.

27

The word "endeavor" in the passage is closest in meaning to

A. mechanism
B. work
C. composition
D. effort

For the artistic professions, work in a "recognized field of artistic endeavor" includes such industries as music, writing, the theater, and graphic arts.

28

The word "ensuing" in the passage is closest in meaning to

A. promoting
B. guaranteed
C. subsequent
D. major

The ensuing rapid expansion of commerce, especially after the 10th and 11th Century, transformed the economy of the Mediterranean peninsula.

29

The word "escalated" in the passage is closest in meaning to

A. intensified
B. supported
C. provided
D. verified

Following the Rodney King verdict in Los Angeles in 1992, riots escalated into a five-day war that resulted in over 50 deaths.

CONTINUE

30

The word "flawed" in the passage is closest in meaning to
A. plenty
B. specific
C. early
D. incorrect

Though some activists have called the process flawed, Turkey is still implementing their agreement with the European Union regarding immigration policy and practice.

31

The word "gifted" in the passage is closest in meaning to
A. accustomed
B. talented
C. self-sufficient
D. sophisticated

During the Second World War, a gifted individual named Albert Einstein was recruited to take part in the Manhattan Project.

32

The word "graphically" in the passage is closest in meaning to
A. vividly
B. decently
C. recently
D. freshly

Denise Brown's graphically accurate descriptions of her sister's relationship with O. J. Simpson were the basis for her advocacy work against victims of domestic violence.

33

The word "humble" in the passage is closest in meaning to
A. truthful
B. palpable
C. obvious
D. modest

It is not uncommon to find artifacts of exquisite qualities in humble Roman households in remote and isolated villages.

34

The word "innumerable" in the passage is closest in meaning to
A. countless
B. mixed
C. conflicting
D. diversified

According to Darwin's theory, evolution happened gradually over time; however, we cannot observe this process in its integrity because of the innumerable gaps in fossil findings.

CONTINUE

35

The word "pale" in the passage is closest in meaning to
A. lose significance
B. turn white
C. lose face
D. support

The destructions caused by the natural phenomena, like the Indian Ocean tsunami of 2004, pale in comparison to the human-made destructions.

36

The word "prolonged" in the passage is closest in meaning to
A. heavy
B. boring
C. widespread
D. lengthy

Areas in India have started flooding due to the prolonged monsoon season.

37

The word "relevant" in the passage is closest in meaning to
A. influential
B. applicable
C. dominant
D. functional

The really relevant experimental details were those which might provide clues in constructing molecular models.

38

The word "seek" in the passage is closest in meaning to
A. grab
B. change
C. attempt
D. seize

The research team will seek to discover viable solutions for eradicating extreme poverty in Sub-Saharan Africa.

39

The word "seeps" in the passage is closest in meaning to
A. takes off
B. flows slowly
C. keeps out
D. spills copiously

The water seeps underground and forms subterranean currents.

293

CONTINUE

40

The word "sensible" in the passage is closest in meaning to
A. famous
B. talented
C. reasonable
D. experienced

The first step to any sensible decision is to approach the matter objectively—separating the facts from the fiction.

41

The word "sequence" in the passage is closest in meaning to
A. order
B. system
C. part
D. link

The researchers plan to record the DNA sequence of hundreds of patients, so as to create a database for their study.

42

The word "severing" in the passage is closest in meaning to
A. saving
B. delaying
C. ceasing
D. cutting off

By refusing to reduce oil consumption governments are currently severing the opportunity of a sustainable economic development.

43

The word "spearheaded" in the passage is closest in meaning to
A. led
B. missioned
C. created
D. ran

Merchants, who spearheaded the guild movement became pioneers in their industries, although they did not have a close bond with either nobles or peasants.

44

The word "splendid" in the passage is closest in meaning to
A. bright
B. magnificent
C. essential
D. flawless

The splendid architecture greatly impressed the visitors of the 1889 World's Fair and later became the symbol of France.

CONTINUE

The word "sponsored" in the passage is closest in meaning to
A. estimated
B. praised
C. envied
D. supported

Sculptures, paintings and literature became very popular among the noblemen of the time, thus artists who could paint, sculpt and write enjoyed a quite high status and they were often sponsored by aristocratic families.

The word "termed" in the passage is closest in meaning to
A. expressed
B. portrayed
C. known as
D. marked out

The ability of a gem to propagate light within itself is termed refractive index.

The word "transform" in the passage is closest in meaning to
A. convince
B. change
C. charge
D. move on

The accumulation of rocks causes them to transform into metamorphic rocks sediments because of the continuous pressure over time.

The word "trivial" in the passage is closest in meaning to
A. similar
B. inaccurate
C. small
D. crucial

In ancient Rome, trivial matters, such as trespassing or public indecencies, were settled by the local council.

The word "whereas" in the passage is closest in meaning to
A. all the time
B. although
C. even so
D. for all

Whereas the European parliament sees the measures as the only way to save the precarious economy of Greece; the Greeks view them as a punishment.

CONTINUE

50

The word "seclusion" in the passage is closest in meaning to

A. concern
B. isolation
C. characteristics
D. interpretation

Farm dwellers in their seclusion not only found it harder to locate companions in play but also, thanks to the unending demands and pressures of their work, felt it necessary to combine fun with purpose.

END

1

The word "desolate" in the passage is closest in meaning to
A. deceiving
B. deserted
C. revealed
D. open

More than 400 million years ago, when plants as we know them first appeared, the land was infertile and desolate.

2

The word "enigmatic" in the passage is closest in meaning to
A. ancient
B. dangerous
C. mysterious
D. magical

Unlike dinosaurs, whose features were later preserved in birds, the enigmatic species of pterosaur met its evolutionary dead end.

3

The word "imaginative" in the passage is closest in meaning to
A. astute
B. creative
C. funny
D. academic

Andy Warhol is largely regarded as the most imaginative artist of the 20th Century because of his bold fusion of pop art with celebrity culture.

4

The word "infrequent" in the passage is closest in meaning to
A. rare
B. significant
C. sophisticated
D. uncommon

Early in the 19th Century, European art was influenced by Victorian style, resulting in infrequent citing of movements such as Futurism.

CONTINUE ➡

The word "legendary" in the passage is closest in meaning to
A. factual
B. historical
C. famous
D. timeless

The Battle of Waterloo, where Napoleon confronted the Duke of Wellington, is legendary.

The word "locations" in the passage is closest in meaning to
A. places
B. attitudes
C. guidances
D. statuses

There are roughly a few hundred vases from the Greek period at the British Museum that come from different locations all over Greece.

The word "momentous" in the passage is closest in meaning to
A. of average significance
B. very important
C. not fully understood
D. destructive

Although the changes in climate were subtle in the region—changes in snow and rain patterns; these cycles had momentous impacts on the civilizations living in the area.

The word "posed" in the passage is closest in meaning to
A. established
B. proved
C. entertained
D. presented

When animals evolved they faced an array of challenges posed by the terrestrial environment of that era.

The word "prospect" in the passage is closest in meaning to
A. problem
B. decision
C. possibility
D. change

The prospect of her losing the election terrified her supporters, considering her opponent was known for being a racist and bully.

CONTINUE

10

The word "transition" in the passage is closest in meaning to
A. opportunity
B. benefit
C. change
D. journey

The effects of this transition have not been fully analyzed yet, but it is clear that the people living close to these areas were impacted the most severely.

11

The word "authenticity" in the passage is closest in meaning to
A. improvement
B. pragmatism
C. genuineness
D. repetition

One of the things that still most impress the audience of realistic painters is their commitment to authenticity.

12

The word "accidental" in the passage is closest in meaning to
A. incremental
B. unintentional
C. practical
D. uncommon

The accidental killing of a Dutch diplomat on American soil sparked a major international incident.

13

The word "ample" in the passage is closest in meaning to
A. real
B. convincing
C. plentiful
D. unlimited

Insects are incredibly easy to find and contain ample nutrients, thus experts have suggested that they should be inserted in our diet.

14

The word "contention" in the passage is closest in meaning to
A. investigation
B. growth
C. debate
D. interpretation

Whether Kant's idea of justice is acceptable is open to contention, and some authors have recently pointed out flaws in his reasoning.

CONTINUE

The word "cramped" in the passage is closest in meaning to
A. isolated
B. secured
C. attached
D. confined

Volterra was founded in the 8th Century BC; a small village settlement of cramped, squared-based huts with straw or clay roofs.

The word "allusions" in the passage is closest in meaning to
A. conclusions
B. stories
C. illusions
D. references

In modern scientific literature there are frequent allusions to a current mass extinction event.

The word "assured" in the passage is closest in meaning to
A. caused
B. guaranteed
C. affected
D. conceived

Further reduction of the use of fossil fuel is not assured, especially since technological advantages in new sources of energy are still far from satisfying.

The word "circumstances" in the passage is closest in meaning to
A. finances
B. communities
C. conditions
D. regulations

The circumstances that had allowed natives to acquire some of the main features of the British culture, also led the self-sustaining British community in India to embrace some of the local customs.

The word "compulsorily" in the passage is closest in meaning to
A. by submission
B. according to ethics
C. by requirement
D. by limitation

Guilds were required to provide for military equipment, in case of an attack, while normal citizens were to serve compulsorily when needed.

CONTINUE

20

The word "conversely" in the passage is closest in meaning to
A. if not
B. for all I know
C. on the contrary
D. in that case

Conversely, water that ordinarily would be of good quality may be unsafe for irrigation.

21

The word "elaboration" in the passage is closest in meaning to
A. outcome
B. opening
C. development
D. image

According to Sigmund Freud, dreams are the result of an elaboration of our daily existence, wherein daily life is played out in our imaginations while we sleep.

22

The word "engraving" in the passage is closest in meaning to
A. printing
B. carving
C. reproducing
D. releasing

The University spokesperson announced that the research team has discovered signs of engraving in a Neanderthal cave; this is an extremely significant finding.

23

The word "enjoys" in the passage is closest in meaning to
A. owns
B. dominates
C. absorbs
D. experiences

Following his critically acclaimed success with Broadway's Hamilton, Lin-Manuel Miranda currently enjoys multiple offers from Hollywood producers looking to make a film version of the award-winning musical.

24

The word "erode" in the passage is closest in meaning to
A. put on
B. dress down
C. wear down
D. withstand

In the 19th Century, geologists started to observe that tectonic plates erode at different speeds depending on how they are positioned and violated.

CONTINUE

25

The word "frictions" in the passage is closest in meaning to
A. puzzles
B. paradoxes
C. conflicts
D. illogicalities

When not engaged in battle, generals would make sure that the troops maintained a high morale, so as to avoid frictions and riots.

26

The word "fringes" in the passage is closest in meaning to
A. composure
B. borders
C. handles
D. rules

Settlers to the New World resisted confinement in small spaces; thus, they decided to expand beyond the fringes of early American colonies and head West.

27

The word "gains" in the passage is closest in meaning to
A. breakthroughs
B. developments
C. increases
D. recurrences

The technology might not be ready yet, but it promises great gains, such as substantial greater power for stimulation of chemical reactions and, possibly, machine learning.

28

The word "heterogeneous" in the passage is closest in meaning to
A. consistent
B. singular
C. crowd
D. varied

The most inexperienced archeologists are preoccupied with the task of sorting out heterogeneous residues (rocks, dirt, soil deposited there after the findings).

29

The word "instructive" in the passage is closest in meaning to
A. accurate
B. authentic
C. informative
D. precious

Thomas Hobbes's 1651 work entitled *Leviathian* was an instructive exploration of political philosophy in the 17th Century that still holds merit to this day.

CONTINUE

30

The word "intense" in the passage is closest in meaning to
A. steady
B. equitable
C. extreme
D. famous

The intense heat caused by rapid climate change resulted in Boston's Great Molasses Flood in 1919, which killed 21 people when two million gallons of molasses melted into the streets of downtown.

31

The word "legible" in the passage is closest in meaning to
A. distinct
B. recognizable
C. singular
D. graphic

Medical doctors are often criticized because their writing is not legible, which can result in hospital nursing staff giving the wrong dosage of medication to their patients.

32

The word "option" in the passage is closest in meaning to
A. control
B. power
C. choice
D. right

Nomadic populations can move seasonally and avoid shortage of resources, while sedentary civilizations do not have this option.

33

The word "outdated" in the passage is closest in meaning to
A. inappropriate
B. corrupt
C. worsening
D. old-fashioned

Venice stuck to its outdated building methods, while the Dutch whose pioneers switched to lighter and more easily handled ships, which is why Venetian merchants started losing their competitive advantage.

34

The word "practical" in the passage is closest in meaning to
A. usable
B. sturdy
C. certain
D. ultimate

Solar energy becomes available in a practical form when solar panels process light from the sun through photovoltaic effect.

CONTINUE

35

The word "pristine" in the passage is closest in meaning to
A. sincere
B. transparent
C. honest
D. pure

Pristine water, is extremely hard to find, and is nowadays mostly near mountain springs and rivers that run with snow melt.

36

The word "reasonable" in the passage is closest in meaning to
A. more than abundant
B. sufficient
C. superfluous
D. barely enough

Before children can take fully part in our society, they have to accumulate a reasonable amount of experiences.

37

The word "reluctant" in the passage is closest in meaning to
A. unwilling
B. unnatural
C. scared
D. nervous

The research team was reluctant to admit that the experiment was not successful and they would need to redesign the study.

38

The word "resume" in the passage is closest in meaning to
A. reproduce
B. restart
C. commence
D. reuse

If the seizure is severe enough, a nurse will intervene, so that the patient can resume his sleep.

39

The word "resurgence" in the passage is closest in meaning to
A. reply
B. placement
C. comeback
D. emergence

In the decades following the Second World War, European countries that had been devastated by the war began an economic resurgence that made them into well developed nations.

CONTINUE

40

The word "revise" in the passage is closest in meaning to
A. change
B. ameliorate
C. quote
D. comment

Archeologists proposed to revise the date of the discovery of America based on new and fascinating discoveries.

41

The word "shift" in the passage is closest in meaning to
A. change
B. chance
C. charge
D. concern

The different samples from the excavations allowed archeologists to observe the shift in the eating habits of the Neanderthal men from predominately animal-based diets to plant-based ones.

42

The word "sovereign" in the passage is closest in meaning to
A. master
B. conqueror
C. expert
D. champion

The cities of Elis and Olympia had Zeus—god of the sky and sovereign of all other gods, as their patron god.

43

The word "superseded" in the passage is closest in meaning to
A. replaced
B. triumphed
C. followed
D. acquired

Although small airplanes still continue to be used for shorter flights, Boeings and Airbuses have superseded all of their competitors for long-distance flights.

44

The phrase "tentatively identified" in the passage is closest in meaning to
A. identified without certainty
B. positively recognized
C. well known
D. without positive confirmation

The cause of several major infections, occurring in the Medieval Age, has been tentatively identified with the arrival of new populations.

CONTINUE

45

The word "terrestrial" in the passage is closest in meaning to
A. lotted
B. land
C. partitioned
D. inherent

Terrestrial deposits are full of residues and fossils, which could shed some light on the earth's composition during the Cretaceous Era.

46

The word "therefore" in the passage is closest in meaning to
A. on the other end
B. in the end
C. as a result
D. reasonably

The politician decided he could not continue in the race for presidency, therefore he called a press conference and announced he was suspending his campaign.

47

The word "threatened" in the passage is closest in meaning to
A. scared
B. controlled
C. endangered
D. worried

It has been estimated that more than half the world population is threatened by this condition.

48

The phrase "accustomed to" in the passage is closest in meaning to
A. deprived of
B. envious of
C. insisted on
D. used to

After several generations, the bacteria had become accustomed to its environment and started reproducing much more rapidly than it had before.

49

The phrase "apart from" in the passage is closest in meaning to
A. except for
B. together with
C. compounded by
D. generally with

Apart from a short power outage, the storm caused little damage or inconvenience to the residents of Atlanta.

CONTINUE ➡

The word "accumulation" in the passage is closest in meaning to
A. growth
B. pile
C. deposit
D. quantity

When the professor came back from her fall break, there was an accumulation of papers stacked on her desk for grading.

词汇练习
List ⬀ *19*

1

The phrase "course through" in the passage is closest in meaning to
A. rise through
B. heat up in
C. run through
D. pass by

This is the same system used in an old-fashioned watermill, in which the water stream passes back and forth so as to let water course through the turbines.

2

The word "extended" in the passage is closest in meaning to
A. was eternal
B. elevated
C. prolonged
D. endured

An extended mild period was required to form rivers, lakes and oceans.

3

The word "fracture" in the passage is closest in meaning to
A. crack
B. attempt
C. crash
D. report

In many places across Oklahoma, the Arbuckle rests on fragile, basement rocks, which can fracture along major faults under stress.

4

The word "intrinsically" in the passage is closest in meaning to
A. traditionally
B. aesthetically
C. fundamentally
D. immensely

Because of its vastness across multiple continents, the Empire, although very wealthy and heavy populated, was intrinsically frail.

CONTINUE ➡

The word "legitimately" in the passage is closest in meaning to
A. properly
B. falsely
C. totally
D. gently

A bee hive can be legitimately recognized as a superorganism because its connection system is highly interconnected so that the hive works as a whole colony.

The word "paradoxical" in the passage is closest in meaning to
A. legendary
B. problematic
C. equal
D. contradictory

Her argument was paradoxical, demonstrating her lack of intelligence regarding the differences between quantum mechanics and relativity.

The word "paradoxically" in the passage is closest in meaning to
A. clearly
B. surprisingly
C. inevitably
D. firmly

Although urban areas have more access to water compared to rural areas—which rely on rainfall only, issue of water availability were paradoxically more severe in cities.

The word "repudiated" in the passage is closest in meaning to
A. rejected
B. despised
C. avoided
D. blamed

The servant was bound to its master by much more than just a contract that he could have repudiated at any time.

The word "signal" in the passage is closest in meaning to
A. escort
B. communicate
C. appear
D. confirm

Some species signal members to advert the others of possible dangers.

CONTINUE ➡

10

The word "suppress" in the passage is closest in meaning to
A. dissolve
B. stop by force
C. step away
D. divorce

Romans did not believe in using violence to retain control over their provinces; however, it is known they stationed troops in every major city to suppress major rebellions.

11

The phrase "analogous to" in the passage is closest in meaning to
A. predicted by
B. expected of
C. similar to
D. simultaneous to

The question related to the orbit of satellites is very closely analogous to a question that astronomers have discussed for thousands of years, concerning the movement of Earth around the sun.

12

The phrase "assists in" in the passage is closest in meaning to
A. initiates
B. provides to
C. helps with
D. sets up

Graphology, the study of physical characteristics and patterns of handwriting, assists in the identification of a specific writer; in particular, it helps with indicating a psychological state at the time of writing, or evaluating personality traits.

13

The word "afford" in the passage is closest in meaning to
A. provide
B. spend
C. devoid
D. absorb

Perhaps the biggest unmet promise of the newly issued tax-law is that it was supposed to afford many people with cheap insurance, yet, the majority has not received such benefits.

14

The word "credible" in the passage is closest in meaning to
A. helpful
B. believable
C. valuable
D. uncommon

Behavioral sociologists established that children believed that the characters used in animated movies represented real life characters, thus children accepted such characters as credible sources of values and advice.

CONTINUE ➡

The word "consensus" in the passage is closest in meaning to
A. authority
B. responsibility
C. tradition
D. agreement

Achieving consensus within the political sphere, and across parties, is at the core of one major issue which surfaced during the assembly.

The word "contexts" in the passage is closest in meaning to
A. mixtures
B. influences
C. environments
D. requirements

Importance of low reliefs is directly related to the functions of Greek temples and the contexts in which the buildings were set up.

The word "core" in the passage is closest in meaning to
A. material
B. shape
C. center
D. frame

The Earth's inner core is the Earth's innermost part and, according to seismological studies, it is believed to be primarily a solid ball, with a radius of about 1220 kilometers.

The word "deceiving" in the passage is closest in meaning to
A. opposing
B. discrediting
C. denying
D. misleading

Numbers may be deceiving, yet, statistics show that, in only 125 years, we have used almost half of the Earth oil reserves.

The word "depiction" in the passage is closest in meaning to
A. aim
B. wandering
C. fabrication
D. portrait

Brazilian actor Wagner Moura's recent depiction of Pablo Escobar was met with international acclaim for its highly emotive and artistically provocative exploration of drug trafficking in Columbia.

CONTINUE

The word "deviated" in the passage is closest in meaning to
A. removed
B. departed
C. refuted
D. challenged

When reward methods failed, ancient societies successfully kept control over members by threatening to reject or ostracize those who deviated from social norms.

The word "drastic" in the passage is closest in meaning to
A. obsessive
B. unmerited
C. extreme
D. bias

When the economic crisis happened in 2008, the federal government took drastic measures to avoid another financial depression by offering over $700 billion to bailout American banks.

The word "empirical" in the passage is closest in meaning to
A. based on observation
B. produced through dialogue
C. followed pure logic
D. theoretical

Until Dr. Etminan disseminated his findings in the *Journal of Clinical Psychopharmacology*, doctors had no empirical evidence of whether the drug Abilify caused extrapyramidal symptoms in patients.

The word "endowed" in the passage is closest in meaning to
A. guarded
B. promoted
C. provided
D. stated

AI devices may one day be endowed with traditional human attributes such as awareness and emotional intelligence, enabling them to perform the most complex human activities.

The word "ethic" in the passage is closest in meaning to
A. legal action
B. a set of moral principles
C. training exercise
D. tradition

Since their rise to power, merchants and business owners have had a strong meritocratic ethic, which promoted values such as hard work and dedication.

CONTINUE

25

The word "illuminate" in the passage is closest in meaning to
A. light
B. justify
C. reorganize
D. shield

Various species of phytoplankton are known to be bioluminescent, and their glowing bodies illuminate beaches all around the world.

26

The word "immobile" in the passage is closest in meaning to
A. motionless
B. lifeless
C. ice-cold
D. solid

Even when confined within an underground layer of permeable rocks, water cannot remain immobile, and maintains continuous fluidity.

27

The word "impediments" in the passage is closest in meaning to
A. wrongdoings
B. illusions
C. misbelief
D. obstructions

Because of numerous impediments to implementation, the new laws will not go into effect until after the President-elect assumes office early next year.

28

The phrase "imposes on" in the passage is closest in meaning to
A. places on
B. regards as
C. puts up with
D. relies on

John Nash is known for his belief that rational thought actually imposes limits on an individual's ability to engage his surroundings fully and optimally.

29

The word "inflate" in the passage is closest in meaning to
A. enlarge
B. pull
C. distort
D. hold out

It is part of a peacock mating ritual to inflate his plumage to impress the female counterpart.

CONTINUE

30

The word "interlocking" in the passage is closest in meaning to
A. frozen
B. sudden
C. linked
D. intermediate

The interlocking tunnel between Britain and France promotes shared transportation, and increases import and export between the two countries.

31

The word "interplay" in the passage is closest in meaning to
A. show
B. interaction
C. game
D. acceptance

This scientific achievement and its progresses underline the crucial interplay among surveys, forecast, and trails required for academic research.

32

The word "likewise" in the passage is closest in meaning to
A. separately
B. variously
C. partly
D. similarly

The final stage of its evolution is likewise not predictable nor can be deducted by further studies.

33

The word "meager" in the passage is closest in meaning to
A. watery
B. thin
C. varied
D. intermittent

Comparing to other planets in our universe, the Earth has a very meager atmosphere, which exacerbates climate change challenges such as ozone depletion.

34

The word "neglected" in the passage is closest in meaning to
A. failed to do
B. renounced
C. left
D. gave up

To be clear, their evaluation of the 1945 World War II causes is not completely off; however, they neglected to take into consideration the impact of the Great Depression on European countries.

CONTINUE

The word "norms" in the passage is closest in meaning to
A. policies
B. rules
C. truths
D. powers

Community norms usually have great impact on individual's behaviors, however, they do little for those individuals who are committed to causing harm.

The word "overshadowed" in the passage is closest in meaning to
A. distracted from
B. shamed
C. embraced
D. avoided

In the mountainous region, disastrous environmental effects caused by Mountaintop Removal are overshadowed by the profits accrued by the coalmining companies that execute these removal methods.

The word "postulated" in the passage is closest in meaning to
A. challenged
B. summoned
C. hypothesized
D. postponed

Hanna Arendt postulated that the anti-Semitism which characterized the Second World War was triggered by fear, resentment and anger.

The word "potent" in the passage is closest in meaning to
A. extreme
B. inspiring
C. creative
D. powerful

The first, and most potent limitation, to Artificial Intelligence will be its ability to harm humans.

The word "prediction" in the passage is closest in meaning to
A. expectation
B. inheritance
C. opinion
D. faith

A big concern, especially for areas at risk, is that the prediction underestimated the rate of sea level rise.

CONTINUE

40

The word "prestige" in the passage is closest in meaning to
A. role
B. wealth
C. front
D. status

In Egyptian culture and religion, the cat was an animal of enormous prestige, and thusly greatly revered for its prominence.

41

The word "progressive" in the passage is closest in meaning to
A. increasing
B. notable
C. occasional
D. rapid

After the decolonization, the various countries tried to maintain peace and carry out a progressive process to develop democratic societies.

42

The word "quantifiable" in the passage is closest in meaning to
A. truthful
B. measurable
C. worthy
D. undeniable

Empirical data are collected and used as quantifiable indicators of positive responses to new stimuli.

43

The word "regarded" in the passage is closest in meaning to
A. claimed
B. respected
C. praised
D. considered

Although, since the 1980s, the movie industry has developed at an impressive rate, none of the new movies have been regarded to be as noteworthy as the old ones.

44

The word "reveal" in the passage is closest in meaning to
A. amaze
B. surprise
C. confuse
D. show

Different types of sediments preserved in various layers reveal the different soil composition and biota (animals and plants) during the Pliocene epoch.

CONTINUE

45

The phrase "size up" in the passage is closest in meaning to
A. confront
B. evaluate
C. criticize
D. pick on

Face-to-face meetings held with the company's competitors allow the executive committee to size up the opposition's potential for growth and development.

46

The word "substantiated" in the passage is closest in meaning to
A. confirmed
B. confronted
C. challenged
D. coped

Although there have been claims that there is a certain regularity to the distribution of black holes in the universe, these declarations have not been substantiated.

47

The word "trend" in the passage is closest in meaning to
A. habit
B. tendency
C. idea
D. result

Although there is a general trend towards urbanization, the process is generally region-specific.

48

The word "verify" in the passage is closest in meaning to
A. show one's cards
B. explain an idea
C. experiment on a theory
D. establish the truth of

Comments based on a non-empirical quality of an object, such as its beauty or comparative advantages, are based on one's opinion; thus, they are difficult to verify.

49

The word "adept" in the passage is closest in meaning to
A. competent
B. skillful
C. proficient
D. capable

Raccoons aren't stupid nocturnal nuisances; they are quite adept at navigating their way through the landscape, rural and urban, to find new sources of food.

CONTINUE

50

The word "flow" in the passage is closest in meaning to

A. movement
B. exchange
C. recovery
D. decline

The diffusion of agriculture and iron was accompanied by a great flow of people who may have carried these innovations.

END

1

The word "concept" in the passage is closest in meaning to
A. power
B. reality
C. struggle
D. idea

The free market theory is based on the concept that the economy and competition will regulate themselves through a system of supply and demand.

2

The word "deliberations" in the passage is closest in meaning to
A. examples
B. discussions
C. notices
D. warnings

Ecologists contend that scientists must include in their deliberations the multiple variations of appreciable impacts that human behavior has on climate change.

3

The word "despondent" in the passage is closest in meaning to
A. faulty
B. proper
C. inappropriate
D. unhappy

How can someone tell when others are happy or despondent? Because joy and sadness are experienced by everyone in every culture worldwide, and experts argue that such emotions may be universal.

4

The word "instigated" in the passage is closest in meaning to
A. granted
B. caused
C. supplied
D. satisfied

The fine products were so appreciated that they prompted a whole porcelain style, called Bone China, which instigated competition between imported and national products.

CONTINUE

The word "invoked" in the passage is closest in meaning to
A. moved on
B. caused
C. believed
D. called upon

In her deposition to the senate committee, she invoked her right to remain silent on the issue of whether or not she was aware that her company was involved in illegal activities.

The word "plugged" in the passage is closest in meaning to
A. covered
B. filled up
C. increased
D. completed

The gaps between bricks have been filled years ago, yet not all of them were properly plugged and now the cracks are compromising the structural integrity of the building.

The phrase "so much for" in the passage is closest in meaning to
A. more than necessary
B. plenty of
C. that is the end of it
D. that is enough about

So much for transparency: the government has yet again promoted a policy which protects them from public scrutiny.

The phrase "amount to" in the passage is closest in meaning to
A. identify
B. differentiate
C. comprehend
D. total

Strategies to restore manufacturing jobs in one country will amount to destroying them in another, in a worldwide zero-sum game.

CONTINUE

The phrase "an English innovation" in the passage is closest in meaning to
A. a new development introduced by the English
B. a type of business found only in England
C. a type of agreement negotiated in English
D. a new practice based on English law

Radio communication is an English innovation that radically changed the course of the First World War and of the world at large.

The phrase "keep pace with" in the passage is closest in meaning to
A. exceed
B. match the increase in
C. increase the rate of
D. slowly assimilate a technique

Cities nowadays have great difficulties to keep pace with the fast growing urbanization— unprecedented growth of urban population.

The phrase "mutually beneficial" in the passage is closest in meaning to
A. helpful to one another
B. generally practical
C. efficiently balanced
D. originally recognized

While parasites can have a mutually beneficial relationship with their host, many parasite-host relationships only benefit one organism or the other.

The word "agency" in the passage is closest in meaning to
A. shape
B. problem
C. force
D. change

Martin Luther King Jr. was one of the biggest agency of change in modern history. His actions and speeches changed the course of United State's history.

CONTINUE

13

The word "aggregated" in the passage is closest in meaning to
A. finished
B. completed
C. counted
D. combined

Within 72 hours, the head scientist at the lab said that responses were aggregated, and sent them to doctors, who could then determine whether the patient was responsive or not to a particular treatment.

14

The word "agitated" in the passage is closest in meaning to
A. emerged from beneath
B. created movement in
C. arranged by
D. made it as if

The man who worked in harsh conditions began to agitate for better working conditions.

15

The word "appreciate" in the passage is closest in meaning to
A. suppose
B. understand
C. approve
D. anticipate

Doctors have stated it is possible that the Zika virus may cause subtler damage that researchers cannot yet appreciate.

16

The word "assistance" in the passage is closest in meaning to
A. criticism
B. power
C. help
D. approval

In 1885, Gustave Eiffel presented the project for the Eiffel Tower. The impressive tower was projected by two brilliant engineers, Maurice Koechlin and Émile Nouguier, with the assistance of the company's architect Stephen Sauvestre.

17

The word "championed" in the passage is closest in meaning to
A. changed
B. debated
C. developed
D. supported

The most widely influential theory, championed by many psychologists in the early to mid-1800s, envisioned that one could determine an individual's psychological attributes by merely observing and feeling the skull.

CONTINUE

The word "channel" in the passage is closest in meaning to
A. produce
B. remove
C. direct
D. supply

It is thought that because of a series of waterways, the government is trying to channel water through the valley, all the way down to the deserted area.

The word "compelled" in the passage is closest in meaning to
A. assisted
B. advised
C. selected
D. required

Scientific evidence compelled scientists to recognize that climate change caused few natural disasters.

The word "compression" in the passage is closest in meaning to
A. elimination
B. crush
C. show
D. reveal

Data compression is a process that minimizes the size of a file, so that it takes up less space on the hard drive and is also easier to transfer.

The word "concur" in the passage is closest in meaning to
A. suppose
B. agree
C. acknowledge
D. understand

Most criminologists concur with Lombroso's theory that facial features are representative of a person's true personality and inclinations.

The word "diverse" in the passage is closest in meaning to
A. organized
B. decisive
C. varied
D. efficient

Scientists who conduct research in the Amazon rainforest contend that its diverse flora and fauna contribute to its unique sub-tropical and temperate climates.

CONTINUE

23

The word "document" in the passage is closest in meaning to
A. book
B. influence
C. issue
D. record

Johnny Saldana's seminal work *The Coding Manual for Qualitative Researchers* is considered the best resource for researchers who aim to document data collection in an ethical manner.

24

The word "erratic" in the passage is closest in meaning to
A. difficult
B. curious
C. secretive
D. unpredictable

Many people living in Africa are denied hope for a better life due to global warming, which has caused a decrease in food production due to erratic weather changes.

25

The word "expanded" in the passage is closest in meaning to
A. varied
B. rejected
C. enlarged
D. improved

The artist wanted to engage the spectators in different ways, so its collection showed both real-size images and expanded ones.

26

The word "fastidious" in the passage is closest in meaning to
A. demanding
B. unclear
C. confusing
D. specific

Tony Award winner, Bob Fosse, was known as a fastidious choreographer, earning a reputation as a driven artist with exceedingly high expectations of all his dancers.

27

The phrase "gathered some momentum" in the passage is closest in meaning to
A. made progress
B. acted on impulses
C. got angrier
D. reduced velocity

The Futuristic movement gathered some momentum in the aftermath of the Industrial Revolution, because it celebrated the changes in the society of that time.

CONTINUE

The word "gratifying" in the passage is closest in meaning to
A. inducing
B. granting
C. satisfying
D. influencing

The work that Malala Yousafzai has done on gender equity has been gratifying to many females who live in countries where they have been denied education based on gender.

The word "illusory" in the passage is closest in meaning to
A. miscalculation
B. misleading
C. underrated
D. wrong

Because all of the species are herbivorous (feeding only on plants), many scientists held the illusory perception they would have similar diets.

The word "immeasurably" in the passage is closest in meaning to
A. inconsiderably
B. universally
C. greatly
D. pointlessly

During his tenure as President of the United States, John F. Kennedy Jr. immeasurably enhanced the powers and scope of the presidential office.

The word "inclinations" in the passage is closest in meaning to
A. therapies
B. theories
C. tendencies
D. satires

Despite Charles Darwin's personal inclinations towards organized religion, his scientific projects were not based on personal faith convictions.

The word "logical" in the passage is closest in meaning to
A. satisfactory
B. modern
C. reasonable
D. mundane

During times of extreme crisis, the brain automatically tries to generate the most logical explanation it can.

CONTINUE

33

The word "methods" in the passage is closest in meaning to
A. oppositions
B. causes
C. circumstances
D. ways

The art students had different methods of sculpting: carving, molding, modelling and casting.

34

The word "obligation" in the passage is closest in meaning to
A. confidence
B. safety
C. responsibility
D. advantage

Upon taking the Hippocratic Oath, medical doctors have an ethical obligation to do no harm towards their patients.

35

The phrase "out of sight" in the passage is closest in meaning to
A. hidden
B. indirect
C. mysterious
D. coded

Only for now, these negotiations are happening out of sight to avoid the appearance of discord before the party has formally selected a nominee.

36

The word "overlie" in the passage is closest in meaning to
A. offer
B. cover
C. fake
D. describe

In the counties surrounding the area, any spot on the ground may overlie what once was the bed of a river that has since become buried by soil.

37

The word "penchant" in the passage is closest in meaning to
A. hope
B. devotion
C. inclination
D. obsession

Unfortunately, a penchant for fantasy and human imitative capabilities alone are not enough to guarantee good theatrical performances.

CONTINUE

38

The word "phenomenon" in the passage is closest in meaning to
A. adventure
B. risk
C. occurrence
D. attack

This phenomenon cannot be explained by using existing theories, because they all fail to account for some part of the situation.

39

The word "precious" in the passage is closest in meaning to
A. idolized
B. valuable
C. skilled
D. proficient

Although the artifact was found incomplete, such ceremonial vases can offer precious details on the life of Etrurian noble families.

40

The word "preposterous" in the passage is closest in meaning to
A. undeniable
B. unreliable
C. awkward
D. unbelievable

Galileo presented the court with his idea that it was in fact the Earth to revolve around the Sun, and not the other way around, which most people found to be preposterous.

41

The word "prestigious" in the passage is closest in meaning to
A. highly regarded
B. publicly envied
C. poorly paid
D. temporary

Milan is recognized for its prestigious fashion designers, many of whom are the foremost in international design.

42

The word "prone" in the passage is closest in meaning to
A. correct
B. respectable
C. complete
D. likely

In tropical regions, the soil appears to be more fertile because it is less prone to parch—it snows less and the abundant rain keeps the soil moist.

327

CONTINUE

43

The word "propulsion" in the passage is closest in meaning to
A. transition
B. moving fast
C. race
D. moving forward

The propulsion system of any rocket is mostly based on the application of Newton's third law of motion—for every action there is an equal and opposite re-action.

44

The phrase "provided that" in the passage is closest in meaning to
A. at this time
B. as long as
C. in addition
D. on the other hand

Provided that all of the equipment was functioning, the process would only take about 17 or 18 hours.

45

The word "rated" in the passage is closest in meaning to
A. contained
B. planed
C. adjusted
D. judged

The participants who undertook the test rated their experience as significantly unpleasant.

46

The word "ratio" in the passage is closest in meaning to
A. time
B. fairness
C. proportion
D. extent

The ratio between school teachers and students has increased, as fewer teachers are entering the profession and more students are coming into the school system.

47

The word "squander" in the passage is closest in meaning to
A. refuse
B. waste
C. deny
D. take for granted

Humans cannot squander all of their energies on work; experts sustain that leisure time is equally important.

CONTINUE ➧

48

The word "static" in the passage is closest in meaning to

A. noisy
B. confusing
C. preserved
D. unchanging

Although many believe that ice is static, in fact, it is not: it not only moves around, but is an integral part of the water cycle.

49

The word "status" in the passage is closest in meaning to

A. height
B. level
C. qualification
D. importance

The function and status of ceremonial vases in ancient Rome have changed from one dynasty to the other—mainly accordingly to religious and traditional beliefs.

50

The word "accrete" in the passage is closest in meaning to

A. accumulate
B. come together
C. increase
D. augment

It is necessary to occasionally remove ships from the water so that minerals do not accrete on the hulls and inhibit their seaworthiness.

END

练习答案

List 01

题号	1	2	3	4	5	6	7	8	9	10
答案	C	D	D	D	D	D	A	C	D	D
题号	11	12	13	14	15	16	17	18	19	20
答案	B	C	B	B	D	C	B	C	A	C
题号	21	22	23	24	25	26	27	28	29	30
答案	B	D	B	C	B	D	A	B	B	D
题号	31	32	33	34	35	36	37	38	39	40
答案	C	D	D	D	B	A	A	B	C	C
题号	41	42	43	44	45	46	47	48	49	50
答案	D	B	D	C	C	A	D	B	C	B

List 02

题号	1	2	3	4	5	6	7	8	9	10
答案	C	C	B	B	A	A	D	D	D	B
题号	11	12	13	14	15	16	17	18	19	20
答案	B	C	A	D	A	B	D	D	B	B
题号	21	22	23	24	25	26	27	28	29	30
答案	D	D	B	C	A	B	A	A	A	A
题号	31	32	33	34	35	36	37	38	39	40
答案	A	A	A	C	A	C	A	B	A	B
题号	41	42	43	44	45	46	47	48	49	50
答案	D	B	A	B	C	B	C	D	A	A

List 03

题号	1	2	3	4	5	6	7	8	9	10
答案	D	D	C	C	C	D	D	A	C	A
题号	11	12	13	14	15	16	17	18	19	20
答案	A	C	D	B	A	C	A	B	B	D
题号	21	22	23	24	25	26	27	28	29	30
答案	A	D	B	D	B	A	B	C	D	A

题号	31	32	33	34	35	36	37	38	39	40
答案	B	C	D	D	B	D	B	B	C	A
题号	41	42	43	44	45	46	47	48	49	50
答案	A	C	D	B	A	C	B	B	A	D

List 04

题号	1	2	3	4	5	6	7	8	9	10
答案	B	A	A	C	B	D	D	C	A	A
题号	11	12	13	14	15	16	17	18	19	20
答案	A	C	D	D	A	B	C	D	A	A
题号	21	22	23	24	25	26	27	28	29	30
答案	D	A	C	C	D	C	C	A	B	C
题号	31	32	33	34	35	36	37	38	39	40
答案	D	C	A	C	B	A	D	C	C	A
题号	41	42	43	44	45	46	47	48	49	50
答案	B	D	A	C	A	D	C	A	C	C

List 05

题号	1	2	3	4	5	6	7	8	9	10
答案	B	D	C	A	D	B	A	A	A	C
题号	11	12	13	14	15	16	17	18	19	20
答案	C	C	B	B	D	C	A	A	A	A
题号	21	22	23	24	25	26	27	28	29	30
答案	B	D	A	A	B	C	C	A	C	B
题号	31	32	33	34	35	36	37	38	39	40
答案	A	B	D	A	D	B	B	B	A	B
题号	41	42	43	44	45	46	47	48	49	50
答案	A	A	B	B	A	C	A	B	A	C

List 06

题号	1	2	3	4	5	6	7	8	9	10
答案	C	B	C	B	C	C	C	A	B	A
题号	11	12	13	14	15	16	17	18	19	20
答案	D	C	D	D	A	D	B	A	A	B

题号	21	22	23	24	25	26	27	28	29	30
答案	A	D	A	A	C	B	A	C	B	C
题号	31	32	33	34	35	36	37	38	39	40
答案	A	A	C	C	A	A	C	A	B	A
题号	41	42	43	44	45	46	47	48	49	50
答案	C	C	C	C	A	C	A	A	D	C

List 07

题号	1	2	3	4	5	6	7	8	9	10
答案	B	A	D	C	D	C	A	B	C	D
题号	11	12	13	14	15	16	17	18	19	20
答案	C	D	C	C	C	D	B	D	C	A
题号	21	22	23	24	25	26	27	28	29	30
答案	D	A	A	D	B	C	A	C	D	C
题号	31	32	33	34	35	36	37	38	39	40
答案	B	B	A	D	C	D	B	B	A	D
题号	41	42	43	44	45	46	47	48	49	50
答案	C	C	A	D	A	A	D	D	D	B

List 08

题号	1	2	3	4	5	6	7	8	9	10
答案	B	D	C	D	C	A	C	B	A	B
题号	11	12	13	14	15	16	17	18	19	20
答案	B	C	C	C	A	D	B	B	C	A
题号	21	22	23	24	25	26	27	28	29	30
答案	D	C	D	D	B	C	C	B	D	C
题号	31	32	33	34	35	36	37	38	39	40
答案	D	D	C	C	B	A	B	D	D	D
题号	41	42	43	44	45	46	47	48	49	50
答案	C	D	C	C	C	C	D	C	B	D

List 09

题号	1	2	3	4	5	6	7	8	9	10
答案	A	A	D	A	A	B	B	B	D	B

题号	11	12	13	14	15	16	17	18	19	20
答案	B	B	A	A	B	B	A	A	A	C
题号	21	22	23	24	25	26	27	28	29	30
答案	B	B	A	B	A	D	C	C	C	B
题号	31	32	33	34	35	36	37	38	39	40
答案	B	A	A	B	A	A	B	A	A	A
题号	41	42	43	44	45	46	47	48	49	50
答案	C	B	B	B	B	D	C	C	B	C

List 10

题号	1	2	3	4	5	6	7	8	9	10
答案	B	A	A	A	D	A	B	A	A	A
题号	11	12	13	14	15	16	17	18	19	20
答案	B	C	D	C	C	C	A	C	B	A
题号	21	22	23	24	25	26	27	28	29	30
答案	C	D	B	C	D	C	A	D	D	B
题号	31	32	33	34	35	36	37	38	39	40
答案	A	A	C	A	D	C	B	D	A	D
题号	41	42	43	44	45	46	47	48	49	50
答案	C	B	C	B	B	A	A	B	B	A

List 11

题号	1	2	3	4	5	6	7	8	9	10
答案	B	A	D	C	B	A	D	C	B	A
题号	11	12	13	14	15	16	17	18	19	20
答案	B	C	B	C	A	D	A	A	C	B
题号	21	22	23	24	25	26	27	28	29	30
答案	D	A	A	A	D	D	A	B	D	B
题号	31	32	33	34	35	36	37	38	39	40
答案	D	A	D	A	C	B	C	C	C	C
题号	41	42	43	44	45	46	47	48	49	50
答案	D	C	A	B	D	B	B	D	C	B

List 12

题号	1	2	3	4	5	6	7	8	9	10
答案	A	A	A	C	D	D	D	D	C	A
题号	11	12	13	14	15	16	17	18	19	20
答案	C	A	C	D	C	C	B	A	B	C
题号	21	22	23	24	25	26	27	28	29	30
答案	B	C	A	D	C	B	C	B	C	D
题号	31	32	33	34	35	36	37	38	39	40
答案	D	D	D	C	B	A	B	D	B	B
题号	41	42	43	44	45	46	47	48	49	50
答案	B	A	C	C	A	A	A	A	B	B

List 13

题号	1	2	3	4	5	6	7	8	9	10
答案	D	B	D	D	A	A	C	B	C	C
题号	11	12	13	14	15	16	17	18	19	20
答案	B	C	B	A	A	C	B	D	C	A
题号	21	22	23	24	25	26	27	28	29	30
答案	B	C	A	A	B	B	B	D	C	D
题号	31	32	33	34	35	36	37	38	39	40
答案	A	D	B	B	B	A	A	B	B	A
题号	41	42	43	44	45	46	47	48	49	50
答案	B	D	D	C	C	B	D	D	C	C

List 14

题号	1	2	3	4	5	6	7	8	9	10
答案	D	A	A	A	B	B	C	A	A	C
题号	11	12	13	14	15	16	17	18	19	20
答案	A	D	A	D	C	A	B	A	C	B
题号	21	22	23	24	25	26	27	28	29	30
答案	C	C	A	A	D	A	B	B	C	A
题号	31	32	33	34	35	36	37	38	39	40
答案	C	C	B	A	A	A	B	A	D	C

题号	41	42	43	44	45	46	47	48	49	50
答案	C	C	C	A	D	A	A	A	A	B

List 15

题号	1	2	3	4	5	6	7	8	9	10
答案	B	A	B	D	B	D	C	D	D	A
题号	11	12	13	14	15	16	17	18	19	20
答案	B	C	B	A	B	A	B	B	B	B
题号	21	22	23	24	25	26	27	28	29	30
答案	D	B	C	A	B	C	A	B	B	A
题号	31	32	33	34	35	36	37	38	39	40
答案	A	A	D	B	C	B	B	B	A	A
题号	41	42	43	44	45	46	47	48	49	50
答案	A	B	C	A	C	A	B	A	B	A

List 16

题号	1	2	3	4	5	6	7	8	9	10
答案	C	D	A	A	B	A	C	D	D	C
题号	11	12	13	14	15	16	17	18	19	20
答案	A	C	C	A	C	A	C	C	D	A
题号	21	22	23	24	25	26	27	28	29	30
答案	B	D	A	A	A	A	B	C	B	A
题号	31	32	33	34	35	36	37	38	39	40
答案	D	A	B	D	A	B	D	D	C	B
题号	41	42	43	44	45	46	47	48	49	50
答案	A	D	B	A	C	D	A	B	C	A

List 17

题号	1	2	3	4	5	6	7	8	9	10
答案	C	D	D	C	D	D	A	A	A	B
题号	11	12	13	14	15	16	17	18	19	20
答案	B	C	A	A	D	D	D	C	C	A
题号	21	22	23	24	25	26	27	28	29	30
答案	C	A	C	A	A	C	D	C	A	D

题号	31	32	33	34	35	36	37	38	39	40
答案	B	A	D	A	A	D	B	C	B	C
题号	41	42	43	44	45	46	47	48	49	50
答案	A	D	A	B	D	C	B	C	B	B

List 18

题号	1	2	3	4	5	6	7	8	9	10
答案	B	C	B	D	C	A	B	D	C	C
题号	11	12	13	14	15	16	17	18	19	20
答案	C	B	C	C	D	D	B	C	C	C
题号	21	22	23	24	25	26	27	28	29	30
答案	D	B	D	C	C	B	C	D	C	C
题号	31	32	33	34	35	36	37	38	39	40
答案	B	C	D	A	D	B	A	B	C	A
题号	41	42	43	44	45	46	47	48	49	50
答案	A	A	A	A	B	C	C	D	A	C

List 19

题号	1	2	3	4	5	6	7	8	9	10
答案	C	C	A	C	A	D	B	A	B	B
题号	11	12	13	14	15	16	17	18	19	20
答案	C	C	A	B	D	C	C	D	D	B
题号	21	22	23	24	25	26	27	28	29	30
答案	C	A	C	B	A	A	D	A	A	C
题号	31	32	33	34	35	36	37	38	39	40
答案	B	D	B	A	B	A	C	D	A	D
题号	41	42	43	44	45	46	47	48	49	50
答案	A	B	D	D	B	A	B	D	B	A

List 20

题号	1	2	3	4	5	6	7	8	9	10
答案	D	B	D	B	D	B	D	D	A	B
题号	11	12	13	14	15	16	17	18	19	20
答案	A	C	D	B	B	C	D	C	D	B

题号	21	22	23	24	25	26	27	28	29	30
答案	B	C	D	D	C	A	A	C	B	C
题号	31	32	33	34	35	36	37	38	39	40
答案	C	C	D	C	A	B	C	C	B	D
题号	41	42	43	44	45	46	47	48	49	50
答案	A	D	D	B	D	C	B	D	D	B